# LINES IN THE SAND

# LINES
## — IN THE —
# SAND

*An American Soldier's Personal Journey in Iraq*

# F. SCOTT SERVICE

*Mill City Press*
*Minneapolis, MN*

Mill City Press, Inc.
322 First Avenue N, 5th floor
Minneapolis, MN 55401
612.455.2293
www.millcitypublishing.com

ISBN-13: 978-1-63413-574-0
LCCN: 2015908544

Editing by Geoff Smith
Author Photograph by Two Roads Photography
Book Design by Sophie Chi

*Printed in the United States of America*

The following is based on the handwritten journals I kept while serving with the United States Army in Iraq from 2003 to 2005. However, in most instances names and identifying details have been changed to protect the privacy and/or anonymity of individuals and places.

The political, social, and cultural opinions, observations, and/or speculations expressed in this work are solely those of the author and do not necessarily reflect fact. The author does not make any guarantee for the correctness and/or completeness of that information.

This work would not have been possible without the inestimable help of Jay White, who reached out a hand when I needed it the most, Gary W. Messecar, whose wisdom and mentorship has helped me chart a new course, and my editor, Geoff Smith, who's truly a magician with the written word.

My eternal gratitude is given to my parents for their support and encouragement in everything I've attempted in my life.

I would also like to express sincere thankfulness and appreciation to all the good folks at Mill City Press who worked so hard to make this book the best it could be.

Most of all, I wish to thank the soldiers, seamen, airmen, and Marines of any war, for without their sacrifices none of us could understand how precious life really is.

For dreams that have yet to be realized…
For anyone not allowed a voice and who needed to be heard…

For my First Sergeant who told me, "You better write that fuckin' book."

# Contents

# Foreword

*Naturally the common people don't want war; neither in Russia, nor in England, nor in America, nor in Germany.*

*That is understood.*

*But after all, it is the leaders of the country who determine policy, and it is always a simple matter to drag the people along, whether it is a democracy, or a fascist dictatorship, or a parliament, or a communist dictatorship.*

*Voice or no voice, the people can always be brought to the bidding of the leaders.*

*That is easy.*

*All you have to do is to tell them they are being attacked, and denounce the pacifists for lack of patriotism and exposing the country to danger.*

*It works the same in any country.*

—Hermann Goering, 1946

THERE COMES A TIME when every service member must face the ultimate test of their commitment. It's often long after they chose to raise their right hand in some dank gray Federal office building in sight of a wrinkly American flag taped to a cinderblock wall and pledge their utmost devotion and allegiance to a president and a populace the vast majority of whom they will never meet. It is the part that requires them to dig deep within their psyche into the complex labyrinth of their own self-defense mechanisms, fears, trepidations, morals, values, and beliefs.

It is the part when they are deployed to war.

Going to war is difficult and frightening enough. *Surviving* a war is often much more traumatic—it can force you to examine everything you had become accustomed to relying on in your previous everyday life. A war zone's constant reality of lethal threat can throw you into utter confusion. Established values and beliefs often wilt like a solitary flower baking in the desert sun.

A soldier's base human survival instincts are usually jump-started with a force that takes many by surprise. A deep recess of the mind conditions you to instinctively drive on no matter the consequence to your psyche; it eventually consumes every thought or feeling and very nearly forces soldiers to extinction as human beings. In the process, a new identity is created even while you desperately attempt to cling to previous images of yourself—your lifelong beliefs, values, and motivations—as if they were still sincerely yours. In reality, you are being spiritually killed by a force that is just as real as the physical bombs and bullets flying around you.

We grow up in America being taught to believe in the "Golden Rule." We do our best to do unto others as we hope they would do unto us. We hold the door for people. We cover our noses when we sneeze. We say "please" when we want something and "thank you" when we get it. We are supposed to treat others with dignity and respect. We are taught that these ideals are the basis of a civilized society—our society. And we *definitely* don't kill people. Is that not an ultimate betrayal of the morality we were brought up to believe in? With few exceptions, we don't do it. And when we do kill, those who are found guilty of such a crime pay a hefty price according to the laws we have crafted as a culture.

However, as a nation we have also become accustomed to think of war as an exception to this code. It becomes automatic and instinctual to consider oneself "under orders"—obeying the rules of engagement formulated by men thousands of miles away who insist it is permissible to act violently—to break that sacred Golden Rule. And a soldier often has the means—at the very least the standard load of ammunition and an M-16 rifle.

Some may ask, "Will I do it? If I have to, will I shoot someone?" Some have answers, some don't. When they answer "yes," changes begin. Their foundational beliefs have just received a giant whack to the head, and it leaves them reeling with the consequences of not only their actions but their dearly held beliefs as well.

From the comfort of "Ft. Living Room," for some it's easy to say, "Yeah, we ought to just go kill all those motherfuckers." But for a veteran, it is a weighty charge and a jarring realization that the Golden Rule is just a shibboleth that evaporates in the harsh reality of war. I don't believe any of us are really ready for the ramifications of having our moral foundation leveled.

What I have just written is but a mere glimpse into what a soldier is forced to grapple with, not only during war but after returning home, when the struggle of reintegrating into "normal life" begins. As people of a civilized society, we are still striving to understand the infinitely complex changes that someone who has survived a wartime experience will undergo. We invent convenient labels such as "shell shock," "combat stress," or "post-traumatic stress disorder" to slap on another in order to ground ourselves with an explanation, some sort of narrative that could explain what that person is experiencing. And more than anything else, we take comfort within the justification that *this war was a good war, a just war, a war worth all the pain and suffering for*—a war worth fighting.

I first met Scott in 2009, four years after he returned from Iraq, after he called my office at a local Veteran's Center seeking help for the problems he had incurred while serving overseas. I was and still am a mental health counselor, and since I am also an Iraq War veteran it was felt that meeting with me specifically would significantly increase Scott's comfort level during an initial conversation. We met on a gray December afternoon in a small parking lot in the van I had requisitioned from the Veteran's

Center—the van being the only place he felt comfortable, away and out of sight of people.

It didn't take me long to discover that Scott is a brave person. He is a deeply abstract thinker, which as beautiful as that is and though it makes for wonderful conversation, can be burdensome when confronted with the trauma that war inevitably inflicts and the expectation of recovering from that trauma. Like most veterans, his recovery has been slow and painful. He is brave because not only has he truly tried to integrate his war experience into his life, he has actively, honestly stared at himself in the mirror and asked who he is and how he might rebuild himself to become better.

It's funny. You might not pick him out of a group as an Iraq War veteran. I'm not sure I would have when I first met him. He wears his hair long and usually has some form of a beard growing. He doesn't seem to pay much attention to his appearance—not out of neglect, it just doesn't feel important to him. He makes himself unnoticeable, often preferring to stay anonymous in the shadows.

He has been slow to come out of his self-imposed shell. I have watched that shell slowly begin to dissolve through careful, compassionate nurturing, but normally he prefers to isolate, spend time with a stray cat he adopted rather than approach people and be social. It is here that he finds safety. A few years ago, isolation was all he knew. He never came out of his apartment—not for a long time and even then only when necessary to buy groceries or run an errand. He does now, albeit with many restrictions and some pretty heavy trepidation. On the surface, this may seem irrational, crazy, or even lazy.

But there are reasons for his choice of lifestyle. Scott has been permeated by post-traumatic stress. Not only has Scott endured difficulty in the combat theater of Iraq, in Kuwait, and in the years following his return, he did so with tremendous upheaval at home, having received the infamous "Dear John" letter and losing everything he had built in his civilian life. When he came home, he decided to stand up for his beliefs, salvaging what was left within him to make a statement as to why war is futile, ugly, and unworthy of the pain and confusion of being forced to sacrifice cherished morals and beliefs.

Army Regulation 600-43, "Conscientious Objection," is an evaluation process in which the soldier must be deemed sincere in his overall demeanor to object to such conditions as war and the effort of killing. Scott had to be noble and honest with himself to even consider applying—in military life, and in life in general, there seems to be some sort of unwritten code that discourages taking this sort of stance, of being bold enough to step away from the herd, to be the black sheep, to deviate from the accepted norm.

There is definitely the risk of being ostracized. What if the application is not approved? What would life in the military be like if the application failed? How would a comrade view that black sheep? And what if his status was accepted? Would his friends stay away from him? Would they consider him disloyal, even a traitor? These questions must have weighed heavily on Scott's mind as he tried to balance his disgust for war with his innate feeling of duty to his fellow comrades in arms.

As you'll read in the following pages—the diaries Scott kept while serving in Iraq—he had a choice. He had a choice both before and after his deployment to Iraq, but it was only after his deployment had ended when he finally applied and was granted conscientious objection status.

Why would anyone make the choice to go to war? There are different reasons for each person, but for Scott that motivation revolved around having to confront a broader picture than his own fears or dislike for war. He was forced to realize there were others who might need him and it was his duty to honor them above all else.

"There was honor in honoring them," he would tell you, and if he hadn't gone it would have been a betrayal of not just them but of his own sense of loyalty and commitment. For Scott, war has meant much more than fighting for a cause. War has meant an opportunity to not only face the darkest fears that we're all afraid to confront but to develop a greater understanding of who he is, what he stands for, how he wants to approach the world, and what he might have to offer those around him.

He did what he thought was a great thing when he enlisted with the Army. He surrounded himself with less than one percent of the American population. He fought a war, became a veteran... and a conscientious objector. That is where the truth of his character is truly projected.

Fighting in Iraq and becoming a conscientious objector was the beginning of a personal and moral journey for Scott that allowed the seed of his ideas and views of the world to become a full-grown tree. He chronicled his way through Iraq. He wrote in his journals about his everyday experiences even as mortars fell around him and is now presenting a firsthand, front-row ticket to the realities of war.

War and moral injury are the veteran's common, yet unique story. This book is about heartache and loss, courage and fear, loyalty and betrayal, commitment and abandonment, self-reflection and redemption. It is about the deconstruction and deliverance of the human soul.

Jay White
January 2013

# PROLOGUE

# SHAKEN AND STIRRED

*A mighty flame followeth a tiny spark.*

—Dante Alighieri, *The Divine Comedy*

ON NOVEMBER 23, 2003, the Sunday before Thanksgiving, I received a phone call from Chief Warrant Officer Donald Brown—a phone call that changed my life. After the usual courtesies, he explained that 38 members from my Montana Army National Guard unit were being notified of an impending deployment to Iraq in support of Operation Iraqi Freedom, and as the only Aircraft Hydraulic Systems Specialist in our unit at Ft. Harrison in Helena, I had been chosen to be one of them.

It was about 1100 hours. I had just finished showering and was ready to enjoy a Sunday off from work, hoping to spend some time with my wife, Rita, perhaps putter around my newly built house, watch a movie, or read for a while. In short, I had been looking forward to a lazy day.

At the time, I was employed at a small company in Montana and had settled in somewhat, enjoying writing, image manipulation, and designing web pages for the company's various products. I was as settled in as much as I had been at any other job before. *This one* felt good. It was a family-oriented workplace that nurtured an inner feeling that I was on the right track. I had finally found something that would bring contentment to my life and allow me the time and energy to address some of the issues that plagued me—mainly a lack of direction and stability after graduating from college that had caused a fair amount of friction between my wife and me.

I remember being told to report to the armory for what Chief Brown called the SRP, or Soldier Readiness Processing. I don't remember much of the rest of our conversation other than the sickening, leaden sensation developing in my stomach. I hung up the phone and collapsed into a kitchen chair. I wondered how on earth I was going to tell Rita about this new turn of events in our life—our life of nearly ten years together.

I called her cell phone but she didn't answer. That wasn't surprising since she was at work, but I left a number of messages telling her it was imperative that she call me as soon as possible. I think it was about 30 minutes later when she called back and I broke the news. She didn't believe me at first—a natural reaction considering that even my unit's platoon sergeant had recently assured us that we would *not* be deployed. Rita came home shortly after and the day rapidly blossomed into a surreal blur of distorted, disjointed conversations as we began to discuss what this news might mean to our life together. I felt a shock blending with a sense of anxiety and it crept into each of us as the day wore on.

It was bewildering and unreal to say the least and I remember breaking the news to my employers the following day. I told them I would be taking the rest of the week off and would have to quit my job. They were very kind and offered to help in any way they could, all the while reassuring me I would have a place in the company when I returned from my service to our country. I left the office that day feeling somewhat more comfortable, as if they had offered some tangible assurance that a deployment might not be all that bad.

Thanksgiving with Rita's family was somber, our vain attempts at being cheerful fooling none of us. I tried to enjoy it as much as possible, but who could with that kind of news hanging over your head? The following week I was in Helena at Ft. Harrison attending the SRP, still feeling as if the whole experience was unreal. I remember a floating sensation, as if I were dreaming.

The Army leaves little time for such reflection, however, and I dutifully closed off my mind, determined to do the required paperwork and sit through classes and briefing upon endless briefing. Since I lived a good ninety miles to the south, I was required to stay in Helena for the duration of training. I was assigned a room at the barracks on base that couldn't have been more than ten by ten feet wide with drab concrete walls, a bare concrete floor, and one narrow window with a pane of wire mesh. It felt like a prison cell and should have foreshadowed what would come.

I tossed my duffel bag on the bunk and slumped onto the hard mattress, exhausted by the day's activities. I had stayed at Ft. Harrison during drill weekends so I was well acquainted with the accommodations. The rooms are plenty warm in the winter, the heat works wonderfully, and in the summer they stay cool fairly well. I lay down and quickly succumbed to a fitful sleep.

Out of the seemingly endless reams of paperwork we filled out during the SRP, there was one questionnaire in particular that would irrevocably change my life. It was a simple form with mostly "fill in the bubble" answers, one that every soldier must complete in order to be deployed. I remember it clear as day, hunched in a chair, trying to finish the form while filling in those bubbles on one knee. (For some reason, the Army never provides a writing surface.) Hidden among all the others was one simple question: "Are you a Conscientious Objector?"

To be quite honest, the question caught me by surprise. I even chuckled to myself thinking, "Well, now. That's a fine time to be asking me this." I had never considered it. My recruitment sergeant had never mentioned it. I had never seen it on any Army form before and it threw me at first... but it sparked something. That one little question would set in motion a sequence of events that would change my life permanently and profoundly. Everyone else had already handed their forms to the duty officer while I still sat there musing upon the prospect.

Was I a conscientious objector? It *felt* right. My gut *told* me I was. It was as if some flickering light within me was now suddenly, brilliantly lit up, flashing like neon lettering beckoning me in the pitch dark of night.

It told me to be true to my heart.

Most people thoughtlessly fill in the bubble for "No" regardless of how they might feel. However, my compulsion to not do that seemed overwhelming. Something in my heart told me this war was wrong—that war itself was wrong. And yet there could be consequences I wasn't entirely sure I could live with if I answered "Yes."

That one question ultimately sparked the beginning of a war that has taken place inside me ever since—my own private war of right and wrong, a war that has continually shaped and reshaped my views of society, culture, politics, and myself. That five-word question hidden in a sea of other questions would be the genesis of an ever-evolving formulation of a new *me*.

After a brief pause, I answered "Yes." I felt I just couldn't lie.

You see, before I was notified of my deployment, Rita and I had been closely following the news every evening and had discussed our country's situation at great length on many occasions. Both of us were convinced that invading Iraq was wrong, that the evidence couldn't justify a foreign war, a war we weren't sure America could afford, morally or financially, no matter our leaders' assurances that it would go smoothly and quickly. We concluded that our government wasn't weighing the consequences as thoroughly as it should and were not a bit surprised when the invasion found itself on shaky footing and events began to conspire against a speedy, easy victory.

Anyway, I answered "Yes" and a warrant officer with utterly

disbelieving eyes asked if I would like to file paperwork on behalf of that belief. He seemed uncomfortable and referred me to the JAG[1] office where another warrant officer solemnly printed out the document—Army Regulation 600-43. I remember feeling slightly uncomfortable myself. It's never easy going against the grain—in the Army or anywhere else for that matter. Peer pressure is a potent force and I was now swimming against the tide.

Filing for conscientious objection status is a difficult task. Regulation 600-43 contains pages upon pages of questions, all of them in essay form, designed to scrutinize every aspect of your morality, ethics, and beliefs. It can require literally pages upon more pages of documentation pertaining to how you initially formed your current belief system and how it has evolved over time.

But most of all, they are looking for sincerity. There are also medical and psychological examinations that must be performed with a supervising officer to determine your physical and mental state. It's a rigorous and daunting procedure that's difficult to find in the first place, being buried as it is among piles of other regulations.

I gave the completed application to my commanding officer, Captain Ronald Davis, and he read it carefully, taking his time, the furrow of his brow deepening with each answer. After he

---

1    Judge Advocate General, a legal officer and adviser in the U.S. military

spoke with Chief Warrant Officer Brown, the two officers swiftly met with me. It was a protracted, strenuous conversation with me sitting at one end of a long conference table and the two of them scowling from the other end. It was very tense and grim, their hard faces plainly showing their displeasure.

After asking "just how serious I was" about my application, Capt. Davis seemed satisfied and said he'd pass it up the chain of command to be processed. But first he led me into the arms room and handed me an M-16-A2 semiautomatic assault rifle. Looking at me intently, lips pressed together, he asked, "Do you think you can kill another human being?"

I had grown up with firearms—my grandfather taught me how to shoot his battered old Savage .22 bolt-action rifle when I was young—and feeling the weight of that rifle and knowing its potential, the raw power I was wielding confirmed my beliefs. Again he asked me whether I could kill, this time more tersely. "How do you feel about the children in Iraq?" he continued without waiting for an answer. "Do you think we could actually end up doing some good over there regardless of how you might feel right now? Do you think we could possibly help the needy? You might be letting your unit and the people who need you down if you back out. Is that okay with you?" Finally he said flatly that I "might ultimately end up regretting this decision."

His eyes never left me.

I resisted, stubbornly maintaining my position, but the final straw came after Capt. Davis, satisfied with my answers, left to pass the application up the chain of command. As I paced the lobby of the armory agonizing over whether I had made the right decision, I overheard our CSM[2] (I don't remember his name), talking with Chief Brown and he said, "Well, if this asshole wants to weasel out of the deployment then let him do it. You won't need a man like that anyway."

That was the clincher. My sense of duty, honor, commitment, and obligation kicked into overdrive and I began to feel conflicted—conflicted because I would be letting my comrades down, conflicted because I might ultimately play an important role if I stayed on. I was obligated to those people—I *owed* them my support as they endured the hardships of a deployment.

The honor of my word was at stake.

I found Capt. Davis and asked for the application back. He had yet to pass it along and watched as I tore it up and threw it in the wastebasket.

From then on, I was committed to the deployment.

About a week later, after we had finished the SRP process, which consisted of medical examinations, ID processing, and lots of paperwork, we were sent home for a brief rest with our families. When I reported back to Helena a few days later, I was notified that my unit was now under what is called "Title 10"—meaning we were now an active-duty Army unit instead of a National Guard unit. It was December 15, 2003, and we

---

2   Command Sergeant Major

had a lot to do. At this point we were scheduled to fly to Ft. Knox before Christmas—I think we were set for December 20, but deployment dates continually change during wartime because circumstances are continually under question and readjustment.

The list of training exercises my unit was required to complete was extensive. We refreshed our knowledge from basic training and took classes including: "First Aid Techniques," "Nuclear, Biological, and Chemical (NBC) Training," "Rifle Marksmanship," "Rifle Maintenance," "Mine Field Extraction," and "Explosives Identification." We were even afforded some time with the Army's new computer-simulated rifle firing range.

When I tried to qualify for rifle marksmanship for the first time in years, I failed on the first go-around. But I scored very well on my second attempt, so I guess I was just out of practice. We also had to conduct night firing exercises. I don't remember what I scored and I'm not even sure it mattered to the command personnel who watched all of us with folded arms and stern faces. I was beginning to suspect that the Army was so desperate for any able body that they would've taken just about anyone who could pick up a rifle and was willing to go.

I must admit that I daydreamed a lot during the training, which was terribly repetitive. One thing that stood out was "Family Day," which took place on December 18. Your relatives are invited to the base, in part to meet fellow members of your unit but mostly to take care of certain legalities: Your spouse fills out a Power of Attorney so he or she can conduct business on your behalf while you're deployed. IDs are processed to give your family access to the base and its facilities. Life insurance paperwork—what they call SGLI or Soldier's Group Life Insurance—is put in order. I learned that both Rita and I were fully covered under TRICARE, the military's version of medical insurance, the day my unit was officially under Title 10.

Rita drove to Helena for the 18th. She got a room at a hotel and I ensured that I was authorized by my commander to stay with her. Truth be told, I would've left the barracks anyway, but the authorization was a comfort. I think we were both a little overwhelmed. Deploying to a war zone is no easy thing. In some ways, the lead-up is as stressful as the actual deployment, perhaps more so because the unknown is always lurking in the corner of your mind. As much as the Army tries to take care of business, it offers little comfort when it comes to the emotional stress that you and your loved ones endure in the face of a yet-unfamiliar danger.

So Rita and I sat together through endless hours of lectures and presentations on handling any and all affairs that might present themselves to the family members staying behind. Generals arrived and made grandiose speeches about how proud they were of those of us who were deploying, how we were representing our country, our nation's values—our freedom. They spoke majestically of how each and every relative should be strong for the men and women who were placing their lives in danger for the sake of liberty and democracy. That we should all be proud of the sacrifices we were making for our country.

After the meetings, Rita and I adjourned to a small Mexican restaurant, a favorite of ours. They served the best enchiladas I can recall having in my entire life. I distinctly remember the soft sounds of guitar and maracas; the dim, romantic, almost erotic lighting; the vivid red, orange, and green dried chili peppers hanging from the rafters; old black-and-white pictures on the walls of Mexican heroes proudly displaying their rifles; the crackle of fajitas being sautéed in the kitchen, their searing aroma pricking the nostrils and creating a sense of comfort and belonging. I remember my wife talking about how she was feeling and what the future might bring. Everything would be okay. We would make it through this deployment together. It was comforting. I felt love and support that I truly needed for truth be told, I was scared shitless of the unknown and what it might bring.

Let's face it. When you know that you're leaving, you begin to appreciate what you have a whole helluva lot more. Suddenly every touch of the person you love feels like it could be the last and I feel that taking things for granted has probably been one of my biggest mistakes in life. It's all too easy to become trapped in complacency as we go about our daily lives but war changes that. It's one thing that makes a deployment beneficial and it's a lesson that should never be overlooked or forgotten.

Perhaps that's one reason there is an inevitable unspoken bond that forms between those who have suffered the hardship of war, no matter their personal differences or where they were stationed, what their job was, what their unit was. More often than not veterans have had their eyes forcibly opened to how fleeting life can be and appreciate every day in an entirely different sense. The effects of war are as indelible as a permanent marker—no matter how hard you try to erase them with other life experiences or ideologies, they will always be faintly visible through every layer of ink. Yet, it always seems as though you learn lessons in life too late—too late to take back harsh words or silly arguments.

But I remember those special moments with Rita. Every detail lives in me now and will likely live in me for the rest of my life. I remember how beautiful she was. I remember her soft, supple brown hair with its strawberry highlights. I remember the warmth of her breath, the smoothness of her shoulder, the glow her eyes, the furrow of her brow, and the gentleness of her voice. Then, just like that she was gone, driving back to our home. At least my date of departure had been pushed back to January 4, so we'd have New Year's Eve together.

By then we had been issued our "black boxes"—large black plastic containers that constituted the new Army foot locker and would hold our belongings—our lives—for the next year. Anything non-military that we wanted to take could go in there, and people filled them with all sorts of keepsakes—

whatever might remind them of home or make their lives more comfortable while in Iraq. I picked out books and Rita and I shopped for essentials like toothpaste and shampoo. We even bought a portable DVD player and a case for some movies I wanted to take.

I'm not sure we really knew what to expect or how to handle things. We just took care of business, blindly occupying ourselves, buying things we thought might ease the pain of my deployment. It had to be done and allowed us to focus on a task rather than face the anguish of being compulsorily separated. I honestly can't recall us talking about anything emotional, just the business at hand. Perhaps we were merely speechless, I don't know.

It's kind of crazy how those days in Montana are a blur in my mind. I remember some things vividly, others not so much, some not at all. I don't remember being overly frightened but I did have nervous pangs about going into entirely unknown territory in my life.

I *do* clearly remember the day I left Montana for Ft. Knox—the real beginning. It was filled with speeches, formations, equipment inventories, tearful good-byes, and nervous anticipation. There was a final formation in which we were given praise, sincere wishes of good luck, and an admonition that our honor and duty bade us to do this job we were undertaking. I remember seeing Rita out of the corner of my eye as we stood rigidly at attention. She was standing to the side, her face contorting with a kaleidoscope of emotions—nervousness, worry… sadness.

We broke formation for a last chance to say good-bye to relatives who had gathered in clusters. There were tears and long kisses as if the world we knew was ending and a new one—a world unknown to us—was to begin. Rita and I hugged for what seemed like hours, clinging to each other, melting together, desperate for reassurance that everything would be okay, that we would see each other again in a world overflowing with sunshine. I remember when we finally parted, looking into each other's eyes—hers streaming tears, mine filled with fear but stolid determination.

"I love you more than the world itself," I told her, and she broke down, wiping her cheeks with the sleeve of her fleece.

We kissed—a long, passionate, deep kiss. I remember the texture of her lips as they softly wrapped themselves with mine. I felt as if I could've stayed there forever, secure in the warmth of our love. But before I knew it, I was slinging my duffel bag over my shoulder, treading to the flight line where my 37 comrades were already boarding. I turned once, saw Rita waving to me, then whirling and stiffly striding out of the hangar, never looking back. For the first time in nearly ten years, this woman—my wife, my lover, my best friend, my partner—and I had parted from each other.

Soon I would be leaving the country for the first time in my life. That notion wouldn't set in until I watched Cape Cod disappearing from my airplane window and I turned forward to greet the broad expanse of the Atlantic Ocean.

I will never forget those moments for the rest of my days.

# PART ONE

# SO... WHAT I HEAR YOU SAYING IS...

*In the middle of the journey of our life I found myself within a dark wood where the straight way was lost.*

—Dante Alighieri, *The Divine Comedy*

*Fighting for peace is like fucking to save your virginity.*

—Anonymous soldier in Iraq

M Y DEAR WIFE,

Well, I've been here in the fabulous resort of Ft. Knox for two days now. This is the real beginning of my deployment. Soon my unit will be flying into hostile territory to do our part for the United States of America, to participate in another war instigated by our country's interests abroad. Our destination is Iraq—to confront a culture largely unknown to us, a people with thousands of years of tradition vastly different from our own. How this epoch will conclude is anyone's guess, but in the meantime let me catch you up on how things are going.

As you know, we left Helena and the peacefully majestic slopes of the Rocky Mountains on Sunday a little after 1100 hours. We were delayed, and although the extended time allowed me to say good-bye to you properly, it also made our farewells much more exquisitely painful. I have to say, leaving you was the hardest thing I've ever had to do. Plunging into this deployment and a war zone filled with people who would like nothing better than to blow my head off, made it seem as if every moment I spent with you on that frigid morning was the most precious of my life. I hope we will be reunited someday soon, that this duty of mine will be fulfilled swiftly. Until then, however, I'll have to speak with you by writing in this journal I have vowed to keep. I am determined to chronicle this experience—the greatest, most challenging event of my life.

The 38 of us Army National Guardsmen who left Montana—the 38 who were chosen for a variety of reasons, most importantly our professional military occupations, which would complement and fill empty positions within our new parent unit previously notified of deployment—had an uneventful flight to Kentucky to meet our new comrades-in-arms. Most of us were fairly quiet during the flight, either because of nervous anticipation or because we already missed loved ones—or both. I spent my time dozing and trying to wish away my fears and sadness. Images of you flickered through my mind like a movie. Memories I had previously forgotten surfaced and quickly became my only thoughts.

We landed at Louisville International Airport and were greeted by a bus with a welcoming party from our new mother unit. My first impression of Louisville was that it stank of car exhaust. Perhaps the pollution was trapped by the overwhelming humidity but after living in arid Montana for so many years, I've discovered I'm not at all accustomed to the stifling environment of the South. It was warm as well, another stark change to Montana's winter. You know that wet, warm city stink that stings the nose and makes you feel slightly slimy? Needless to say, I found myself immediately missing and appreciating the fresh, crisp Rocky Mountain air.

After our gear and duffel bags had been unloaded, we left without delay for Ft. Knox and upon arrival spent the rest of the night unloading our baggage, eating dinner, socializing, and settling in.

Ft. Knox, as you may or may not know, is about 39 miles south of Louisville. The base is absolutely huge—more than 100,000 acres of sprawling training ground nestled among the Kentucky hills. It houses the Army Human Resources Center of Excellence, including the Army Human Resources Command, the Army Cadet Command, and the Army Accessions Command. At one time it was the home of the U.S. Army Armor Center and the Army's Armor School, which have since been relocated to Ft. Benning in Georgia. Ft. Knox was once used by both the Army and the Marines to train crews on the M1 Abrams, our main battle tank. They have a museum here commemorating General Patton's career and the history of the United States' Cavalry and Armored forces. It's quite a base, with an extensive history to say the least.

While I'm at it, let me take a moment and describe to you our living conditions here. Our barracks are not quite disgusting... but they're pretty close. My room has hard tiled flooring scarred with cracks and stains—mostly hardened clumps of blackened bubble gum. The paint on the walls and windows is flaking off. The windows have no screens and scream in protest when you open them. The yellow-stained ceiling tiles are filled with holes that I can only guess came from endless hours of flipping pencils in an attempt to make them stick into the soft material—doleful testaments to the tedium of Army life. Nothing but a despondent piece of peeling duct tape holds the vent onto our meager heater.

There are three of us crammed into this 10 by 20 foot room on bunks old enough to be condemned for rust damage. My stained mattress sags so badly that I've found myself grasping the edges to keep from being sucked into the black hole in its center. The drab olive green wool blanket with "US" stenciled in the center that I've been issued provides little comfort for my weary body. It doesn't cover my feet when I stretch out and smells like a century of mold. In fact, everything in here smells like must, mold, and too many years of body odor, the bleach they use to disinfect the place barely masking it. My pillow is hard, any fluffiness it once had long since beaten out by the weight of a hundred other heads.

The bathroom—or latrine as we fondly call it in the Army—has three showers. The hot water faucets aren't working, so I took a cold... no, make that a frigid shower the first morning I was here. Needless to say, it's not up to your standards of cleanliness. Soap scum and hard water stains are permanently etched into the fixtures. The walls were a faded sickly orange and the one washer/dryer available to us is barely hanging on by sheer mechanical will power.

In typical military fashion, wake-up the day following our arrival was early—0400 hours—with a company formation at 0515 hours. For breakfast, I had what can only be described as an ice cream scoop of wet scrambled eggs, a pile of soft bacon, and some kind of "orange drink"—there being no milk or juice of any kind. The long lines and bland breakfast reminded me of basic training at Ft. Leonard Wood. Amazing how everything in the Army is the same everywhere you go.

After everyone was accounted for at formation, we clambered onto old forlorn white school buses parked in front of the barracks and were taken to an auditorium on base to undergo the SRP once again. It began with a briefing on TRICARE Health Insurance despite having already sat through hours of those in Montana.

But... a soldier is not supposed to question. After the not very informative lecture, a captain began a—oh gosh, PFC[3]Pete Butler, one of my roommates here, just came into our humble abode after an ice-water shower. You should see him: His lips are blue and he looks really, *really* awake. It would be quite humorous if I weren't going to suffer through the same very soon.

Anyway, a captain gave a lecture on terrorism that almost immediately had me struggling to keep my eyes open. I know I should have paid more attention but I'm sure that I'll become increasingly acquainted with the notion of terrorism as time passes. After this briefing, we tramped to our buses and were driven back to our accommodations. I spent the rest of the morning lying on my bed, staring at the rusted grate of the bunk above me.

At around 1230 hours, we boarded the buses again in order to conduct our medical processing. It began with a perfunctory

---

3    Private First Class

dental check that lasted all of two minutes—a quick poke here, a quick poke there, followed by a hasty scraping. Then I went to have my eyes checked. According to the doc, I have 20/20 vision, which is surprising considering I actually have 20/40. After this came the inevitable blood drawing.

Here, a young specialist informed me that I was actually *not* enrolled in TRICARE. I adamantly disagreed, having enrolled with you while we were in Montana. (You remember, don't you?) After giving me this news, he casually sat back in his chair with a grin, offering no assistance and I must admit it angered me. After much debate a staff sergeant intervened, called the TRICARE main office, and supposedly re-enrolled me. My Lord, the debacle begins. These foul-ups are so commonplace in the military, it's a wonder we actually accomplish anything.

But my blood was finally drawn. And I received vaccinations for smallpox, hepatitis A, hepatitis B, yellow fever, spotted fever, even anthrax (which I have been told will require a series of injections)—the procession for injections was almost comical if you could discard the grim faces. It's all so mechanical, methodical… like an assembly line or a factory. You stand in a line stretching clear down the hallway, and there are two stations opposite each other in the shot room, two medical personnel at each station. When it's your turn, you walk up to the first station and both of your arms are peppered with injections. Then you move five steps forward to the next station, where another two medical personnel inject each of your arms again.

It's a continual cycle: stepping up, stopping, injecting. It's amazing—efficient, yet so... eerie and the infirmary reminded me of something I would see in a creepy movie. By the time I was finished, my arms were so sore I was barely able to lift them for the rest of the day, a typical reaction to the chemicals in your body. At the last station was a doctor who signed my paperwork and sent me on my merry way—so much for the medical examination. I guess the Army has deemed me worthy, healthy, and two pounds heavier due to vaccinations.

We got on the buses again and drove to another building where we were compelled to make the rounds at nine different stations in an old basketball gym. The people there, mostly civilians sitting behind tables at each station, looked through some files, asked a few questions, and signed more paperwork. The Red Cross handed out small hand towels and some generic fresh-mint toothpaste—a consolation gift, I suppose. Oh, and they fed us some dinner while we waited on the bleachers—one small burnt chicken leg, an ice cream scoop of potatoes, and a handful of overcooked corn on a small Styrofoam plate.

But the night was not over yet. Next we went to the identification card building. I guess the National Guard ID they gave me in Helena wasn't good enough. Now I have an official Active Army ID. By the time we returned to our humble slice of Shangri-La, it was a little after 2300 hours and I was surprisingly thankful to slump into my black hole for the night and disappear from the world for six hours.

After getting up early again this morning we listened to the full-blown lecture on terrorism—guess I didn't miss that much yesterday after all—then a lecture on Arabic culture. I almost fell asleep a few times since wake-up was at 0500 and we were on the buses by 0700 after choking down our daily portion of soggy eggs and orange drink. We got back to the barracks around 1200 and were released for the rest of the day.

Alas, my siesta was interrupted. I was told that I had not yet completed everything the previous day, which I promptly refuted as bullshit, adamantly insisting it was not my screw-up. After some debate, everything was worked out and I am quite relieved to be free for a spell.

So here I sit in my black hole at 2000 hours, a day before my 32nd birthday, writing you when what I really want is to be lying next to you in your warm embrace. Pete and I are quietly passing the time, awaiting yet another day of the mayhem that is the United States Army.

I'll write more tomorrow. My hand is tired, my brain is fried, but my feet don't stink… yet.

P.S. I have just been informed that I have to go through the SRP for a *third* time tomorrow. I'm a specialist who is a hydraulics mechanic… who is really a writer… who is being run in circles by the Army.

I love and miss you.

## January 8, 2004

Well… another day, another dollar. Or "SSDD" as they say—same shit, different day. To celebrate my birthday, I treated myself to a piece of vanilla spice cake after dinner from the mess hall. It was a somber birthday as I spent it repeating the SRP. Some pencil pusher didn't do his job and, as a result, I wasted a morning correcting the mistake. The rest of the day was pretty boring. We had to attend a class and be tested for field first aid techniques... again.

Yesterday a rumor began floating around that a camp close to Balad, Iraq (Camp Anaconda), about 35 or 40 miles northwest of Baghdad, was heavily shelled by mortars. Apparently the attack killed one person and wounded about 35 others. Scary shit. The news set everyone on edge as the reality of what we are about to do is beginning to inhabit our minds. People are talking in small groups everywhere, speculation spreading like a virus. Some are saying we aren't going to Balad. Others are saying that no one has any idea where we're going. I was told that convoys traveling north from Kuwait have more than a good chance of being ambushed somewhere along the way. It's a topic of great debate since it's also rumored we might have to convoy to get to our permanent duty station.

Honey, I must admit that I'm on edge. It's scary. There is no way to find concrete information because anyone who might actually have answers—the "higher ups"—is never going to tell you a fragment, let alone the entire story. All I know for sure is being kept in the dark is excruciating.

Today after lunch we had a formation and our company's commanding officer, Major John Burns, tried his best to instill in us that we are going into a war zone, emphasizing that our lives will be in jeopardy and that we'll need to come together as a unit so we can depend on the person next to us for safety. It was a stern speech and I overheard a couple of people disagreeing with our commanding officer's strategy, privately muttering they don't believe in scare tactics to get us in order. I also overheard them opining we won't be in Iraq for 24 months—another rumor floating around.

I finished an NBC class about a half-hour ago. Throughout my time with the Army, that has probably been the scariest training I've ever participated in. That we could be attacked by biological or chemical weapons is so frightening I don't even want to think about it. Further, to think people would even consider concocting or intending to use these weapons in the first place does nothing to boost my faith in the human spirit. I guess I've never found anything I believed in strongly enough to justify the utter devastation of a population using such ugly means. It's appalling.

Why do humans find it necessary to go so far? To wreak ghastly effects on the body such as lesions, blisters, respiratory failure, nausea, or even burning the body from the inside out? It's too disgusting to think about.

I am deliberately *not* telling you these things right now baby, only writing them in this journal. I would rather you read these thoughts later than have you bear the burden of fear while I am away. I hope you will understand. There doesn't seem much point in placing more stress on you than you already feel, with little hope of consolation. I know if you were facing these perils,

I would be worried sick.

I wish I could come home.

A vague, barely coherent thought has passed through my mind as of late. It's dawned on me that perhaps it was selfish of me to join the Army. I should have thought more about you and us when the recruiters were filling my head with their sales pitch. It's not fair to you and I apologize with all my heart. When I think of the very real possibility that I might never see your face again, I am filled with bitterness, remorse, and a great sense of dread. I have begun to truly appreciate you and the life we have shared together.

P.S. Last night I overheard a soldier arguing with his wife on a cell phone. He seemed in great pain, pleading for a second chance and to not be barred from seeing his children when he gets back from Iraq.

I wept for him.

### January 9, 2004

Tonight I am going to be brief. This morning we went to the NBC chamber, the infamous gas chamber where they expose you to tear gas in an attempt to better acquaint you with the effects of chemical warfare—not that tear gas is anything compared to what we could be subjected to in Iraq. It was about 0730 when the entire company boarded the buses and drove to a small concrete building that reminded me of pictures I've seen of Nazi concentration camps. Upon arrival we discovered that no one was in attendance and had to wait about 45 minutes until the safety personnel showed up.

This was my second time in the gas chamber. It wasn't that bad, certainly not as stressful as it was in basic training. We basically just walked around a big concrete room filled with tear gas and made sure no gas was getting through our masks.

In basic training we had to remove our masks and take a deep breath, then recite our social security number for the drill sergeants before they would let us breathe clean air. I can barely describe the feeling of the gas defiling your lungs. It burns your eyes, your stomach convulses and you vomit uncontrollably, snot runs in streams down your face and neck—the effects are so potent you can barely think. I can't decide which is worse, that or being pepper-sprayed while I was training at the State Police Academy. Either way, I'm tired of being put through these various tortures that I've somehow volunteered for.

Naturally, I can't blame anyone but myself. I signed on the dotted line. I don't know what drove me to. Was it a thirst for adventure? If so, what provoked that feeling in me? Am I a glutton for punishment? What a selfish person I am. All I want now is to have a family with you, my dear, but I have to dig out of this hole first.

The cell phone charger and your note came in the mail today. It brought a tear to my eye. Thank you. Of all the things I've done in my life, meeting you was the best thing I ever did. I love you. I love you more than you'll ever know.

The overall mood of my company is somber. I see many faces etched with fear, tension. Occasionally there is a nervous chortle. Some are depressed. Most are pushing the sum of their worries to the back of their minds, burying them in an effort to maintain an outward semblance of control.

I have begun to wonder where this long road home will take me.

### January 15, 2004

The end of another day.

Today was actually quite nice, fairly mellow and not rushed. My platoon conducted a map-reading class and short compass course in the morning. I had fun, was able to go outside and get some fresh air and exercise. Then SFC[4]Michael Garcia, my platoon sergeant, gave us the afternoon off. A group of us reserved one of the three company Chevy vans and went to the local Walmart to pick up necessities. We feasted at McDonald's, which was, believe it or not, a welcome relief from Army food. I had a Big Mac and a McChicken. They were a delight for my taste buds.

It was really nice to get off this base for a while, to look at the civilians going about their business, mostly oblivious to our presence with the exception of a few stares. Just another day for them. No war, no fear, no uniforms, no formations, no shots, no tear gas… no bullshit. They're free.

I think one of the biggest battles for me is not being free to

---

4    Sergeant First Class

do as I choose—to come and go as I like. I am so used to my independence, sometimes I want to crawl out of my skin here. I think if we get a couple of days off I'm going to rent a hotel room and just vegetate, be myself again. I am beginning to realize active Army life is not for me, but I guess that's why I joined the National Guard.

There *was* some good news, however. We were authorized two hours of "liberty" last night to go to the bar next to our barracks, a small bar with two pool tables. That was nice. We deserved it. Maybe we'll get to go there every night—if only to relieve the tension we all feel.

I'd like to take a little time to describe my platoon. We have four squads. SFC Mike Garcia is in charge. Capt. Daniel Berry is our immediate commanding officer—our platoon leader. SFC Lance Hall is first squad leader and in charge of the sheet metal shop; SSGT[5]Jakob Stewart is in charge of second squad and the engine shop; SGT[6]Ken Bond is in charge of third squad and the hydraulics shop; SSGT Randolph Clark is in charge of fourth squad and the prop/rotor shop. Together we comprise the Component Repair platoon—or as they say, the "back shop" people. Our entire company is split up into platoons, each according to their duties and responsibilities—including Avionics, the Motor Pool, Maintenance, Supply, Production Control, Quality Control, and Administration.

---

5    Staff Sergeant
6    Sergeant

I'm in third squad, along with SGT Ken Bond, SGT Malcolm Schaffer, PFC Darnell Travis, and PFC Elias Thompson. It's a pretty small squad, but I have word that more personnel are due, the Army drawing the personnel they need from various other places to fill our gaps—they just haven't arrived yet. Most of us in the squad are in aviation hydraulics except for Ken and Elias, Ken being a professional soldier who's been deployed before, and Elias being a welder.

Despite all the madness here, I really do love our platoon. We spend every morning together talking about anything and everything. We are really coming together, much of that due to Mike being an exceptional, compassionate leader who exudes a confidence we can believe in—it's almost like he's a father figure. The other day he organized a surprise party for our newest birthday boy, Elias. We bought a cake and sang "Happy Birthday" to him as a platoon. It was invigorating and I felt as if I was part of my platoon "family." Still, I'm not sure if I fully identify with anyone around me yet or if I will make any real close friends. I guess time will tell.

I love you...

### January 16, 2004

Today we were scheduled for some preliminary convoy training. Yep, it looks as if we'll be driving to where we're ultimately going to be stationed in Iraq, although no one truly knows for sure. Few of us have ever done this before. The class dealt with how the driver and co-driver should properly engage enemy targets. It's going to be difficult, given how packed in we'll be with all the equipment we'll be carrying.

Picture being stuffed in a Humvee or a five-ton truck crammed with sandbags and heavy steel armor to deflect explosive shrapnel, your rifles, radios, and a host of other things while wearing combat vests filled with armor plating, ammunition magazines, and first aid gear. All while driving down the road at an average speed of 40 mph and trying to defend yourself against someone who *really* wants to kill you. In that confusion you'd be lucky to hit a barn.

It's scary, baby. I don't want the burden of knowing I killed someone on my conscience for the rest of my life—the thought weighs on me. Or what if I get killed by a freak explosion or a bullet from someone I might never even see? It's almost unbearable to think I might never see you again. This is as real as it gets, baby, and I'll have to be stronger than I ever thought I could be to survive the physical and mental stress.

Why do people feel compelled to fight? Why do they feel the urge to kill each other?

Sounds kinda stupid, don't you think?

We had some new arrivals today—SPC[7]Jeanelle Griffin and SPC Gary Myers from Kentucky. Jeanelle is a Hydraulics Specialist and Gary is an Engine Specialist. The ranks are filling up.

On another note, I am feeling a bit irritable and

---

7    Specialist

claustrophobic. I guess I have a hard time relating to people sometimes. Maybe I always have. All my life, I don't really think I've fit in well anywhere. It seems so rare that I find someone to relate to or feel at ease with.

Sometimes after training has finished for the day, I go downstairs to our makeshift "dayroom" and watch a small TV, lounging on one of two sagging, stained couches that provide relief to tired legs. Or I end up pacing the halls aimlessly, no one to talk to and no place to go. I feel like a caged lion and not even daily PT[8]sessions have helped alleviate my restless feelings that are slowly building to the point of suffocation.

Maybe I just need to vent to someone, but I really don't know to whom yet. Most people are too immersed in their own problems to care little for another's troubles—I'm certainly guilty of this too. Maybe I'll just keep all this in my journal and read about it later on my porch, with the sun setting and a warm breeze touching my face, refreshing my life, and enlivening my soul.

I wish I could be free. I want to dance in a field under the stars to some rock 'n roll. I want to take a walk on a tropical white-sand beach at sunset in a loose Hawaiian shirt, floppy pants, and sandals. I'd like a margarita or a rumrunner. That sounds so pleasant right now.

I love you... always.

---

8    Physical Training

### January 18, 2004

We've gotten some bad news lately. Last night our first sergeant, Leyland Rice—we call him Top because he's at the top of the enlisted food chain in our company—called us into a formation at 1930 hours and informed us that "Family Day" is still up in the air. We also received a truly wonderful lecture about keeping the genders segregated.

Morale is low. Faces are grim. We feel like prisoners. We're prisoners to the whims of the Army and some politician hundreds of miles away. There are occasional outbursts—a man yelling in the hall, a grumble in a room, or a private conversation you overhear when you walk by. Everywhere people are bitching about how much they hate this deployment.

I can't help wondering if all this lockdown will ultimately help these soldiers or if it will drive people to desperation. When you get desperate, you start to do crazy things. I wonder if there will be any AWOLs. It's a possibility at least.

We have training in a few minutes so I have to suffer through a bit more before I am released to my black hole.

You are in my dreams.

### January 19, 2004

Today the members of my platoon and I organized our equipment and, to our dismay, discovered we are missing two hydraulic toolboxes and one power plant toolbox. I have no idea how those toolboxes went missing or where we are going to appropriate any more equipment. It's a sickening feeling to realize we are vastly underprepared for this deployment. What were the politicians in Washington thinking when they undertook this debacle of a war?

Anyway, organizing and accounting for our equipment took just about all day, but we got the job done and our equipment is now sitting in an Army warehouse here on base awaiting transport overseas.

A few more members of our platoon arrived today. They should be the last members to fill our ranks, though there may yet be more to come.

I spent the evening playing cards with Jeanelle. We had a good, in-depth conversation about what we'll have to face in the coming months. It was nice to connect with someone on a personal level. After Jeanelle and I finished playing cards, I came back to my little room and stared at the walls for a while. I am all too aware that I am lonely and in need of companionship. I miss and love you so much it hurts.

We are hearing that we'll have this weekend off, the first two days I've had off in weeks now. I haven't decided how I'm going to spend it yet. And I don't know what I am going to do for the rest of tonight either. Maybe I'll watch a movie. Goodnight my dear, and never forget that you are always in my thoughts.

**January 21, 2004**

Today was unusual. The scheduled training was grenade practice, something I admit that I've always enjoyed. I like the explosions, the adrenaline—it's a blast, if you can pardon the pun. It was scheduled for the morning so my platoon dutifully got on those big white buses and headed to the grenade range way out on the other side of the base. After standing around outside in the frigid Kentucky air for about a half-hour freezing to death (yes, the weather has turned for the worse), we were told that since we didn't have a medic with us we would have to postpone the training until we could scrounge one up. So we all went back to the barracks and ate lunch—so much for grenade training.

At about 1230 hours, we appropriated a medic (from where, I have absolutely no idea) and got on the buses again. Despite the morning's fiasco, everyone seemed to be in high spirits. I think it was largely because we're getting this weekend off, or perhaps it was because we have become resigned to our situation. Who knows, maybe we were all just in a good mood for once, something that seems to catch me off-guard when it happens.

Anyway, we received instruction on the four basic throwing techniques, two of which are in the prone position. Throwing hand grenades is an art. Some would think, "Who cares? Just lob it out there and hope for the best." But it's not just a matter of tossing the damn thing out there, hoping to hit your target while not being blown to bits in the process. You have to get into a proper stance and sight your target before letting the grenade loose. It works very well when done correctly.

So we practiced our techniques with some dummy grenades. That was the only part that disappointed me. I wanted live munitions to have fun with. The only time I have ever thrown a live grenade was in basic training. Talk about an adrenaline rush. A typical hand grenade has a kill radius of five meters and an effective injury radius of around 15 meters, so if you fuck up it's likely you're going to have a *very* bad day.

I'm looking forward to having this weekend off. I might book a hotel room but I haven't decided yet. I could stay here and go to that bar next to the barracks. Ken and Derek are thinking of joining me either way. Like me, they're desperate for a breath of fresh air from the outside world. A decent dinner would be nice, and a shower with hot water would be a blessing. I'm thinking about a real steak instead of that brown, spongy, unidentifiable stuff the Army claims is meat.

On a side note, my smallpox shot is in good shape. It's scabbing up nicely and itching like hell today. You're not supposed to scratch it, but it's driving me nuts. Don't ask me where that came from, just a random thought.

So that was today.

I love you so very much and I can't wait to come home.

### January 26, 2004

"Hey, it could be worse," Jakob Stewart said this morning. "It could be raining."

"It *is* raining," Nate Hughes replied.

I found that quite hilarious.

I overheard a sergeant talking to himself as he paced the hallway with boundless restless energy: "Dear Iraqi insurgent. I am distressed to inform you that I will not be able to engage you in a firefight today due to inclement weather."

A few common sayings around here:

"You'll get it at the MOB[9] station."

"This is not your bus."

"We can go to war, but we can't go to Walmart."

"You're not authorized think pay."

"You're not authorized chow here."

The last one was caused by a dispute that broke out recently concerning where we can actually eat. Some people in authority are apparently upset we accidentally intruded on their mess hall and ate their lousy, greasy fried chicken, as if that's something to be protective of.

Finally, "I'm in Hog Heaven."

This past weekend was the first official time we've had off since we got here. I spent the weekend in a drunken stupor, gorging myself at Red Lobster and the local steak joints. I spent a little too much money, but I feel I can justify it by acknowledging and indulging the need to quell an overwhelming sense of deprivation for a bit. After living off Army food for some time now, I've discovered food with actual flavor is exceedingly delectable. That combined with several shots of tequila each

---

9    Mobilization

night made me feel human again. As they say, I was in "Hog Heaven."

Today we woke up at 0415 hours to draw rifles from the arms room. We were supposed to qualify on the rifle range and the buses were to leave at 0700. So I took a shower, ate a bowl of cereal, grabbed my rifle—and waited. While I cooled my jets, I glanced outside and was awestruck by the remnants of a fairly serious ice storm that had rolled through and covered everything with two inches of beautiful clear ice. I was sweating under my cold and wet-weather clothing and felt like some kid whose overprotective mother had wrapped him up in everything she could before sending him to school.

Well, 0700 rolled around and we were told we'd be delayed until 0900. So I took off all my gear and promptly dozed off. After dressing again, we were told we'd be delayed until 1100. Same thing, I took everything off and dozed for a while. At 1100, after getting dressed again, we were told that we weren't going at all. So I took everything off for the third time and lounged until lunch, which consisted of an MRE[10]because the mess hall never opened since we were supposed to be outside. So much for a productive morning!

Then we were released and I headed to the gym with Malcolm, SGT Jacob Shelter, and Elias Thompson to play racquetball. What a tension release, banging a ball against a wall with primal fervor. Remember when we used to play at the

---

10   Meal, Individual, Ready-to-Eat. A U.S. military field ration.

university courts when we were in college? I really loved those times with you. We played for about 45 minutes and I felt so relaxed when I was finished. I had worked up a really good sweat and was smiling because of our memories.

I have determined to get in shape during this whole experience. I've lapsed into too comfortable of a lifestyle, living the good life—fat, dumb, and happy—watching the latest movie with my wife, snug in the confines of my world with you. Getting in shape seems worthwhile, something to at least distract me from my current situation and the increasing pain of missing my life with you.

Tomorrow is just one day closer to seeing you again. You are the best part of me. No one else knows me like you and I don't want them to. You're a beautiful person filled with creativity and warmth. I *will* get through this deployment. I *will* come home to you so we can spend the rest of our days wrapped in tender embrace.

Goodnight.

### January 27, 2004

Today we got up at 0430 hours again, and this time we actually made it to the rifle range. I was going to skip the zeroing range but decided it couldn't hurt to check out the sights on my rifle just to ensure they weren't fucked up. Well, my suspicion was unsubstantiated and with one small adjustment to the windage setting I was satisfied. I zeroed perfectly within 10 rounds.

From there, we clambered into our white buses and were driven to the qualification range, the Kentucky wilderness serenely drifting by. It seemed like a decent range and proved to be so. I scored 35 out of 40 targets, which earned me a Sharpshooter badge. The night before, Lance Hall told the platoon that he'd buy a beer for anyone who beat his score. He shot a 32. Looks like I'm gettin' me a beer... if we ever get the chance to go to the bar again.

From the general qualification range, I went to the NBC qualification range. I didn't do so hot there, but you know what? I'm not so familiar with firing a rifle while wearing a gas mask. It's more difficult than you might imagine, the mask getting in the way all the time and no clear sight through the goggles. I missed the minimum 11 out of 20 by two, but from what I hear the regular qualification is the most important and the only one you really need to be deployment ready.

By this time it was late afternoon and the weather, which had never really been great, was turning uglier. The wind chill was in the negatives and snow was beginning to fall steadily. Yes, it was a nasty day to be standing out in the cold. I was still frozen to the core even with all my cold-weather clothing. When they decided to shut things down for the day it was a blessing for I was losing feeling in my fingers.

There was, of course, the usual snafu.[11] When we got to the NBC range, we waited for more than an hour for the range

_____

11   Situation normal: all fucked up

personnel to show up with ammunition. Then when it was time to leave, we had to wait in our foxholes for another half-hour before they began to take us off the range in small groups. All this pissed Lance off so much that when we got home he took off his shirt and threw it and his gear across the room. I've never seen him lose his temper before but I think the inefficiency of this place is getting to him. I heard we had four cold injuries today with one case of actual frostbite.

I love you.

### February 1, 2004

It's been a while since I have written anything. So many things have happened.

First, a couple of days ago it was finalized that we'll be stationed in Balad, aka Camp Anaconda, an airbase about 35 miles north of Baghdad. The major made the announcement in a morning formation and I know little about it other than it's a "hot" base that's continually under attack. That news naturally unnerved me, but only time will tell how bad it actually is.

Second, Mike and I had a private heart-to-heart a few days ago. He told me he wanted to entrust me with an assignment—taking part in the convoy my unit will be conducting. He said he felt I was suited for it and could trust me to do the job right. He insisted it was strictly voluntary, but I agreed to participate because I didn't want to let him down. Truth be told, I felt as if I was a vital, integral part of my unit and I must say that sent a rush through my heart.

According to the initial plans I've been given, I am going to be driving a Humvee, the lead scout vehicle, through Baghdad into Balad. From what Mike has told me, this is a good thing because technically I won't be part of the convoy. Instead of being jammed together with all the other trucks—which would surely make us a bigger target for an IED[12]—our vehicle will be scouting up ahead and largely on our own.

They've also assigned my traveling companions. Captain Berry will be in the passenger seat with his M-16 and 9-mm pistol. Pete Butler will be carrying the machine gun. Malcolm Schaffer will be the fourth man in our little wagon. He'll be carrying an M-16 with a grenade launcher. Finally, we're supposed to be getting a fifth man who is Combat Lifesaver qualified. If so, we'll have all the bases covered and be good to go.

Mike told me he wouldn't have put me there if he didn't have the utmost confidence in me and during our heart-to-heart the other day, we vented about our situation—the frustration we both feel about this deployment. We both agreed it is stressful enough being away from home and our loved ones that we hardly need the added strain and aggravation of how disorganized the Army can be.

I feel as if we became a notch closer to knowing each other. Then he surprised me by telling me to have you come down to Kentucky to visit and... I am so glad you're here now, I can

---

12  Improvised Explosive Device, aka a roadside bomb

hardly believe it. You flew in this afternoon and I can barely wait to see you tonight when I get off duty. Having you here for a few nights calms my heart so much.

Lately I've felt as though if I didn't see you one last time before I leave the United States, my last moments on earth would be unbearable if it came to that—and let's face it, it very well could.

We're doing some good training now, getting down to the nitty-gritty of it. Yesterday we learned how to clear a room, an urban assault type of thing. Although I don't think I will get that hardcore and we didn't drill for nearly long enough, I think it was valuable to at least practice the techniques once.

I've realized the attitude of some of the soldiers in my unit frightens me, the ones who think they're some sort of commando cowboys or bad-asses. I'll give you two examples. Today as we practiced convoy operations, we were ambushed by enemy fire. So we all got out of our vehicles and took cover. We were receiving fire from the 11 o'clock position when two guys spontaneously abandoned their vehicle, and us, to go chase a sniper up a hill. That's against protocol—it's reckless to abandon your vehicle, to say nothing of running off and abandoning your comrades for a glory kill. And what if there were a lot more of the enemy up there? They also didn't tell anyone, leaving the rest of us in the dark.

Second, I overheard a conversation with a couple of guys discussing their combat first aid training. During the training, some of our guys were "wounded" while there was some uncertainty about the direction of fire. In the resulting confusion, these guys said "Fuck it, you got in the way. You can just die," abandoning the wounded and the medic. Can you believe it? Suppose they up and abandon me. This unit needs more cohesion and less macho bravado.

It seems we have a fair amount of people who only look after themselves, which could mean the death of someone. How can our own people be like that? I don't know, but I *do* know I will be watching my back. There is so much confusion and lack of communication. We desperately need more convoy training. We could have been training all this time instead of "rockin' on our nuts," as Derek is fond of saying.

Tomorrow we get to learn about vehicle searches, should be interesting if nothing else. I'm just glad we'll have some time together.

I'm out of words for now.

I love you and I can't wait to see you tonight.

### February 4, 2004

You left today, headin' back to the life we have built together and I miss you dearly already. I'm so glad we had the opportunity to see each other one last time before I head into the unknown, unsure of when I'll see your sweet face again, if ever, and I wouldn't trade the last few days for anything in the universe. I'm not trying to be melodramatic, but the danger I might be placed in before we are reunited is pervading me ever more deeply with each passing day. I needed to see you and remember what it was like to talk, laugh, and feel complete again. As your soul mate I don't feel right when we're apart.

I can't help but feel that the core of our relationship thrives on a complex underlying level beyond the articulation of words or physical contact. There's an undercurrent of understanding, of connectedness. I love you with all my heart, my best friend and wife, and hearing you say "I love you" in person one more time made the world seem right.

I ran after you as you were driving out of the parking lot. You didn't see me but that's all right. I suddenly felt compelled to savor one more taste of the harmony I feel when my lips touch yours and I felt part of my heart leave with you; it was agonizing no matter how content I felt from your visit. I can't wait for the day when I am released from my service, destined to live the rest of my days in peace.

I have visions that are so clear—of us laughing together on a boat, in the mountains, in a car, in a resort somewhere, snorkeling, hiking, and reading in a mountain meadow, sharing our thoughts, running my fingers through your hair. I remember so many details of you right down to the way you gently slept, the way your breath lightly escaped from your lips.

Gosh, what a heavy yet light heart.

I pray you are home safe in the house we built, safe with our family and friends. I pray I will join you soon but if not, you will be in my dreams and my heart.

We leave for Ft. Campbell in a couple of days for live fire convoy training.

I love you.

**February 10, 2004**

We're getting ready to leave.

From what I've heard we'll be getting on the plane on the 15th of this month. Ayup, the big long ride to Iraq is right around the corner. I've learned I will be allowed one personal bag and that's nice because the flight will take about 17 or 18 hours; I'll need to pack a couple of books to help me pass the time. We are allowed one MRE to eat for the trip, but Mike hooked me up with an extra beef with mushrooms entrée which was very kind of him and with some Tabasco, it should be all right. When in doubt with Army food, hot sauce'll save the day.

Anyway, we got back last night after a couple of days at Ft. Campbell. It was a three-hour drive on the highways and byways of Kentucky and we crossed into Central Time while getting there. We took three buses—the same old (now infamous) white buses that we've been riding in ever since we came here and were followed by a semitrailer loaded with all of our necessary gear.

When we arrived, we were quickly taken to Camp Hinsch, a small training camp on the outskirts of Ft. Campbell. Camp Hinsch isn't much—eight open-bay barracks, a tiny mess hall, a shower and laundry, a soda machine that wouldn't take dollar bills, and a few small offices. That's it... that and the Kentucky woods that seem to stretch eternally.

I had a brief chance to unpack some of my stuff before about 20 of us were required to spend the rest of the afternoon learning the aspects of Hazardous Material Shipment Procedure, although I'm still not sure why. But, in the end I was awarded a certificate supposedly authorizing me to drive this stuff around. It was supposed to be a 40-hour class but I got the condensed version—approximately four hours.

So at about 1700 we were bused back to the good ole camp and I gratefully crashed in my bunk for the evening. You should have seen us, all crammed into these barracks. With about two feet on either side of the bunks and about a three-foot walkway down the center, it felt like what summer camp must have been like for those who went as kids.

The only drawback was that the showers were a good 100 yards away. They were open bay as well, about eight to a side, and if you didn't get there quickly enough, the hot water would run out and it felt as if you had leaped into the Jefferson River.[13]

There were five personal sinks and four stalls. All of this served about 100 guys, crowding around or waiting in line. Like at Ft. Knox, there were concrete floors, chipped paint walls, and the floor in the shower area was always muddy because we had to hike so far, usually in uniform, to get there. It was too cold to go in anything less and you would likely have gotten in trouble for walking around in less anyway.

The first night at the camp was actually quite amusing. I didn't get more than three hours sleep total. I never knew we had so many people prone to snoring in our company. Let me describe a typical five minutes of our night's slumber. The heater rattled loudly and obnoxiously on and off about every

---

13 A tributary of the Missouri River that flows through Montana

two minutes, and everyone was coughing because we were all sick due to the weather. And every night one of our companions let forth sounds that I have literally never, and I mean *never*, heard a human make before. We are talking about full-volume gurgling, snorting, growling, panting, tongue clicking—anything you can imagine.

I never knew a person could snore like that—the poor fellow sounded like he had a dying water buffalo stuck in his throat. Eventually everyone was laughing hysterically until he woke up wondering what was so funny. But he was merely one instrument among the orchestra. It seemed that the symphony played its best to the irregular rhythm of the heater. But we made it through each night, getting back to the barracks at around 2000 hours and waking at 0430 hours. I normally fell into a fitful sleep at around 0100.

One day we were bused way out to a rifle range with bellies full of runny powdered eggs, expired two percent milk, and orange drink. Our gear consisted of a combat vest with armor plating, Kevlar helmet, gas mask, and all the cold-weather gear we could don as it was absolutely frigid.

We arrived at the range and were briefed on the day's activities. It was decided we should break up into three platoons and form a wedge and move up to the firing line in turn, where we would shoot at pop-up targets. The whole thing lasted until about 1400, most of the time spent waiting for the other platoons to take their turn. We stood in the cold because the only warming facility was a small tent housing a tiny space heater connected to a propane bottle on the floor. When we got back we had our usual meetings and then were dismissed to do the nightly routine once again.

The next day, after a breakfast of sour milk and orange drink with boiled sausage patties, we were bused about 45 minutes to another range, the convoy driving range. We had a metal shed with no electricity as a warming hut this time, but they did provide a burn barrel stoked with a healthy fire to nourish the frozen soul.

Anyway, we were broken up into the same platoons, and this time the wait between training cycles was even longer. They brought in a dozen Humvees and a two-and-a-half ton truck for the exercise. When it was the second platoon's turn, we all got in our vehicles. I was a driver in the second Humvee with Captain Berry; Pete Butler was the gunner. Anyone not directly assigned a vehicle piled in where they could. We drove a dirt road loop that was about five miles long.

There were some great puddles, a couple of rivers to cross and some tight turns, always fun in a Humvee, those vehicles being virtually indestructible. About three-quarters of the way through, we were ambushed at Checkpoint 8. It was an unblocked ambush, so the procedures for convoy operation dictated that we keep driving. We did as we were trained and the passengers shot a few blanks here and there as we sped down the muddy trail. At about Checkpoint 12 we came across a roadblock so the convoy halted according to procedure, our team in Vehicle One trying to clear the road. Then we were ambushed again. It was quite realistic, so far as I can tell.

The ambush consisted of our trainers calling on the radio to tell us it was time for an ambush. At the roadblock pop-up targets appeared suddenly on the side of the road. Training dictated we dismount, take up our positions, and take down as many targets as we could. Even though our rifles were loaded with blanks it was still kind of fun.

The people in charge got to do a lot of talking on the radio. Our training supervisors came over to various people on the road, tapped them on the head, and said they were wounded, which gave us the opportunity to practice first aid and load the wounded onto stretchers.

After all this, we stood around for a good two hours after a review of our performance by the guys in charge. Then we went back to our barracks for another fun-filled evening of cold showers and the ceaseless snoring ensemble.

The next day was the same, only we got to use real ammunition. I hit a few targets, which made me feel better. I think the exercise went more smoothly and everyone got more out of it than the first time. When we got back to camp, we loaded up, and about three hours later we were on the road back to Ft. Knox.

That was it—training was over just like that.

Ahhh sleep, blessed is sleep and those who have the opportunity to enjoy it without a five-piece rock 'n roll snoring band.

I love you, baby.

**February 13, 2004**

Well, I am finally validated to go overseas once and for all. What that means is we all stood in line waiting to sign a piece of paper with the major's declaration that we have been properly trained and are officially prepared for war. Amazing. I find it terribly amusing how it all comes down to one signature. Just like enlistment, a mere shred of a tree changes everything irrevocably.

Yesterday and today were designated "Family Days." I wish I could have seen you. My loneliness felt like a pile of lead weights. Since I didn't have anything better to do, I went to dinner and had drinks with a few people. That helped make me feel better and I was able to pass the night a wee bit more comfortably.

Apparently everyone but about 20 of us will be flying to Camp Doha in Kuwait soon. I have to stay here and take care of some last-minute details and then, after the convoy, meet them in Balad. We have some new trucks coming in and God knows what else. When I get to Balad, I am going back down to Kuwait to link up with the trucks and equipment then convoy back up through Iraq. It feels kind of convoluted to me but I am assuming they have their reasons for it.

I heard a young woman crying in the hallway just a minute ago. Good-byes can be so tough. Also, a new guy arrived. His name is Bob Graves; I just met him while having a cigarette outside. He seems to be a great guy, perhaps someone I will become friends with.

I love you.

P.S. There are not many people here to trust and confide

in. I have many acquaintances but friends are few and far between. There are so many here who treat this whole thing like a boarding school.

## February 16, 2004

I'm sad, honey. Two things have hit me in the last two days.

Yesterday the majority of the unit—all but 28 of us—left for Kuwait. There were many anxious faces and more than a bit of crying, the good-byes being tense and somewhat fearful. I tried to say good-bye to most of the people I know but just couldn't get to all of them. The reality of what we are about to embark on has really set in, the beginning of a journey into an uncharted realm of unparalleled dangers, trials beyond our imagining, and facing our darkest enemy buried deeply within, hopefully to emerge born anew, with more experience, more wisdom... if we emerge at all.

Captain Berry's family left right before the rest of the company departed. I found him sitting in his room, silently crying with his head in his hands. Shortly after, I found Mike in the hallway. He had just gotten off the phone with his wife and kids and was watery eyed. I spoke with him briefly and my own eyes began to tear. I felt as if we were all kin at that moment. I know I'll be joining them in a few weeks but I didn't realize how close I had become to each of them. Seeing them depart worries, even saddens me. I don't want to be without them, to not be there for them if they need help.

It's strange. When you're with your comrades, they get on your nerves and you just want to be left alone. Then when they go, part of your heart goes with them. I hope my friends stay safe. I'm sick of war already. I see how it tears people apart. Damn the assholes who create these situations. The world must learn a better way to handle its problems.

For the 28 left behind, it's only a matter of time. We have all resolved to make the most of this gift of time because it *is* a gift.

It's so quiet here now.

I moved my belongings to the first floor with the rest of my remaining company. Brandon Carr and I took Room 114. Brandon is tall with broad shoulders and has been a good friend so far. He's a little sloppy but he respects my space and personal items. He's an E-5[14] and is very friendly and fun, a person you can hang out and laugh with.

I'm living in luxury now. Brandon brought down his laptop, color TV, and coffee maker, and we set the room up really nicely. Astounding what a few creature comforts will do for the soul. That brings me to the other reason for my sadness. We have a color TV in our room, complete with a cable hookup bootlegged from the remnants of someone else's "backyard" connection. I managed to catch a movie yesterday evening and it was set in Montana. God, it made me feel homesick. The images of the mountains, trees, the shining swift water of a mountain stream,

---

14  A sergeant in the U.S. Army

the openness of the big blue sky and the expanse of wildflowers tugged at my heart and made me cry. I miss the quiet of the meadows with the aspens shimmering in the sun, the smell of fresh pine, a chipmunk darting out in front of me on a trail.

I loved getting your email today. I agree that life is about the little things like our Friday nights on the couch, our walks, our once-a-week movie tradition, and the road trips we've taken. I've felt comfort looking at you and knowing exactly how you're feeling and thinking—even if my certitude sometimes pisses you off. We really *do* get each other don't we? You're the best, baby. I wish I could hold you.

I miss walking with you too. I long to lie in a field with you and watch the clouds drift by. I want to sit on a rock, close my eyes, and feel the peace of the fresh air, the clean sunshine. I want to watch a thunderstorm steadily advance across a valley. To feel the charge when a lightning bolt strikes miles away and the sudden drop in temperature that heralds rain. Seconds later the thunder hits, grumbling in your bones and the breeze begins to bluster through the grass.

Serenity.

I want to drive on some lonely back road with you. To break the crest of a hill, a lone house appearing among the fields stacked with bales of hay, a dust cloud billowing from behind the tires of our old truck and your smile glowing in the passenger seat. I feel as if my life can begin again when I come home.

Speaking of home, before the others left, I happened to have a conversation with Jakob about the politics of the Montana

Army Guard. It seems as if certain people in our unit back home are weaseling out of their deployment, as my CSM put it. But I'm not going into it. It's just not worth it. I've never liked politics. I never will. I don't like bureaucratic mouthpieces either. Leave me out of their petty little games. So they are not worth one more word in my journal. At least they've helped me reaffirm that I made the right choice when I decided to support my comrades.

I found out that Mike told Jakob about the conscientious objection paperwork I tore up before we left Helena. He said he respected the fact I had the guts to stand up for what I believe in. He said courage would carry me a long way and I hope he's right. And he asked why I didn't go through with it. After a moment's pause I said I didn't want to let down the people who are going to Iraq. I'll stand by him and the others through thick and thin regardless of my personal beliefs. Jakob said he was impressed.

I love you.

### February 25, 2004

Well, here I sit on duty. I'm pulling a CQ or Charge of Quarters shift—12 fucking hours (1800 to 0600) of sitting here in the dismal office we have haphazardly put together, manning the phone and listening to NPR on a portable radio.

The Texas people, more personnel who are supposed to supplement and complete our ranks, have just arrived. Better late than never I suppose. There are about 20 or so in all. I haven't really talked to any of them so I don't know what they're like.

Some of the boys are watching porn, just passing the time.

The remaining trucks and equipment are ready.

*We* are ready to go.

I love you.

# Part Two

# Road Trips

*Do not be afraid; our fate cannot be taken from us.*
*It is a gift.*

—Dante Alighieri, *The Divine Comedy*

## March 10, 2004

GOD, IT SEEMS AS IF it's been forever since I have written anything in my journal. I'm in Kuwait now. We left two days ago, a morning flight, and it went like this:

On March 6, we were ordered to have all our bags ready to go by 1900 hours the next day. So on the evening of the seventh we stood in formation, our previously merry, drunken faces now sobered by the prospect of entering the unknown. After the formation we broke up into small groups, chatting and smoking until the MPs[15]arrived at midnight with German shepherds. We watched as the dogs methodically snuffled our bags, confirming we weren't carrying any sort of contraband.

At 0100 hours our old white buses arrived for a final time and drove us to a gymnasium. Here we waited for an hour or so before we were driven to the airport. It ended up being a long night of waiting, isolated and confined due to security precautions. They didn't want any of us getting into trouble—drinking, hiding last-minute contraband, perhaps even going AWOL. Eventually we were allowed to board and the plane left the ground at 0800.

What an incredibly long flight.

---

15   Military Police

First we flew to New Jersey to pick up an outbound MP unit from Ft. Dix. That filled our MD-11[16] to the maximum and I believe we all felt a bit cramped. Then we flew from New Jersey to a joint U.S./NATO air base named Rhein-Main in Frankfurt, Germany, the flight taking about 9 hours. It's an immense ocean, the Atlantic and I remember looking out the window, acutely absorbing the last scenery from the United States that I suspect I'll see for a long time.

I watched Cape Cod slowly drift by from 30,000 feet, the landscape clearly visible, until my nose was pressed up against the window, vainly trying to memorize the last speck of land as it disappeared from view. Below was the endless Atlantic Ocean, the big pond, small white breakers dotting the rich blue waters. I settled back in my seat, closed my eyes, and felt surprisingly calm.

We were headed into an unfamiliar, dangerous foreign land, but I felt only a speck of fear deep in the pit of my stomach. There was no turning back now, nothing left to do but live out the deployment, do my job, and support the people around me the best I could. There was no point in worrying about it any more—I was on my way. My mission now was to come home alive and well.

Rhein-Main, established in 1945, is often called the "Gateway to Europe." It supports us transients on our way to distant lands—these days, mostly to the Middle East. We spent about two hours at the base while our plane was refueled. Then

---

16   A jetliner similar to a DC-10

we reboarded to make the six-hour flight to Kuwait.

As we got closer and closer to the Middle East, I watched the sun rise over the desert. I had never seen such an expanse of flat tan and brown before. Among that ocean of sand and rock were miniature blotches of green or an occasional tree—perhaps signaling an oasis being fed by an underground spring for there was barely any water to be seen, only a small river here and there snaking its way through the landscape. It was mesmerizing. The sun was so bright, so golden, bathing the countryside in a transparent cloak of light; it took my breath away.

We landed at Camp Wolverine in Kuwait at about 1000 hours.

Camp Wolverine, ahh what can I say—it's a glorious place. Perched right on the Persian Gulf, the ocean water stinging the arid desert air with its salty smell, Camp Wolverine is the main entry point for most if not all of the U.S. forces in the region. It was about 120 degrees when we landed—it felt like I was sticking my head in an oven. It was *so* hot. There's no vegetation of any kind and no animals—only people, dust, heat, and endless tents. It's a hot, bleak place and I wasn't sorry to see it disappear behind the horizon.

We were immediately bused to a tent some ways from the airfield where our baggage was unloaded and we received a safety briefing. The major and Top soon arrived to welcome us. Our baggage was loaded onto buses and we drove to Camp Virginia some ways away.

Camp Virginia was established with a combat-ready

battalion of soldiers shortly after Operation Desert Storm back in the '90s as part of our mission to protect Kuwait. It also trains service members for possible future wars against Iraq. That's where I am right now, but it looks as if my traveling days aren't over. In a couple days I will be going to Camp Doha near Kuwait City, where I will be helping with the equipment and trucks due to arrive by ship on or around the 18th. After that mission has been completed, I'm pretty sure I'll be convoying up to Camp Anaconda. That's the plan—for now at least. We'll see how it goes; things always change.

I have to admit, I'm incredibly awe-inspired by my travels so far. I've never traveled overseas before and it felt as if I was stepping onto the moon when we landed in Germany. It was like a whole different planet—writing on the bathroom walls in English *and* German, strange uniforms, accents, smells, even the chairs felt different somehow. I'm sure I had that "deer in the headlights" look.

I've learned these camps are called *kabals*. It's an Arabic term for "fortress" and here are some things I've observed so far in Camp Virginia and Camp Wolverine:

1.  Invitations scrawled on the port-a-john walls from men to women to have sex at varying times and places.

2.  An old Mercedes truck used to clean the port-a-johns that had a battered Arabic license plate on it, orange background with black lettering. I had never seen an Arabic license plate before.

3. The long, jostling, sweaty, body odor-filled bus ride to Camp Virginia from Camp Wolverine, the driver blasting Arabic music for our entertainment.

4. Arabic servers yelling in their native tongue in the mess hall.

5. Rows upon rows of tents and equipment pitched on a never-ending sea of wind-rippled sand.

6. Soldiers playing cards on a bunk to pass the time.

7. Carrying a rifle everywhere I go and casually hanging it next to my bunk as if I did that every day.

8. Watching the sand blow across the tops of the tents, twisting dust plumes angrily rising high into the air.

9. A blood-red, monstrously huge sunset that rippled on the horizon with the last blazes of the day's heat.

10. A cool evening with a full bright moon, my profile clearly shadowed on the ground.

11. The constant hum of an Army generator.

12. Endless lines to the phones, the mess hall—everywhere.

13. Constant activity even at 0300.

14. An occasional lone palm tree or shrub alongside the thin two-lane road through the middle of nowhere.

15. A blazing sun filtered through the dust.

16. Waiting for a truck to fill the shower trailer's water tanks.

17. A five-ton personnel truck rumbling by with grimy, grim-faced soldiers in the back.

18. Newly formed couples strolling along improvised gravel trails.

19. The American flag billowing in a steady, dusty breeze amid a sea of tents.

20. Hundreds of water bottles stacked on pallets.

21. Hand sanitizer dispensers by every port-a-john station.

22. Soldiers checking weapons, carrying pistols.

23. Sandbag guard stations with armed soldiers.

24. Concertina or "razor ribbon" wire fences.

25. Humvees driving by with a couple of soldiers on some errand.

26. Soldiers busily modifying their trucks with steel plates in an effort to protect themselves from IEDs planted along a convoy route.

27. The light from the sun seeming different somehow—brighter, whiter.

28. The clunk of my boots on the plywood flooring of our tent.

29. How my boonie cap[17] and sunglasses are more than essentials in this place.

---

17  A floppy wide-brimmed hat often worn by the U.S. military in hot climates

30. The smell of the mess hall's unfrozen breaded veal patties drifting over the desert air.

31. The overwhelming moisture and steam from the mess hall.

32. A soldier squatting in his sandbag guard station and glaring as if he hated the world around him.

33. The silhouette of a camel on the horizon.

34. The beads of sweat on everyone's brow.

35. Coughing in the wake of a Humvee's dust.

36. Smiling when the sun sets—it's blessedly cool!

I'm not entirely sure I've wrapped my head around being here yet. It's all so absolutely fucking amazing. They are saying this is the biggest troop movement the U.S. has undertaken since World War II. I am part of living history.

I just got word we are going to be here at Camp Virginia for at least a couple more days and will be traveling to Camp Doha soon—a solid date is still to be determined. I kinda figured that was the case. Since the dockyards are close by, it will be very convenient for us to get our trucks and equipment ready after everything has been unloaded. In the meantime we're going to play a lot of cards and wait in the desert heat.

I love you.

**March 13, 2004**

Well, I have moved to Camp Doha. I should be here for two or three weeks, waiting for the ships with our equipment and trucks to be docked so we can unload them and prepare for the trip north. The shipyard is about an hour and a half west of here on the Persian Gulf.

A few more thoughts about Camp Virginia:

It's out in the middle of nowhere, about a two-hour drive from Kuwait City. The camp is surrounded by desolate sand with the occasional clumps of dry grass, shrubs, perhaps a small tree. There are a few nomadic shepherds outside the perimeter with camels and/or flocks of sheep numbering sometimes more than 50. They typically wear cloth hats and long robes and recently I saw one carrying a tall staff or walking stick. The desert is the dominant landscape and is so incredibly flat that you can see for what seems like 50 miles, maybe more if the dust doesn't make the horizon hazy.

It's astoundingly crowded with soldiers and obscenely long lines anywhere you go. The base is comprised mainly of tents with a few trailers scattered here and there. The trailers comprise the PX,[18] the Cyber Café where we are allowed 15 minutes of Internet use at a time, a barbershop, the mess hall, a small ice cream parlor, a small sandwich/Chinese take-out restaurant, and telephones. Everything else, including the finance building and post office, is in tents. The trailers and tents are air-conditioned

---

18   Post Exchange—retail stores on U.S. military bases

and powered by huge Army generators that hum with an unwavering consistency. Some people find it irritating, but I have found that the hum combined with the heat puts me to sleep rather quickly.

The barracks tents can easily hold 40 people each and if you look down one of the hastily graveled roads in that area of the camp, it seems as if there are never-ending rows of them. They're open bay with plywood flooring that is always covered with a thin layer of dust. The bunks are the cheapest, ricketiest metal things I have ever seen. You close your eyes wondering if they will collapse on you in the middle of the night.

The wind blows incessantly, which makes those beautiful ripples of sand but is a real nuisance when you step out of the shower trailer and you're dirty within two minutes. There is always dust and grit in your ears and it often turns your hair a different color, however, the dust does make for beautiful sunsets because of all the particles in the air. The shower facilities are trailers with big tanks that have to be filled nearly every day by a Mercedes semi driven by Kuwaiti nationals. Inside there is always mud on the floor and the water runs out about half the time. They just can't keep up.

The toilet facilities are port-a-johns scattered everywhere on base and they are nothing to brag about. Toilet paper has become a precious commodity and there are hand sanitizer dispensers outside every port-a-john. It's a good idea to use them.

The Kuwaitis here on base do a lot of the menial tasks. They also run a few makeshift stores where you can buy Zippos, singing stuffed animals, stuffed camel dolls, watches, necklaces—any little trinket they can sell. They are mostly firm on their prices but are *sometimes* willing to negotiate if you happen to be a savvy haggler.

The Cyber Café is neat. There are about 50 computers along the wall and you can use them for free. You have two options: make an appointment and come back or stand in line for hours. (I chose to make appointments.) You are allowed about 15 minutes to a half-hour, but the computers are so slow it can be difficult to send a single email before your time is up. I didn't bother with the phones—it's expensive on the old calling card and the lines are more than obnoxious.

The PX has a very limited supply of things—PT gear, sodas, music, and a few snacks. Again, the line is unbearably long and I tolerated it only once. The post office is a huge tent surrounded by concertina wire and can handle any package. Personal letters are free to mail but packages require shipping and handling payments. And they only take cash—something I found amusing because there are no ATMs on base. I don't know anyone who carries a wad of cash around the desert with them.

There are guard posts at each entrance to the base, bunkers fortified with sandbags and plywood and manned by two machine gunners. Concrete barriers are everywhere. They say Camp Virginia is a safe zone but we were warned that the "enemy" is still watching us. It gives you a weird "look behind you, there's someone staring at you" feeling. You're constantly aware that you're under scrutiny of some sort.

Since the camp is a major staging point, there is a constant flow of troops coming in and out. You always see at least one group with their trucks lined up, checking their weapons and equipment and smoking cigarettes. Regardless of the time of day or week, there is constant activity.

I was only at Camp Virginia for a few days before my ride to Camp Doha. We played cards and slept a lot. I think it was jetlag and the strain of being in a new place. On the 11th, about 20 of us were picked up by Top and driven to Doha to wait for the ships. Within the next few days, the remaining people at Camp Virginia were flown to Balad to officially join our company and begin work at our assigned base, so I'm part of the stay-behind crew again. I don't mind though, I'm getting to see so much of the country.

It was just about 1700 hours on March 11 when a small bus with Iraqi plates and a five-ton Army truck arrived to take us to Camp Doha. We knew it was coming and I was already packed. We left the camp and went south, at first traveling along a small road with no lines whatsoever. None of the back roads in Kuwait are lined and it's amusing to see everyone driving in whatever space they want. I've heard there is a speed limit, but I have yet to see a sign.

Anyway, the side of the road is mainly desert with scattered bits of vegetation that feed the nomads' herds of sheep. Most of the landscape was barren and dusty, and there was hardly a mound of dirt to distract from the miles of flat sand. Through most of the drive it was partly cloudy but the sunset was beautiful, a deep orange-red. The moon and sun are so damn big on the horizon here. Astounding.

We eventually came to a main highway—the road signs were in English *and* Arabic, pretty wild. Oh, and I also saw the "Boneyard," the infamous area where all the bombed-out trucks and vehicles were dumped after the Gulf War. Hundreds of scorched relics baking in the desert next to the highway, some almost unrecognizable as the mighty machines of war they once were.

The story is that back in the '90s, after Iraq invaded Kuwait, the Iraqi army was pushed back by American forces along the main road leading out of Kuwait City. It became known as the "Highway of Death" because of all the carnage and I had an eerie feeling that I was passing through a battle zone haunted by ghosts. A prickly, supernatural feeling formed at the base of my neck and I shuddered slightly as I gazed at that immense field of wreckage.

When the fighting was over, the bodies were removed and the vehicles were dumped here in the desert. They had no other place to dispose of them and this was chosen for its remoteness and open space. From what I've heard there are no plans to clean up the mess. Supposedly these wrecks are contaminated with depleted uranium, radiation still emanating from their broken skeletons.

Soon after passing that mournful cemetery I saw a small, dilapidated shop, a kind of convenience store with heaps of junk and garbage around it. Next we came to a huge gathering area where supposedly everyone from the region meets—kinda like a flea market. There were a few palm trees—a welcome sight after so much desolation—and at least a hundred cars parked in a huge lot on the side of the road. Some people were milling around. Others were kneeling on blankets, chanting and praying, prostrating themselves before God with their foreheads touching the ground. It was very dramatic.

Before we knew it, we were on a main highway that led to Kuwait City and eventually Camp Doha. Quite suddenly we were in an urban area, the blank expanse of the desert rapidly disappearing behind us. There were temples, dance clubs, stores, and 10,000-square-foot mansions.

The streets were lined with shrubs and landscaped palm trees. Cars, most of them BMWs, zipped every which way. Gosh, these people just do whatever the hell they want on the roads. We had more than a few near-collisions and anyone who's scared by American drivers should never go to Kuwait.

A car with a Kuwaiti family with two of the cutest children I've ever seen passed us. They were leaning on their father, smiling and waving to us. Occasionally we would see a guy just standing on the side of the highway staring, slack-jawed at the traffic—that was kinda unnerving. The city was lit up brightly and I saw a couple of nightclubs with Mercedes and BMWs parked out front. I could almost imagine the Kuwaiti rich folk clubbin' and partyin' the warm desert night away. Then we passed the security checkpoints and drove into Camp Doha.

Camp Doha.

I honestly didn't know what to expect, but Doha is absolutely huge and the security is highly regimented. There are more than 10,000 people on this base, which has been around for more than 10 years. It has a giant air-conditioned PX with an Arabic rug store, ATMs, a movie theater, and a large food court consisting of a Subway, a Kentucky Fried Chicken, a Starbucks, a donut shop, and a pizza place.

We are staying in a big warehouse—and believe it or not, my bed is fairly comfortable! Best of all there is no wind and dust although you can tell we're on the coast because it's not only hot, but humid. The bathroom facilities are better than at Camp Virginia—I have yet to run out of water and the showers are in trailers that line a street about 100 yards from my warehouse.

You can get your laundry washed and folded by the Filipino nationals who wait outside the laundromats. The price is negotiable and they do a decent job. I gave one man a $10 bill to do mine. I figure Americans have it good enough that I can pay 10 bucks for laundry.

Down the street from us is a little nightclub that shows movies and serves fake beer—there is no alcohol of any kind allowed here. I tried some of the fake Budweiser and it sucked so badly I couldn't even drink it. It tasted like water squeezed through lawnmower shavings.

Just like at Camp Virginia, there is constant activity here. I haven't seen too much of the base as we have been sticking to the warehouse and the PX while waiting for the ships to come in. They should be here soon—around the 18th.

One really nice thing is that I can get on the Internet fairly regularly here. Everything we need is right within a few blocks of the warehouse, so we sit here waiting.

I love you.

**March 14, 2004**

Some thoughts for the day.

I am being indoctrinated into a whole new way of life, a way of life not only foreign to me (I feel so ignorant and overwhelmed) but also to the Kuwaiti people, who have encountered numerous, arrogant, even spoiled Americans at this point. We're all thrown into the mix here, largely oblivious to the whims of politicians hundreds if not thousands of miles away. We are much more focused on the here and now, on what is really important to *us* regardless of the politics involved—striving to make it home or providing for our loved ones. For us, politics is superficial to our everyday reality of just living this thing out so we can get the hell out of here.

Perhaps that's the difference between people who do the dirty work of war and those who dream up policy in an office on Capitol Hill. It seems to me that you can make anything look good on paper, but the result is often quite different when you have to execute it. It's the difference between reality and theory.

It's my feeling that we, as people, should all be continually evaluating our actions. We should always be striving to put ourselves in the shoes of the people in our lives, the people we encounter randomly, or the people we may not even know so that we can be better, more open-hearted people. I think we need to be more aware of the people we may be making decisions for or with—decisions that affect not only the soldiers, seamen, airmen, or Marines but their families, friends, and colleagues—anyone who has at least a rudimentary relationship with those who may serve in a war or are in our lives in general. We need to be more aware of how our decisions will affect the world.

I think what I am reaching for is that ultimately, all of us regardless of ethnicity, religion, culture, or gender must open our closed, often fearful, even angry hearts and have compassion and love for one another. It seems to me that this is the only way for us to pull it together as a species and stop fighting for the exclusive rights to some allegorical water hole. We need to understand that we're ants in the universal scheme of things, that we must compassionately accept everything that makes us different and everything that makes us the same so we can conquer the challenges that will determine our future. We must understand that we're all in this together and that embracing our collective togetherness is the only path forward for us. It's the only path toward a peaceful world and selfishness, greed, ignorance, arrogance, corruption, and warfare don't do anything but contribute to an absolute downfall. I can't imagine anyone wanting that.

I love and miss you.

### March 15, 2004

Well, we are still waiting for the ships to come in.

I have to admit, I've enjoyed this brief hiatus from work and stress, although I am becoming restless. There is nothing to distract your mind here, nothing to do but wait, which can make the minutes seem like hours.

I should be leaving Doha in a week or so, after our equipment and trucks have been unloaded and prepared for the 400-mile convoy through enemy territory.

It might just end up being a long year. Oh well, I'm here now and there is no turning back.

I love you. Tonight I'll dream of a sweet life together.

### March 15, 2004 continued

I wonder what use I'll be when I arrive in Balad. I've been thinking lately and in my four years with the Army National Guard, I have never really felt I fit in, sometimes even feeling useless and on regular drill weekends there was never anything to do. I've felt inadequate, a nagging feeling that seemed to quietly snicker in my ear that my time would be better spent elsewhere. And I've discovered that the feeling is still with me in Kuwait.

Although the Army has been interesting and enlightening in a few ways—I *have* enjoyed the travel and meeting people from all backgrounds—I want to do so much more. What I decide to do will be on my terms as soon as I'm discharged. I want to be free of the confines of an organization that leaves me little fulfillment and sweeps me up in decisions I wholeheartedly disagree with. I want to make smarter decisions about my life.

I feel more strongly than ever that I should continue writing. I want to write these journals for me, for you, for our children when they perhaps decide they too want to join the military. It does run in my family after all. My relatives have fought in every war this country has engaged in right back to the American Revolution.

There is a humongous rock plaque situated outside the town hall where my father's side of the family settled. It's inscribed with the names of every citizen of that town who fought for our country. My father and I visited the plaque one day and he showed me all of our veteran relatives. His name was there too since he fought in Korea. I was amazed. I had no idea my family had shed so much blood for America. There were a couple who fought in the Revolution, a couple in the Civil War, several in World Wars I and II, some in Korea and Vietnam. Okay, so perhaps not every war, but more than enough.

My maternal grandfather also fought. He was a World War I veteran. Now there was a character. Often troubled and restless, he ran away when he was 14 and became an honest-to-God hobo, hopping freight trains and playing poker to make a little money so he could see what was around the next bend of the track. Then he joined the Army and met my grandmother. I've been told he was a good shot with a rifle. Incredible isn't it?

It's important for me to document this. I want us to be able to tell our future children that this experience made our union stronger. You know that I've always enjoyed writing and loved every author who whisked me away to different places in my mind. The books I read as a child taught me to dream and I fondly remember all of them. You know how many books I have, my dear. I wouldn't give them up for anything. They gave me the chance to stretch my imagination—to live adventures in exotic places, to meet strange and interesting characters from all walks of life, to laugh, fall in love, or feel loss. Sometimes their varied perspectives helped me to expand my concept of the world.

Through reading, and writing for that matter, I've come to understand that it's not appropriate for me to think that I'm always right. Honestly considering someone else's opinions leads to a greater breadth of comprehension, compassion, and empathy. In short, books have given me insight and knowledge. Isn't that the magic of books?

I've always dreamed of being a writer. It's been a goal of mine since I was 10 years old, awkwardly pecking away at my mother's old manual typewriter, writing my very first short story. In all truthfulness it wasn't much of a story, but writing it got me hooked.

It's incredible to realize how dreams or goals are often displaced by the challenges of daily life as the years go by. We often become lost—directionless, like I was. I want to change that now. I feel as if I am finding that direction after all the years of trying different things. And to think my direction was right in front of me the entire time since I was a child.

I just want to inform someone who is interested. I want to tell them what it's like to be a soldier, to be deployed—all the feelings, circumstances, activity, pain, sorrow, excitement, boredom, every aspect that could resonate with someone who might want to make a real difference in this world.

I don't know, baby. I can't truly explain why or how I know it's important to keep filling these journals. I just feel it in my bones that this work will become significant in some way.

I love you very much, my wife.

### March 17, 2004

Well, we are still waiting for the ships.

I've heard they will be in tonight around 1900 hours, so tomorrow should be a working day. It's almost a relief.

On another note, I heard that the Air Force dropped a 2,000-pound bomb less than a half-mile from Camp Anaconda. Apparently it scared the shit out of everyone up there. There are also rumors that the base is getting hit by several mortar attacks each day. Once or twice the mortars have exploded within the living area, so close to the trailers and tents that debris flies everywhere. Sounds like fun. I also heard that an Iraqi rebel—sorry, "insurgent"—made it past the second guard post with an RPG[19] and managed to inflict some serious damage, injuring

---

19 Rocket-Propelled Grenade

some soldiers on guard duty. That's not very comforting at all.

We are going to the port tomorrow around 0800. We've been told to wear our full "battle rattle"—full battle gear including ballistic vests.[20]

How did I get myself into this mess?

I love you.

## March 18, 2004

Today we got up early and put on our ballistic vests, grabbed our rifles and helmets, and headed out. We all thought our ship had come in, so to speak. We drove about an hour to the port, circling the Gulf and I got a nice view of Kuwait City from across the water. There were numerous skyscrapers and quite a bit of smog but what stood out most were the massive complexes of power lines strung this way and that. We also passed some oil fields and storage containers, rows upon rows of them, and I couldn't help but wonder just how much money is sloshing around in those tanks.

We got to the port and stood around for 45 minutes waiting for the officers to figure out what was going on. It turned out the ship wasn't even docked yet and they wouldn't start unloading until sometime around 1500. Eventually the officers decided we should get lunch at Camp Arifjan. I had the scallops and rice.

After lunch, the officers were again forced to decide what to do. After considerable deliberation they called it a day and we

---

20   A bulletproof vest

came home to our warehouse at Camp Doha to start the whole thing over again at 0700 tomorrow. Hopefully the ships will be ready by then and we'll be able to get this shit over with. It was a typical Army day and we enlisted folk had fun on the bus. The continual "busting" on the part of the officers was classic; Top just had a ball raggin' on them. And rightfully so—to put it in Army terms, they "gaggle fucked" the entire day.

On another front, I've heard Congress wants to increase our basic pay. I suppose that does *something* to ease the building resentment I feel toward my government for authorizing this war, but I can't quite get over the nagging feeling that all my buddies, family, friends, and I are nothing but cattle to them, nothing but a collection of voters whose only purpose is to get them into office.

Our government officials seem removed from the average American as if they are elite in some way and I often feel as if they think they can play by their own rules, that the rules we average people have to play by don't apply to them. Rather unsettling if you ask me. A government detached from the public is not what our founding fathers intended. Abuse of power and corruption are rampant and that makes me sad for the present and future of my country.

I wish I could do something to stop this war. We all know... all of us over here... that this war should never have been started. We all know that the justification for this war was misleading. Most of us feel the American public has bought into propaganda promulgated by a few in power who've put their egos and/or wallets first.

Now that it has begun, the war machine will inevitably grind on. It's easy to start a war, not so easy to end one. How many people must die for a nonexistent cause? How many years will be wasted? It's my firm belief that this won't be over quickly and that's a shame. America will be involved with Iraq much more intimately from now on, perhaps indefinitely. Imagine that.

This war is likely to have serious consequences to America, the American taxpayer, and all those who are serving. At least in World War II, we fought for a definitive, righteous cause. Over here, we don't feel that and we're confused. It seems this is more of a politician's war than anything else—another Vietnam. And I have no choice but to participate unless I favor the stockade.

It's agonizing to be forced to play a part in something I know is wrong.

I love you so very much, baby.

### March 19, 2004

Today we finally got to the port.

The trucks and equipment were unloaded from the ship last night and deposited in what amounted to a big parking lot. When we arrived, we were supposed to drive the trucks to Camp Arifjan where they will stay until they are loaded onto other trucks to go to Balad. It sounds strange, doesn't it? What are we going to need them for at Camp Anaconda? To go sightseeing through the Iraqi countryside? It seems like a waste of taxpayer money.

Regardless, we have only 20 people and you need two people per vehicle. Since there were 37 trucks to move we had to make two round trips. We got up at 0600 and didn't finish until 2200 hours. It made for a fun day but by the end of it everyone was tired and cranky. Tomorrow I have to help bring five trucks up to Camp Virginia for another unit to borrow. I just can't get over this road tripping madness—back and forth, back and forth.

Oh, and I'm going to make it a point not to forget my sunglasses. I got a bunch of sand in my eyes today. That sucked.

It rained last night. Yes, it actually rained! It woke me up with its insistent, thunderous drumming on the warehouse roof at 0300. It was so loud, I'm surprised anyone could sleep. There was even a good crack of thunder that rattled the walls. The air had an acrid smell, like it smells in Utah or Arizona when it rains.

I love you, baby.

### March 21, 2004

Yesterday I went on a road trip… this time to Camp Virginia. Twelve of us made the trip from Camp Arifjan. It was a beautiful ride. I got to really see Kuwait City, filled with spires reaching for the sky, palm trees, night clubs, shops, vendors, and many stunning houses. There was a ton of traffic—everyone fighting for positions, horns honking, people bustling here and there—it's such an active, vibrant city. Of course we ended up in one of the traffic jams, joining the chorus of horns. To be honest, I never knew there were that many people in Kuwait. I was impressed with the architecture and the people. It was great to be in a foreign land, albeit viewing the culture from a distance, but it was enthralling nevertheless.

I also got to see the darker, "slummier" side of Kuwait City. I'd always thought the Kuwaitis were rich but there is a part of the community that is definitely poor. We saw trash all over the side of the road, people picking through dumpsters. Men in rags were sitting on the stoop of a tremendous house staring vacantly at passersby. It seems no matter where you go there are haves and have-nots. I saw cars littered along the highway, all damaged in some form, one with its entire front end bashed in.

When we got to Camp Arifjan I was to be a co-driver, my M-16 loaded with 30 rounds because even though we are in Kuwait there is always the possibility of some sort of attack. It's easy to become complacent down here and life can be so casual but I am still in a combat zone. We drove a five-ton, pulling a big 50-foot flatbed semitrailer and it was about 80 miles to Camp Virginia, but the ride was pleasant enough.

So our little convoy went north, Top dutifully trailing us in our bus. The highlight of the trip was taking a wrong turn that landed us on a big-ass hill that seemed to overlook all of Kuwait.

We stopped at the top of the hill to figure out where we

were and how to get to Camp Virginia. It turns out this is the highest point in Kuwait and the very road Saddam Hussein used to invade. Wow... you could see clear down to the ocean, a few smoggy cities dotting the horizon here and there. The sky was a beautiful blue right overhead but closer to the horizon it turned whiter with a touch of dingy brownish-grey, the pollution bending the light and causing a refractive glare. And the sun was so bright, almost blinding, like it is in the Arizona desert. I got a picture of me there that I'll have to send to you, honey.

Eventually we sorted everything out and completed the drive to Camp Virginia. The facilities looked the same but it seemed as if everyone had left. Gone were the lines and crowds, the constant grumble of trucks on a mission, and the steady hum of most of the generators had been silenced. It was a barren cluster of empty tents in an empty desert, a despondent wind rippling the sand at every angle. I guess a lot of people had come and gone to wherever they'd been ordered to be. God bless the war machine.

Come to find out, the unit that wanted to borrow our trucks didn't need them with the trailer we hauled—they needed two trailers of a different type. Typical. So after about an hour of debate, the officers scratching their heads, four of their guys got on our bus with us and we went back to Arifjan, but not without getting a little sandwich from their snack bar first. Oh, and we drove by the Boneyard again. I'm still in awe at its sheer size and the utter devastation. We also passed the Ali Al Salem

Air Base, a Kuwaiti base that we'll probably fly out of when our deployment is finally over.

So we arrived at Camp Arifjan and the four guys from the other unit got the right trucks. The sun was starting to set and my ass was tired from sitting all day. They followed us to the main road then turned in their own direction as we took the southern road back to Camp Doha.

My, the sunset was gorgeous. It streaked the sky with a brilliant, shimmering deep orange. The sun looked like a monstrous piece of glowing fruit dropping off the face of the earth with dramatic flair.

I love you, baby. God, I miss you so much. I don't want to waste any more precious moments. You wanna go on a road trip? Let's get in the car and just go somewhere. Maybe we could find a place where there are no people, no crowds—just you and me. Whattya think?

You're such a beautiful person with a great heart, my wife. I do love getting your emails. They warm my heart with your sincerity, your love... our love. Today's was wonderful; it made my heart gush. Now that I've been over here a while, I fully realize how lucky we are—or how lucky I am to have you. Sometimes you seem so far away but I always keep you close in my heart. It consoles me. I can't wait to grow old with you, but that never takes away from my desire to enjoy every moment until then.

And you're right, you know. We *are* the richest people in the world. Others have nothing on us. I thought it was so sweet of you to say you have no regrets, that you would die a happy woman if it happened tomorrow because you know you have been loved by someone more than anyone could possibly love another. It gives me peace and comfort as well, my dear. Like you, I feel we were meant to be together. Our souls are connected. They reached out for each other... found each other. And I agree, my dear—let us never allow the temptations and confusions this world throws at us destroy the connection we have. We truly would be lost, wouldn't we? When people talk to me about the problems in their lives, it helps me fully realize how good we have it.

I wouldn't say we've ever been big fighters and most of our fights have been about stupid shit. I don't want to fight like that any more. Time is too precious. *You* are too precious to me. When I look back on our little arguments, I'm filled with regret—not a single one of them seems necessary or worthwhile now. Oh, here I go getting all mushy again. I can't help it. You know I've always been an emotional one, forever pulled by the tidal passions of my heart.

To lie in bed together and sleep in on a Sunday afternoon, to get up and take our dog for a walk sounds like the best thing I could do right now. I often think about the time just before I left when we were walking her. It was cold and I was throwing snow on her nose, getting her all riled up. I remember you smiling at us as we cavorted under the winter sun. Goddamn, what a pretty girl you are.

I miss and love you with all my heart.

**March 22, 2004**

I spent the day rereading Mark Twain's *The Adventures of Tom Sawyer* and occasionally checking my email to see if you had written. It always makes me melancholy when I check and there's no message from you. I long to hear all the news from home and imagine it's your voice I'm hearing as I read the words. It's as if when I get on the computer, I am with you.

Throughout the days, I find myself daydreaming of our life together. I can vividly see our bedroom, the moon filtering through our white sill window with half-drawn shades. All is silent—a few lights twinkling from homes across the field behind our house. You are asleep, wrapped in that fluffy down comforter you love so much, breathing softly into your pillow. Our cats are downstairs, munching on a snack or sneaking a drink from the water glass I left next to the sink.

I remember all the times I tried to be as silent as possible when slipping into our bed so as to not disturb your peaceful slumber. I'd wrap myself in the warmth of our bed and you'd shift almost imperceptibly. Can you imagine what it's like to relive moments like this on a daily basis, not knowing how long it will be before I can live them again?

Sometimes it's beyond agony to know that my independence has been sacrificed to the war machine known as the United States. Like I signed my life over when I handed over the enlistment paperwork on that gorgeous spring afternoon. I desperately want it back.

My life seems so very far away right now.

A roster was passed around the other day and I put in for leave time. It gave me something to look forward to, some glimmer of hope and light at the end of a long tunnel. Between now and then seems like an eternity, and then there will be yet so many more miles before we can rejoice at our reunion.

For what purpose has God or a higher power sent me upon this road?

Sometimes when I look around me, at the people I live with, at the crowds eating dinner in the mess hall, at the endless streams of Humvees filled with stone-faced soldiers and realize that some of them are going to be killed up north in Iraq—that people are being killed in Iraq *now*, are being killed all over the world—I begin to question.

Is there truly a God?

I know that I've always had some issues with organized religion. I've always felt that human spiritual frailties, maybe our own fears or intolerance, have corrupted, distorted, even denied the message of God throughout human history and have caused an incredible amount of violence and pain. But I've always had faith that there *is* some higher power guiding me, wanting to teach me.

Now I have begun to wonder why God would allow so much warfare and misery. Or have we just become misguided? Have we merely strayed from what God intended for us? When did that happen and why does it seem so hard for us to find the right path? Is it us, not God, who allow such misery in the world because we have strayed from the path we are all supposed to be walking? Have we walked away from God?

This place makes me feel uneasy. That doesn't make any sense, I know, but this place is just... eerie sometimes. I just feel that *something* is going to happen, but I don't know what. Truthfully, nothing over here makes any sense and the voices of the discontent are scrawled on the bathroom walls:

"Politicians suck."

"I hate this fuckin' place."

"Active Army life blows."

"Ten more months and I'm a gone motherfucker."

I've read them all and thought the same.

If so many people don't want to be here, if so many people don't want war, why have we so passively allowed all this to continue?

I love you.

### March 23, 2004

A friend of mine told me something interesting today. We were sitting around playing cribbage when I casually mentioned that the Army is transforming me into a narcoleptic, that it seems to inculcate in me some strange desire to sleep all the time. He looked me dead in the eye and said, "You are under a great deal of stress, that's all."

He then went further, explaining that people in our situation, knowing that combat, injury, or death could literally be around any corner at any moment often exhibit symptoms like mine to deal with the stress of the situation. The body just shuts down every once in a while because the stress is constant whether we are aware of it or not. It was quite a revelation. I hadn't even felt as if I was under stress, and it gave me pause. I began to think of how sly stress can be, how it sneaks up on us, and how it can manifest itself in physical ways as we force ourselves through the days.

I told him that I have developed an occasional twitch in my right eye since being deployed. He patiently explained that is also a sign of being in a high-stress environment and he had noticed it when talking with me a few times.

Here in Kuwait it is relatively quiet, but there has been quite a lot of activity up at Camp Anaconda. We've heard there was a car bombing a while ago, that mortar rounds come in frequently at night, and insurgents try to get into the compound with their RPGs and other stuff on a daily basis.

I talked with some combat engineers in the mess hall who had just survived an attack up there. One of them said an RPG passed by his face less than five feet away. It seems I am going right into the lion's den and I'm beginning to be frightened.

I'll make it a point to watch my ass up there. But you can only do that to a certain extent—odds are you will never know what happened when the mortar that kills you explodes.

My eye just twitched.

However, a situation like this can be liberating in some ways. I eat ice cream freely, if for no other reason than because a sense of fatalism has begun to wash over me. Well, I ate ice cream before too, but now I have no *guilt* over whether it's bad for me. It's as if you almost feel more carefree.

The fact that I carry a loaded rifle everywhere I go is a queasy indicator of how precarious the serenity here is.

Oh well, I don't want to talk about it any more.

I need to have faith and hope.

I love you.


**March 24, 2004**

I've been thinking.

Since I've been in the Army, in fact for my whole life, I've been inundated with talk of the duty and honor to serve… but what does that actually *mean*? Does it mean what we think or is it a manipulation? Do people who typically espouse these codes live in an illusion? Have they allowed themselves to be programmed by other people's agendas? Why do they feel it necessary to lay their lives on the line for what could be someone else's selfish interests? Are they willing slaves of someone else's ideology? Do they even *thrive* on that? Does it give them a sense of security? Are they prisoners of war? Are we *all* prisoners of war? Are we mere sheep? How much of life is merely following the leader?

I'm not sure there are any answers but I feel compelled to ponder nonetheless.

Another ship supposedly came in today, the second one with the rest of our equipment. That means I'm most likely working tomorrow.

I love you.

## March 26, 2004

I sit with nothing to do.

The confusion within the leadership about how to handle our trucks and equipment is really bringing morale down. We ended up not working and people are tense, ready to come to blows with each other. I've also noticed we have all fallen into our little cliques, even with just 20 of us. The black guys are sticking with the black guys, listening to hip-hop. The white guys are hanging around with the white guys, playing cards or bullshitting. Sometimes hardly a word is spoken between the white people and the black people here—it's quite surprising.

When I first began basic training at Ft. Leonard Wood, the drill sergeants told us on Day One that they didn't care who we were, what color we were, or what our backgrounds were. From that time forward, we were *all* green—*Army* green. We were soldiers, members of the greatest fighting force in the world. I'm not sure how many people took the time to digest that and it saddens me. It's a shame we don't like each other very much when we're surrounded by people who don't like us very much either.

Racism is a cancer that sickens the whole Army, not just our unit. Even if it's unspoken, you can see it in so many eyes. Just reading the racial graffiti on the bathroom walls makes me uncomfortable and sad. And I've heard a disturbing profusion of remarks that degrade women.

It seems to me that underneath all the societal facades, humans can be quite base. The beast dwells within us, barely chained by our rationality and integrity, our desire to do good, to love, and to live in a better world. It's right under the surface, always seeking an opportunity to strike, to corrupt us. It's fed by our fears, our disillusionment, our anger, and it seems as if instead of denying it food, we willingly feed it more. Why, I don't know.

Perhaps the real enemy is within each of us and we merely project that outward onto the world. How do we exorcise ourselves and create better energy?

These hateful attitudes contradict everything I believe in. To be among people who don't seem to care about anyone around them makes me so very sad. Where are the noble causes? Where is the sense of duty and respect?

It looks as if I'll be here a little while longer and it's probably about three weeks before our convoy will take place—at least that's the newest plan circulating. From what

I've heard through the grapevine, we are flying some people down from Balad on a C-130[21] to be drivers or co-drivers. I'm not sure, but we might also do some more convoy training.

So, since I will have even less privacy than I do now, I barricaded my bunk. I hung my poncho on the right side and my wool blanket on the left to serve as makeshift walls. At the head of the bunk is my locker. Essentially I have an enclosed space the size of my bunk and it's cozy. I hung my Army flashlight from the bottom of the bunk above me to use as a reading lamp.

I finished *The Adventures of Tom Sawyer* for the second time last night. I have now embarked upon Sir Thomas Malory's tale of the adventures of King Arthur and his knights, *Le Morte d'Arthur*. Books are my solace right now. I can hide within the pages and be instantly transported into another world. Since I can't be where I want, since I don't like where I am and I'm afraid of where I'm going… I go to another place.

It's kinda fuckin' crazy.

I love you, honey.

### March 29, 2004

I am so homesick. I have no energy to write. It came on quite suddenly and has stayed with me for two days now. It's a sickening feeling, filled with worry and uncertainty.

We might be leaving here in a couple of days. There has been another change of plans—we might be flying now. Then,

---

21  A turboprop military transport aircraft

maybe even as much as a month or so later, a detachment might fly back down and drive the trucks up. But you never know, it could change any minute.

I can do nothing but wait.

I love you.

### March 30, 2004

We're still waiting and it's becoming difficult not to be cynical.

I went to the barbershop today and the dude who cut my hair fucked it up. It was kinda funny. I got into the chair and told him I wanted one length longer than skin on the sides and back with just a trim on the top, pretty standard all in all. He nodded dumbly and gave me a haircut that was nothing like what I'd asked for. It doesn't look *that* bad though. What the fuck, I'll live with it, right? Who honestly cares about haircuts that much?

I have also been taking more to fake beer lately. Bitburger doesn't really taste bad; it's far better than the fake Budweiser at least. I can't believe I just said that—fake beer tasting good! Wow, I really must be losing my mind. It's 0.5 percent alcohol so you'd have to drink at least seven just to get one real beer out of it. We sat around last night and tried to figure out how many Bits it would take to get drunk. After intense calculations scribbled on a scrap of paper, we came up with 47. Unfortunately no one is brave enough to carry out that experiment.

Later, we came up with a profound thought—a real thought

provoker that still has us stumbling. It's something that I am sure will drastically affect our lives in years to come. Have you ever wondered why your finger fits so perfectly in your own nose but no one else's? Yes, we are pondering the most important of life's questions.

I'm trying to think what else might be interesting or profound to talk about, but my mind is drawing a blank. I wait. I get orders. I follow them. I wait. Nothing, and I mean nothing, has happened lately.

Okay... there are a couple of things. This morning I saw a detailed ad for sex from a male soldier to other male soldiers on the latrine stall wall.

And I experienced a moment of tranquil beauty recently as I was sitting outside watching soldiers scurry about on what appeared to be very important errands. A certain distinct calm suddenly drifted over me and I felt I could see more clearly, as if the world was brighter, more vivid and colorful. My heart gushed and I drifted into a state of peace. I felt more alive than I have in a long time. It was as if I were seeing the world around me for the first time. I saw beauty in a bird that was drifting lazily on the wind, in the breeze that tickled my neck, in the golden rays of sunlight that illuminated the airborne dust, in the Arabic Coca-Cola can I was holding, in the smell of the desert air salted with the breeze from the Gulf.

It was a transcendental feeling of connectedness to the energy and wonder of the simplicity all around me. It was the sun peeking through a tempest, the moon washing my face with its serene, pale luminescence. It was lying in a meadow watching the clouds drift by.

It was almost as if I was on the threshold of understanding something.

Was it God?

I love you.

### April 1, 2004

Well, the plans have changed... as we'd suspected. Now we are convoying up to Balad again. By my count, our plans have changed at least six times in the past three weeks. Naturally everyone is in an uproar. People aren't trained on vehicles so at least 30 drivers will have to be flown down here. Vehicles need to be prepped and training needs to be completed. Soon we will be moving up to Camp Virginia to sit in tents and probably wait again.

### April 2, 2004

Today we were supposed to leave at 0800 to go out to Camp Arifjan and get the equipment for our convoy from these large shipping containers called Conexes. They contain most of our equipment to outfit some vehicles with gun mounts. Then we were supposed to have some driver training. Well, it's 0930 and we're still waiting for the bus. There was a lot of arguing among the higher-ups last night. Top "wanted to have this shit wrapped up a long time ago" and he was pissed off at the officers for "farting" around.

We are all getting our game faces on now. The convoy will probably take place sometime next week. I have to admit, I'm scared. Those fuckers up north are out for blood. But you know what I'm really scared of? That I won't get the chance to see you again. I can't help but continuously reflect on all the moments with you that live only within my memories now. I want to survive and make more of our life together. I'm scared of being cheated out of that.

If something *does* happen to me, know that I loved you with all my heart and our moments together meant more than a lifetime—they meant the universe to me.

### April 2, 2004 continued

We finally got out to Camp Arifjan to work on our trucks.

Here were the snafus of the day:

First, the revolving ring mounts for the machine guns were buried in the back of the Conexes, so we had to unpack then repack them. Second, the ring mounts are designed for two-and-a-half ton trucks. We have *five*-ton trucks. So we are "mickey jobbing" the mounts to fit them. Third, we have no armor for our trucks. We don't even have sandbags. And the plane from Balad bringing the rest of our convoy drivers down has been delayed. Who knows when it will arrive? Finally, we have to move to Camp Virginia to begin convoy training. Again, who knows when that will happen?

Some quotes from the day, things I overheard people muttering while we were going about our business:

"Huh... fuckers."

"Meanwhile... back at the ranch."

"Me, being who I am..."

"Sons o' bitches."

My quote for the day is "I love you."

## April 8, 2004

Oh gosh, where should I begin?

On the morning of April 3, we were told we were definitely convoying. We drove to Camp Arifjan, got our trucks, and proceeded to our staging point in Camp Virginia. We parked and secured the trucks but it proved to be an all-day event. We didn't get back to Camp Doha until 2100 hours. Along the way, Top got lost and we wound up going through Al-Jahra, eventually ending back up on the highest point in Kuwait (which I have now learned is called Mutla Ridge) again. I didn't mind. What a beautiful view. You can see clear down to the ocean. That's about all there was to that day except for getting my first real experience driving a five-ton truck. They're big and somewhat clumsy, slow to accelerate, but otherwise fun to drive.

On the 4th I left Camp Doha. We needed to pick up the remaining trucks we didn't move the day before from Camp Arifjan and bring them to Camp Virginia. At some point we were supposed to link up with the 30 some people flying down from Balad who were meeting us for the convoy. I must admit, it was somewhat sad to leave Doha. It's such a danger-free area, almost as if it's a surreal Army amusement park.

I had a feeling it was the beginning, the beginning of a long arduous journey, a turning point—or starting point, as the case may be.

Anyway, we arrived at Camp Virginia after getting the trucks and met with everyone around 1200 or 1300 hours. Overall it was uneventful, just a lot of driving around Kuwait. Then of course we had to endure the usual organizational cluster fuck but were eventually told we were going to be on the move again—we had to drive to Camp Udairi for two days of combat and convoy training.

After everyone got organized—gathered equipment, checked their assigned trucks, lined up, started the engines—we were on our way. Dust was swirling, engines were throbbing, exhaust fumes choking the air. Tanned arms hung out of doors, Kevlar helmets were perched on dusty heads, and rifle barrels glinted in the sun. There was the resounding click of a magazine being loaded, discussions of plans and strategy—it was utterly astonishing. A massive movement of trucks and equipment all at once. I had never experienced such a thing.

Just outside of Camp Virginia I saw a whole herd of camels—there must have been about 50. They kept trying to approach our trucks, obviously curious about these funny, noisy contraptions, but a Humvee kept chasing them off. It was really funny. Three rebels separated from the herd and started running toward us, the Humvee in hot pursuit. One camel broke off, and the Humvee chased the other two around and around in circles. Imagine telling your spouse what you do in a combat zone—"I herd camels with my Humvee." Hilarious.

The drive to Camp Udairi was dusty, long, and grueling with little to no scenery but sand dunes—a desolate wasteland baking in the blistering sun. The roads were terrible—hard-baked uneven sand and rock continuously jostling us back and forth in our tiny cab. Occasionally we would drive by a dead camel at the side of the road. One time I saw three dead goats, all in a bunch. I don't know what they died of—thirst? When we finally arrived it was dusk and all you could see in every direction was endless rippled sand dunes—there was absolutely nothing out there as we were just about on the Iraqi border.

After parking our trucks for training the next day, we were told wake-up was 0400 hours and were released to settle in and get some rest. Briefly surveying our surroundings (it didn't take long), we were dismayed to discover there were no facilities other than a couple of port-a-johns. The camp was nothing more than a few tents housing a small contingent of soldiers and a classroom.

The landscape was utterly flat with a few sand dunes scattered here and there, essentially a wasteland. I watched the last remnants of the day's heat shimmer on the horizon before the sun yielded to twilight and eventual darkness. It was like I had stepped onto a whole different planet, light-years from any sort of civilization. It was an anthrophobe's dream.

Our choice of accommodation was either the floor of one of the tents or the trucks. By this time, it was dark and we were all tired. I opted to settle into the cab of my truck—it seemed the most private place to get a little rest and I could stretch out fairly comfortably on the bench seat. All of our baggage was stacked in the back of one of the five-tons and a group of people sorted through them, which of course quickly decimated any organization we had. Think of it, rummaging for two duffel bags, one rucksack, and one personal bag each for 20 people, in the dark, in a big truck—it was virtually impossible to find anything.

Brushing away the fatigue rooted in my eyes, I scavenged through the mess until I found my bags. It was fully dark by now and I was sweaty and sticky when I finally settled into my truck to brush my teeth using a bottle of water, splashing a little on my face while trying to wipe as much sand and dust from my body as I could. I draped my uniform top over the open door of the truck, took off my boots and socks in an effort to air out my feet, ate an MRE, and watched the moon rise over the horizon.

Late that night, perhaps around 0100, I was awakened from a light slumber to the sound of vicious wind whistling around my truck, making it tremble and vibrate. Shaking away my sleepiness, I quickly discovered it wasn't just wind—dust and sand were angrily swirling into my cab and I scrambled to close the windows, coughing through the choking airborne earth. Squinting into the side-mounted rear-view mirror, I chuckled in amazement because I found that I was completely blanketed with dust, the whites of my eyes seeming to glow in the dark.

After taking a few moments to pat myself down, again coughing with the dust billowing around me, I summoned the gumption to crack the window—mainly out of curiosity—and clouds of sand soared in, caking everything. That was enough of that. So... for the rest of the night I kept the windows closed. The stuffiness and dust inside the cab made it virtually impossible to sleep and I ended up propping my head on my uniform top that I was using as a pillow and listening to the wind rattling my truck as I took in my first bona fide Middle Eastern sandstorm.

We woke at 0400 and began training shortly after. Most of us were already awake thanks to the sandstorm. I didn't get a chance to eat or change or even brush my teeth. The wind was still blowing—at least 25 or 30 mph I'd guess—and after a brief formation we all headed out to a little rifle range about 100 yards away. After about an hour of class instruction—all of us clustered in a small circle, the instructors shouting through the scarves covering their faces so we could hear them above the gale—we began some close-quarters combat exercises. We could hardly see, the sand constantly getting in our eyes despite our sunglasses and headgear.

We conducted rifle drills such as shooting while walking, reloading while keeping our target in the rifle sights, and turning and shooting. It was very dynamic, much more so than the typical rifle range at a stateside base, those being merely plastic pop-up targets with the shooter stationary in a foxhole. But we didn't do so well, as most of our rifles jammed at some point because of the dirt.

The training was actually quite good, but it was so difficult to concentrate. I was tired and aching from the night before. Sand was crusting my nose, caked in my ears—there was nothing I could do to keep it out. It was remorseless.

At noon we broke for a half-hour and ate lunch—more MREs. Then we drove the trucks to some nearby tents and parked. We were split up into four groups and had classes in one of the tents. We covered many convoy driving techniques: what to look out for along the way, how to spot suspected insurgents who might be trailing us, and how to identify IEDs alongside the road. I honestly don't remember that much. The tents, which weren't air-conditioned, were so hot and stuffy I was struggling to stay awake after 20 minutes. We sat on backless wooden benches, our instructor standing behind an easel, occasionally handing out photos of IEDs or other devices. We finished around 1730 hours and were given a break for the night.

I ate another MRE for dinner and grabbed one for the next day because they were running scarce. The wind had thankfully died down to a light breeze and I managed to take a sponge bath with a baby wipe. I never thought I would appreciate baby wipes so much. I rooted through the baggage truck again and grabbed some clean socks, underwear, and T-shirt in the duffel bag I couldn't find the previous night.

Then quite suddenly, it miraculously became wonderfully calm. The stars were out, brightly shining, accompanied by a dazzling full moon… it was beautiful. No, that's not quite right. It was stunning, striking… a sight beyond my imagination—so peaceful, clear, still, and silent.

After changing and wiping the essentials, I leaned back in the cab and savored the moment. I watched as the shadows from the trucks shrank as the moon crept higher and higher in the sky—until it illuminated the landscape almost as though it were the sun. This was roughing it in the extreme and the exhilaration of it took my breath away. All you could hear were a few people bullshitting here and there, maybe the sound of an engine for a couple of minutes.

Eventually all was still—completely, deafeningly silent. I was in the middle of nowhere, miles and miles from any sort of civilization, so far out I never even heard or saw a plane flying overhead. It was like an ultimate camping trip.

I began to miss you terribly, yet I felt… soothed. The best way I can describe it is that I felt a comforted loneliness—I was so far from home but I knew that you were with me… I could *feel* you with me.

We got up early, 0500 hours, and began our practical convoy driving training. It took all day. Camp Udairi has a two-mile driving range and we conducted some practice drills in the morning with a live-fire exercise in the afternoon. We learned how to park our trucks in a defensive "box" formation and how to dismount safely and take up fighting positions. We learned how to shoot from the cab and reload while driving, how to set up an emergency MedEvac,[22] and how to effectively get first aid to the wounded.

It was good training.

We finished in the late afternoon and packed up, heading down to Camp Virginia in the late evening to stay for a night. The camp was still as hushed as a ghost town and some tumbleweed was all that was needed to make the scene complete, maybe the creak of a wooden sign as well. I finally got a shower and you should have seen the sandy stream flowing down the drain. It was the best shower I had ever taken.

We stayed for three relatively quiet nights. Essentially all we did was check our trucks, review our training, clean rifles, and rest. The best part was I had the opportunity to get on the Internet and send you a letter, the queue being bearable these days. It felt good to be able to express how my thoughts of you are my light, my beacon, a lighthouse guiding me home. I could almost feel your presence through the computer screen when I read your email.

---

22   Medical Evacuation Site

You're so adorable… you know that, my dear? When you spoke of our nights together, cooking, watching a movie and snuggling, I felt as if my smile would break my face in two. I too can clearly recall those times when you would stand at our kitchen counter chopping the piles of vegetables we were having for dinner. I will never forget all the times you would ask me to mince the garlic as you stood there, a glass of wine in hand, overseeing the operation.

I remember us chatting about our crazy friends while we marinated shrimp together, chuckling about how complicated they made their lives. Still laughing, we'd fire up the wok, sauté our creation, and pile it onto plates and snuggle up on the couch, the cats lounging on the back of the sofa, our dog nestled comfortably on the living room floor.

Please don't worry too much; I'm not going anywhere. No one can predict the future, but I have no plans to leave you or our life together. How strange that you dreamed of the future, a future without me, and regretted it. I wonder what happened that would compel you to dream of that. You'll have to tell me all about it when we can hold each other and take comfort that we are never to be parted again. Now is our time to be strong for each other… *both* of us being a beacon in the night to guide us back to each other.

I love you.

**April 10, 2004**

We left to go north… to Baghdad… to Camp Anaconda—to war—on April 9.

The convoy officially began by 0700 and all I can say is it was a fucking incredibly long drive. I was paired with Major Burns, who had flown down from Balad, and he really took care of me. He made me a bottle of strawberry Tang, practically shoved beef jerky down my throat, and requisitioned a cot for me to sleep on. Top assigned me to drive with him, although I'm not sure why and I have to admit, I felt a bit strange driving my commanding officer around. Overall though, it's been a nice chance to get to know him better.

The beginning of the journey was a long dirt road that took us past Camp Udairi again. It was the same terrible road we had driven before and the bottom portion of my ballistic vest, now weighted down with armored plates, stabbed my kidneys with every lurch of my truck making it difficult to concentrate on driving. Not comfortable to say the least.

Oh, I guess I should mention that the day before we left everyone chalked their trucks with everything and anything, sayings such as:

"Fighting for freedom."

"Freedom ain't free."

"I didn't get that memo."

Anyway, we drove to just shy of the border and pulled over at a fuel station. We were told that when we crossed the border we needed to lock and load our rifles and keep our eyes open. At that point, it was show time—the real deal. We were entering an active combat zone and had to be ready for anything. The major had arranged for an escort of three armored Humvees with machine guns—a welcome sight.

We never did get any armor for our trucks and whatever we had certainly wasn't provided by the military or our government. We scrounged steel plates from scrap heaps in Camp Virginia, scavenging through piles of junk and jerry-rigging anything that might work. After gathering what we could, there was the problem of cutting the scrap to fit our truck doors and perhaps even the flooring. For that task, we "found"—well, "borrowed"—a cutting torch from the camp to complete the job. The scant scrap we managed to gather didn't go very far, so the majority of the trucks were unarmored when we began traveling.

Everyone *did* chip in for a "sandbag party" one afternoon however, but what we were able to make didn't go very far and wasn't very comforting. My truck had just a few sandbags laid on the floorboards and no scrap metal. It was pretty nerve-wracking because the flimsy canvas door of my truck would have done absolutely nothing to stop an AK-47 bullet, let alone an IED. But it was too late to worry about it, the drive had begun and I just hoped everything would go smoothly.

We left the fuel station and drove out of Kuwait, past the demilitarized zone between the two countries that's roughly 100 yards wide and flanked by two rows of concertina wire, with guard posts for each country's entrance. I must admit it felt peculiar crossing the border, almost sinister... you could tangibly feel a change in the air—I don't know how else to describe it but it was real nonetheless.

Shortly after entering Iraq, we came upon a small village. It consisted of a few haphazardly scattered sand-colored brick houses, all of them reduced to shambles by some past battle. A few junked cars stood forlornly next to the houses and a cluster of small children dressed in ragged T-shirts watched us from the roadside. A few of them waved but most just stared at us with a vague curiosity as we lumbered by.

Trenches had been dug between the houses, and a few patches of grass dotted the landscape. There was only one road, the one we were traveling on—a divided six-lane highway, three lanes on each side. Running north, the right lane was reserved for Iraqi citizens. Our trucks were to stay in the middle lane, with the far left lane reserved for our escort. We averaged 45 to 55 mph with the escort slowing down and speeding up accordingly, keeping a watchful vigil over us and the surrounding expanse of desert. Radio communication was strictly limited because it could trigger an IED, so each truck was largely on its own despite each of us silently depending on one another to watch out for danger.

I was driving with my rifle aimed out the window, praying not to have to engage with anyone. But nothing could be left to chance and you never knew who was friendly or out to kill us. Let me tell ya, it's tough driving a big-ass truck with one hand and holding a rifle out the window with the other combined with aching kidneys and a real sweaty ass. I've definitely been on more fun road trips.

Shortly after passing the ruined village, a group of children on bicycles rode by us on the opposite side of the road and I was amused when the lead kid looked right at me and gave me the finger, his dark eyes flashing and smudged face twisting with hatred.

Honestly, I don't blame him.

As we drove on, we saw countless burned-out wrecks of military and civilian vehicles on the shoulder. Whatever houses we came across were in shambles, piles of rubble nestled against their remains. Every child we saw was dressed in dirty rags. Some of them were smoking cigarettes, sitting alongside of the road and gazing at us indifferently as we passed by. They couldn't have been more than 10 years old. Stray dogs rummaged in trash piles, poking noses in tin cans, licking plastic wrappers, occasionally snarling and fighting over a scrap of discarded food. And on the horizon the great steel mazes of the oil refineries reared their cities of pipe and machinery. They glittered in the fierce midmorning sun, gouts of unwanted natural gas burning from their flare stacks, spewing pollution into the air. The contrast between this ruthless extraction of black gold and the poverty all around me took my breath away.

We were told during our training to tailgate and even bump out of the way any vehicle that got between our trucks. We were also told to look for cars pacing us because they were most likely watching us, perhaps even radioing to an ambush up ahead. One car I saw twice (I wasn't the only one who noticed)—a dented white Chevy Caprice that was definitely *not* friendly. It hovered around our convoy until chased off by our escort then returned shortly after, pacing us and watching. There were three Iraqis—two in the front seats, one in the back—*all* with AK-47s. When they passed my truck I braced for an inevitable confrontation. But they sped ahead and were soon chased off again. Thankfully our escorts were good at their job, however, the bottom line was we had been noted and that information was bound to be disseminated. We all knew they would be back... them or someone else.

I must admit I was frightened. I felt a sickening feeling creep into my stomach, the reality of the situation becoming all too clear. I was also dismayed to find that the tic in my eye had returned, which made it difficult to see, to aim, or drive.

Sometime later, I saw a guy selling old Iraqi money on the side of the road and we passed many rundown brick shacks no bigger than four feet square, where the locals had set up stands to sell snacks and trinkets.

The whole way we were tailed by random cars, the white Chevy returning as we predicted. At one point, we were delayed 20 minutes when one of the Humvees busted a radiator hose and I noticed (after we had dismounted and taken up fighting positions) that the guardrails on both sides of the highway had been removed, dismantled either by looters or U.S. forces in an attempt to prevent IED planting. Our escort was hit by an IED on the way down to meet us but no one was injured, thank God.

We never knew when we might be attacked. The enemy could have been around any corner, in any car. There have been a number of drive-by shootings, which is why we were told to level our rifles at *anyone* who passed us.

The Iraqi rebels hide IEDs in virtually anything they can find on the side of the road, even animal carcasses. Some of these bombs are remotely triggered by cell phones. Snipers hang out on the side of the road, waiting to pick off passing Americans. Sometimes people drop grenades from overpasses. Children throw rocks at convoys as they pass. I also found out that when Iraqi civilians know that a convoy is driving into an ambush, they'll often just pull over and wait, making no attempt to warn us.

By early evening we arrived at Camp Cedar II. We'll be stuck here until Monday at least. Camp Cedar II is a tiny cluster of tents surrounded by endless desert. What a surprise. But the mess hall is very nice. The camp has clean shower/latrine facilities—believe it or not, this place is cleaner than Doha or Virginia. On the other hand, we are by no means safe. There is so much activity up north right now that they're not letting anyone through. These are organized attacks and a great number of IEDs have been found along the roadway. Two other units have been delayed with us.

It took quite some time for us to park our trucks, check them for the day, and be assigned sleeping quarters in a cluster of tents about 50 yards from the shower trailers. I'm just beginning to calm down now. Not only was the drive extremely stressful, but as I was securing my truck for the night, I heard some gunfire and then a rather loud, strange thud next to me, about a foot or so away. I didn't realize it at first, but it slowly began to dawn on me that I'd heard a bullet ricochet off something and spin away into the gathering dusk.

Oh my God, honey, my heart began to pound. The thump of that bullet was all I could hear for an instant and it seemed as if time slowed, the seconds ticking by like hours. Before I knew what was happening, instinct had taken over and I was ducking behind my truck, rifle in hand, peeking over the hood. I was the only one there; everyone else had walked to the mess hall just a couple of minutes before. I had stayed behind because I wanted to check a tire one more time before buttoning up my truck for the night.

I couldn't see very well, but I noticed a dust cloud billowing on the near horizon, just on the edge of the camp. It was a Humvee barreling toward what appeared to be a few men silhouetted in the setting sun. More gunfire broke out, what looked like an exchange between the men and the Humvee. There were shouts and more gunfire as the men scattered but in the gathering dark it was impossible to know whether they'd been killed.

It was odd... so very quick, my mind hardly had time to process it. I have no idea whether it was just a stray bullet or whether they were aiming for me, making for an easy target since I'd become separated from the others. I don't know what to make of this latest little adventure and I just want to push it to the back of my mind for now, but I did think it was important to chronicle.

I've never been shot at before, baby. Oh my God, what if they had hit me? What if I wasn't able to come home to you? Weird… to be killed by some errant bullet that was probably never even meant for me. What a meaningless death that would be. The more I think about it, the more shaken up I feel. But I need to keep my wits about me. I need to remember to breathe, remember I'm still alive, and for the time being still able to come home. There will be time to think about this later. Now it's important to focus on my job.

Here we go again. I just heard more fire coupled with an explosion and what sounded like a machine-gun. That's not the rifle range we're hearing this time. Wow, this place is hot.

Oh, some news: I was just told there was a .50-caliber machine gun shooting at our camp. Guards around the base have returned fire and I can still hear the battle as I write this, bullets cracking in the darkness. I think it's going to be a long night, honey.

I also heard that Camp Anaconda got hit last night. Apparently more than 20 mortar rounds hit the base and one person was killed. No one from our unit was injured, thank God. What am I heading into? It seems as if the farther north we go, the worse it gets. We still have a long drive ahead and I wonder what other surprises are in store for us.

The last bit of news I've heard is that the U.S. surrounded and attacked Fallujah, a town near Baghdad, a few days ago and there's a huge battle going on. Rumor has it there are a lot of people dying, on both sides, and that civilian casualties are also mounting up.

I love and miss you.

## April 11, 2004

We woke at 0400 and Capt. Berry, our convoy commander in the lead vehicle, told us we were not driving today. Apparently there's been a tremendous amount of activity up north and the route we're to be taking is too hot right now. So we spent the day waiting and as it wore on, people got more and more anxious. We might be leaving tomorrow. No one really knows. The major told us that by the end of this convoy we will all be combat veterans. I'm not sure what that really means or if that's supposed to soothe our frayed nerves, but if that's what he says, so be it.

There has been an awful lot of talk about getting shot or the possibility of being in combat. People are mulling it over, running through every scenario they can think of. There's a frantic quality in the air and some think they'll be sending us to die if we go tomorrow. A lot are upset, edgy, and aggressive. You can see it in their eyes, their wide eyeballs in the dark of night.

It's only natural for all of us to project, to ponder, to try to carve out some sort of sanity in an insane place in order to help settle thoughts that are quite often dizzying to muse upon. We seem to be taking what comfort we can from each other, unconsciously grouping together as horses do when predators are on the prowl.

I think what's happening here is a fear of the unknown. To face our own worst nightmares—to be injured, perhaps even permanently disabled, to be confronted by something or someone that forces us to change into something we're not comfortable with. We fear that we'll never see our loved ones again, never see home again. We fear the secrets that are buried deeply within us.

I've come to realize that fear is a powerful—if not the most powerful—force in our world. Either subconsciously or consciously, fear is an animating force within each of us, an instinctual motivator that served us well throughout evolution allowing us to survive. Granted, we no longer have to live in fear of being eaten by a tiger in the dead of night, but fear has adapted itself to our modern lives. Now we fear that we can't find a decent job, won't have enough money for retirement, can't afford life insurance for our children, that someone will take away our livelihood or a neighboring country will invade our borders, that we're being spied upon, or even that the new neighbor down the street speaks or looks differently than us. Fear, with whatever justification, insists on choking our lives.

I believe that fear fuels most of the fighting and killing in our world, that anger, ignorance, and prejudice are merely the outward projections of our own inner fears. But maybe it goes deeper than that. Perhaps it fuels greed, corruption, and a lack of compassion as well. It distorts our self-image—we worry about whether we're good enough people, whether we can perform well at our jobs, whether we can be loved by another. Perhaps we are all ruled by fear however it's projected, either inwardly or outwardly and I can't help but feel there has to be a better way to live our lives—there has to be something more.

Ralph Waldo Emerson wrote that "Fear defeats more people than any other one thing in the world." Then again, Napoleon once said that "Men are moved by two levers only: fear and self-interest."

Perhaps they're both right. I'm sure that fear can not only defeat us, but that we can also use it to conquer our obstacles. *That's* what we must do now if we are to survive this trek and reach our destination. In the meantime, I listen to people, I write, and I'm trying to take all this in as best I can without going off the deep end with my own worst thoughts and fears.

I miss you.

Believe it or not, we have Internet access here. It's the last thing I would have expected. So I checked my email hoping for a message and there wasn't one. I felt sad. Where are you? I've been writing when I could and you haven't responded in quite some time. My link to you is so very important right now. It's excruciating not being able to communicate with you when I am so frightened and under so much pressure. I don't want to die without knowing you are there, that we were able to at least write one more message to each other.

I checked over my truck today. It seems all right, but I have a slow leak in the front right tire. I've learned a lot about five-tons lately and I was able to use the truck's air system to put air in the tire. It should hold until I get north… I think.

A couple of more notes. All the sewage in Camp Cedar II is deposited in a big artificial pond right in the middle of camp so there is a smell of rot that sticks in your nostrils everywhere you go. On the other hand, it has one excellent dining facility. This evening's menu was a choice selection of lobster tail and/or steak with wild rice *à la odeur de sewage* for dinner. It's amazing how a bit of decent food can lift your spirits—even in the middle of nowhere, surrounded by people who hate your guts.

I heard an Apache helicopter was hit and exploded during a mortar attack up in Balad last night.

I love you.

### April 12, 2004

We're delayed again. Last night a squad of MPs got into some serious firefights just north of here along the route we're supposed to take, so we're holing up in camp for a few more days. I don't know if anyone was injured, but we're not taking any chances.

I've heard that people are dying left and right in Fallujah, that it's a nasty mess of a situation. I don't really know what to say or think about that right now. I'm feeling so numb that these horrifying things seem ordinary now. My mind seems to be starting to think of violence as a norm… or maybe it's refusing to deal with the specter of violence at all.

There are a ton of flies, sand flies, and sand fleas here. As soon as you step outside, they swarm you. They get in your ears, your eyes, even your mouth—clouds of them follow you everywhere. Despite them, we made an attempt at doing laundry today—the old-fashioned way. A few of us scrounged up a couple of buckets and hand-washed our filthy uniforms.

Some of the soldiers here are really getting on each other's nerves. There have been some verbal altercations in our ranks and one was severe enough that all I wanted to do was get away from the tension. I don't blame them, nor am I surprised. When you put people in close quarters for an extended period of time there are bound to be arguments, even fights. When you add the tremendous stress of being in harm's way, it gets even worse.

With the constant bickering among ourselves, either due to stress or genuine dislike, I feel as if I have bought a ticket for a carnival ride in some insane asylum. I'm distressed by the human spirit, how our high values of peace have found fleeting footing. War can turn good people into savages. I wonder if anyone else feels this way, or if they're just lost in the whirlwind of it all like I am.

A friend of mine once told me, "People at home will never believe the reality of the world we have to deal with."

This is the real world—as real as it gets.

I checked my email again and still no message from you. How very saddening. Amid all these people, I feel alone and scared.

I wish this whole madness would end.

I love you.

## April 13, 2004

It's 1600 and we're getting a whopper of a thunderstorm, an actual desert thunderstorm. The lightning is extraordinary, flashing over the flatness of the brown desert, bolts streaking down to the sand. Believe it or not, it's actually cooled off some. The storm must have brought some cooler air with it. It's in the 90s now, not the usual 100 or so.

Before the storm we practiced some battle drills to keep our minds in the game. The word is we're leaving tomorrow at 0545 hours. Given that we're about an eight-hour drive from Balad, we should get there by late afternoon if everything goes smoothly. I am spending a lonely afternoon in my tent, waiting and wondering what will happen tomorrow. Everyone is eager to get this over with, myself included.

Gary Myers found a camel spider that was taking an afternoon siesta in his duffel bag yesterday. They're big, ugly, creepy, and they like to follow you, scurrying along in your shadow to keep out of the heat. They also like to hide in your boots, a habit that has scared the crap out of more than one of us.

Right now, a few of us are reading, a few playing cards. Some are bullshitting, telling stories of hunting and fishing.

The guys who have come down from Balad, Gary and Bob Graves included, keep talking about all the mortar rounds that are hitting Camp Anaconda. They say the guys who haven't been up there yet are the virgins.

This is one time when I would like to keep my virginity.

I love you.

**April 14, 2004**

We ended up not going today, so we are waiting again.

The convoy staging area here in camp is packed with vehicles. It's kind of amusing how effectively our enemy has clogged the momentum of the United States military. We're constipated.

Uh, oh. I just got word we are leaving tomorrow for sure. They say that every night, and still we don't leave.

By the way, the major was exceptionally kind to me today. He gave me some strawberry Pop Tarts for the ride. I was so dumbfounded I lost my tongue. I have gained some respect for him on this trip and believe he might be a good commander. My faith in him has risen—and not just because of the Pop Tarts.

He does seem to easily command respect and authority. He can be stern at times but he's willing to associate with his men, even to the point of having a smoke with us in the morning over coffee. I like that. I like a commanding officer who's not too detached to be one of the boys. I believe he sincerely cares for our well-being and has a genuine interest in seeing all of us go home alive.

Some quotes I overheard this morning:

"There is no limit to what a driven man can accomplish."

"That would be total tits, man."

I love you.

**April 15, 2004**

We left Camp Cedar II and convoyed to Camp Anaconda today.

I'll start at the beginning.

Wake-up was at 0400. I took a quick shower then hurriedly packed my stuff. By the time I got myself and my belongings out of the tent and down to the trucks, it was close to our start time of 0545 hours. I didn't have time to check out the truck but I felt it was in good shape since I had checked it the day before.

At 0530, we had a quick briefing consisting mainly of how far we might get, what dangers we might encounter, and where we might be stopping. The major reiterated the importance of working as a team and looking out for the soldier next to us at all times—cooperation and communication were just as important as anything else if we were to survive the drive north.

We had a brief equipment check to make sure that everyone had the required amount of ammunition and everything was functioning properly. Finally the major said a prayer with all our heads silently bowed. The mood was somber, our imaginations running wild. We were mostly silent as we climbed into our separate trucks, but resolute. I felt as if I was in some sort of automatic mode, going through my mental checklist as I started my truck, settled in, and waited for the signal for the first truck to begin moving.

We left pretty much right on time. Engines reverberating in the early morning air, we headed north on the highway as the sun's first rays topped the barren horizon. Our gun truck escorts continually roamed, always on the lookout because some KBR[23]convoys had been attacked right outside camp the night before. I hadn't heard anything about that until we were underway. It's hard to keep track of all the bad news, honey. It all seems to puddle into one big blob after a while.

Soon we left the highway and diverted onto a back road made of baked sand and rocks that bounced us up and down in our cabs. We actually began to make decent time, the major and I enjoying a Pop Tart (another interesting balancing act), dust kicking up from the trucks behind us. Then there was a tremendously loud bang. I looked over at the major, who was peering into the rear-view mirror. He turned and told me to stop the truck. We had just had an accident.

It was 0930.

I stopped my truck and we clambered out, rifles at the ready, the morning sun instantly hot on our faces, sweat forming on our brows. The crashed trucks were a little way behind us—about 30 or 40 yards. After briefly surveying the scene, we got back in and turned around, the major obviously deeply concerned. He ordered me to park our truck in front of the crash.

Apparently the dust was so thick that the driver of an

---

23  A subsidiary of Halliburton and formerly Kellogg, Brown & Root. As the largest private contractor in Iraq, KBR provided logistical support to the U.S. Armed Forces.

LMTV[24]had been unable to see the brake lights ahead of him and accidentally slammed right into the ass end of a five-ton at about 35–40 mph. The whole front end of his LMTV was bashed in, crumpled bits of the grill and headlights scattered on the road, steam billowing pitifully from the damaged radiator. (The back of the five-ton was relatively undamaged though, having a solid steel gate for the bed.) By the time I got there, people were already trying to get the injured out of the trucks. It was chaos, with about 10 of us trying to help, the rest taking up fighting positions.

All told, two soldiers were injured in the wreck. Our first aid litter guys were already examining them to determine the extent of their injuries. Top ordered me to set up cots in the back of a five-ton where they could be tended to for the remainder of our journey. "As quickly as possible," he told me tensely. We were in enemy territory and there wasn't a moment to lose. Everyone was on high alert, people acting as security and taking up defensive positions at various places around the scene.

While I was setting up the cots, a British ambulance suddenly appeared from nowhere like some angelic messiah, magically appearing before us through the cloud of dust still hovering around the accident. I still don't know where it came from. I guess I was too wrapped up helping our injured personnel. After a brief discussion with the drivers, our wounded soldiers were loaded into the ambulance and

---

24   Light Medium Tactical Vehicle

away it zoomed, dust billowing, disappearing into the desert again, heading north to the nearest medical facility they could find. Thankfully there were no serious injuries. I don't believe anything was broken, the worst being a gash that would require stitches. When they were gone, we brought the HEMTT (our wrecker truck) forward and hooked up the totally disabled LMTV.

As we were working, an incredibly huge KBR convoy rumbled by, its civilian contractors waving—quite a sight. I was also relieved to see two Apache helicopters buzz overhead, circling us and scouting for any enemy targets. They'd fly by at no more than 60 feet of altitude and disappear into the morning sun only to return, circling and buzzing us again. It was an awe-inspiring sight.

We finally got the truck hooked up to the wrecker and after a brief meeting, the major reiterating the need for alertness and safety, we began driving again. The whole thing had taken about an hour and now that we were driving more slowly for fear of another accident, we began to lose time that we really couldn't afford.

The route we had intended to take was the "long way" around Baghdad and would have taken roughly eight hours. The major began to rethink this strategy and formulate a different plan of action because, as he confided in me as we drove, he felt it wouldn't be wise to travel at night. If we got stuck out in the middle of the desert after dusk, we'd have to pull rotating security shifts throughout the night and people would be tired and not as alert the next day—to say nothing of the possibility of a night ambush.

Fortunately, the rest of the morning was pretty uneventful, just the usual bouncing, numb ass, tired arms, dust, and general discomfort. We got to Camp Scania around 1200 or 1300. Honestly, I can't be sure of the time. My eyes, body, and mind were exhausted.

Camp Scania is a rather large fueling station. Our trucks were low on fuel, so we had stopped there to fill up. My God, honey, you should have seen all the trucks—semi upon semi, bumper to bumper, lines upon lines of them—military and civilian trucks alike. Probably because of all the recent attacks, many roads and routes had been closed, and people just got stuck there.

Soldiers and contractors stood around bullshitting. A few of them took a midday nap on the hoods of their trucks, hats pulled over their eyes, sometimes with an arm dangling over the side. Makeshift canvas shelters stretched between trucks, camping chairs occupied by people smokin' and jokin'. Some were checking engines, tires, and cargo.

The major made the decision to go straight through Baghdad. This would make our trip much shorter but also a lot more dangerous than we'd originally planned for. Basically, it came down to staying at Camp Scania or pressing on for as many miles as possible before the darkness closed in on us.

So after our trucks were filled we made haste and picked up speed. Shortly after leaving we had to stop for some reason

(I don't remember why) and when we were ready to get going again we couldn't because a driver in one of the lead trucks had shut off the engine while we were parked and it wouldn't restart. We pulled another security detail until they fixed the engine—another tense moment done and over with.

The rest of the drive to Baghdad was mainly uneventful. We crossed two bridges that had recently been mortared, the second one apparently *very* recently—a mere 20 minutes before we arrived, I was told. There were huge holes in the structure of the bridge. The engineering crew had hastily cleared a path through the rubble, and our tires clumsily lumbered over the remaining debris. The engineers didn't seem too concerned about any more attacks. Some of them were sitting on the ground, leaning tiredly against their vehicles as they watched us shamble by.

I don't know whether it was just me but there was a different feeling after leaving Camp Scania. I began to see a number of buildings akin to American office parks, some partially bombed. Then, as if out of nowhere, I saw a grove of palm trees with a brick bungalow that must have belonged to some rich person, seemingly undamaged—but upon closer examination I noticed entire chunks of the house missing and a pile of debris in the front yard. Looking around I became aware this house was not the only one, that buildings everywhere despondently bore the impact of war.

We were cruising anywhere between 45 and 55 mph now, whisking down the highway as fast as we could. We were on a main expressway and soon saw our first sign for Baghdad clinging to an overpass, the text in both Arabic and English. The landscape had definitely changed. There was more green than tan. I began to see more clusters of palm trees and more cars as well. It became virtually impossible to keep track of all the vehicles, but our escort was good, sometimes blocking whole intersections as we cruised on through.

We got to Baghdad and I have to say this was the scariest, most stressful stretch of the journey. Suddenly there were cars everywhere, whizzing to and fro. It began to stink worse than you could imagine. The hazy, sticky grey-brown air made me feel greasy and unclean.

Alongside the road were mountains of rubble heaped next to bombed-out buildings, some with entire outside walls missing revealing the rooms inside like a post-apocalyptic dollhouse. People still lived and worked in these immiserated buildings and shops, and there were abandoned cars all over the side of the road. I saw a side street jam-packed with cars, a market street—throngs of people milling about buying food and other necessities. Arabic women, faces veiled, strolled along the streets on some errand. Men sat under the tattered remains of an awning.

Many times there were clusters of cars parked on the side of the highway, people just waiting or bullshitting. I was made aware by the major they were waiting for us to pass, waving at us as if we were friends. This made us really nervous because we had heard about people doing this when they knew there was an ambush ahead. We stuck close together during this time, our intervals being about 25 to 50 meters at the most, and we had to slam on the brakes quite a few times to prevent an accident that would have been disastrous in such a crowded city with so many perils on all sides.

It was hectic city driving and I had a tough time of it—a five-ton truck is not very agile. A couple of times I saw suspicious characters or a car would get too close and I found myself leveling my rifle at them, finger on the trigger, thumb on the safety, ready and intending to use my weapon. This was the first time I had actually aimed a gun at someone and it was the scariest feeling I have yet to experience in Iraq.

A short time later I leveled my rifle at one man with an AK-47 cradled in his arms who was leaning against a car and staring flatly at us as we drove by. I could see his eyes. They were brown, a deep brown like chocolate and… cold, unfeeling. At least that's how I perceived it at the time.

I wonder what mine looked like.

The very notion of killing someone I would never know, taking that person away from his friends and family, is abhorrent to me. But the weird thing is I was ready to kill and had no reservation about it. In that instant, thinking back on it, I realized I just didn't care about pulling the trigger on another human being. I didn't care if that man lived or died.

It felt as if he was no longer human to me. He was merely a hurdle, an obstacle in the way of me going home. It was either kill or be killed and I could have been forced into making a split-second decision that would have violated everything I have been brought up to believe. I would have sacrificed my morals in order to live and I can't shake the feeling that being placed in that position was inherently wrong.

Who are we when we come face to face with the instinct to kill for our own self-preservation? Staring into this primal instinct, I have seen a dark abyss and I wonder... what happens when you discover the *only* morality that exists is *survival* and there's no more room for "Thou shalt not kill?" I can't help but be horrified, repulsed by this new sense of myself, and confused at how contradictory my thoughts are. To think that I was ready and willing to end a person's life. I don't know how to react to that change in me. It's an awful realization.

I have discovered what I am capable of and I'm not sure that I know myself any more.

Who am I becoming?

Just north of the downtown part of the city, we passed into a stretch known as "IED Alley." Alongside the potholed road were more remarkable piles of rubble and burned-out vehicles. This area was especially frightening because a bomb could go off at any moment and you wouldn't know it until you were meeting your maker. We gunned through there as fast as we could and soon we were north of the city.

I felt sad about what had happened to Baghdad. The architecture in the city had once been—and in some places still is—really quite impressive. There are beautiful sculpted spires reaching high into the sky, golden domes glinting in the sunlight. But so much of it was now nothing but gravel, a testament to the U.S. Air Force's awesome destructive force. It's such a shame how we humans feel so compelled to destroy what we create.

As we drove north out of the city, buildings were gradually replaced by farmland—lush with crops, palm trees, and irrigation canals. I saw a family herding goats and a mule-drawn cart carrying some sort of green harvest. It almost looked Amish but for the people driving it. Soon we were on a side road and about 45 minutes later we pulled into Camp Anaconda. The convoy was over, just like that. It was almost anticlimactic given all our worries and doubts, but I don't believe any of us were complaining.

We parked and our bags were unloaded for us. We were greeted with smiles, hugs, and handshakes from a large contingent of our unit. A cooler of soda was brought out. Mike strolled up, shoved me into a Humvee, and whisked me away to find Pete Butler, my new roommate. He was excited and asking every question you could imagine about the trip.

I had the shakes for quite a while and my adrenaline was still flowing at midnight, my eye twitching away, fingers still unsteady. I unpacked a little and made my bunk. Then I actually got down on my knees for the first time in my life, leaned forward, elbows on my mattress, and prayed, fervently thanking the good Lord for delivering my comrades and me to the relative safety of Camp Anaconda.

Part of me still can't believe I actually made it through all that in once piece—and sane.

I've heard that the major is very proud of us. He wants awards and promotions to be given. My promotion paperwork is in. Perhaps I'll be a sergeant soon.

I love you.

# PART THREE

# NO WAY OUT

*There is no greater pain than to recall a happy time while in wretchedness.*

—Dante Alighieri, *The Divine Comedy*

## April 17, 2004

THE NIGHT I ARRIVED AT Camp Anaconda, Pete went to work at 2300, so I was left to my own devices. I hadn't eaten since sometime the day before but I was too wired to feel hungry. I guess it was the adrenaline from the trip—my hands slightly shaking all night, my body exhausted, mind numb. Fortunately all I was required to do was sign the paperwork for my room. I fell asleep after listlessly attempting to read for a while... and was woken up by my very first mortar attack. Wow. What an experience. I had never heard such clamor, so violent were the explosions around me.

I was caught utterly off-guard when out of nowhere the earth shook and the ungodly din of debris began to fall on the metal roof of my quarters, the first explosion echoing in my ears. I was instantly jarred awake, my heart pounding, booms reverberating throughout my body as I peered outside. People were running around haphazardly, some with rifles, some with nothing but the shorts and T-shirts they wore, laces from their untied shoes fluttering around their ankles as they dove into the relative safety of the concrete bunkers placed around the living area of the camp.

Someone ran by—I didn't catch who—his rifle magazines clanging and bouncing, his M-16 faintly glinting in the moonlight. "We're being attacked!" he screamed. "Take cover! Follow me!"

I was transfixed by the sheer whiteness of his bulging eyeballs as he sprinted past in the dim light, and I wondered if my own eyes looked like his. I stepped out of my trailer almost casually and wandered through the compound like a zombie, wincing and ducking at each explosion. Feeling strangely distant, without emotion, I stared in wonder at the commotion as if I were on another planet and observing some strange festival of another species, perhaps their own independence celebrations.

There were flashes here and there temporarily lighting up the night. The noise from one explosion would scarcely leave my ears before the next one tore through the camp. I could feel the concussions in my feet, traveling up my legs like a ripple from a pebble thrown into a pond. I could hear a faint alarm siren all but drowned out by the din of the attack. I smirked a bit as I thought about all the times I've said "Well, now I've seen it all…" to myself during this journey only to experience something new and terrifying once again.

Within 15 minutes it was over, the sudden silence just as deafening and people began shuffling back to their quarters, their shoulders drooping, rifles carried limply at their sides, heads bowed by fear, confusion, and exhaustion. It almost felt as if it hadn't happened… like something you daydream only to shake your head, rub your eyes, and come back to the world around you.

"Welcome to Camp Anaconda," I muttered to myself.

I sat down on my bed and stared numbly at the floor, suddenly convinced that this was where I was going to spend my last days on earth. "I guess I'm not a virgin any more," I said and let out a flat laugh. What a thought and I chuckled again as a sensation of complete absurdity flooded through me. It just didn't seem real.

The next morning I woke around 0800 and took a shower, reveling in the water running down my body. The major had given us the day off so I unpacked and then rested, too weary to want to do anything else. It almost felt like Camp Doha again except that at Doha we never really unpacked. We lived out of our bags.

It's now a day later and the room I'm staying in is one of three to a trailer. It's about 11 by 11 feet with cheap wood paneling and linoleum flooring. There's a wall locker, nightstand, bed, lamp, pillow, sheets, and a comforter—mine is bright pink, an interesting touch. The mattresses are cheap foam like a dish sponge and the doors face the outdoors so each room has its own entrance. One lucky resident has a few wooden steps leading up to his doorway; the rest of us have to climb into our homes.

Along one wall Pete and I have already begun a process of building and rearranging a long shelf to put stuff on. My black box arrived today at 1700 and I was thankful it survived the journey. Even my portable DVD player was still working— astonishing considering the torn-up roads we traveled.

Today I took a tour of Camp Anaconda. I found out where my unit's hangar and workplace is. It's about a mile walk to the hangar, which is called a HAS or hardened aircraft shelter. The base is bigger than I initially thought, roughly three or four square miles and helicopters fly overhead at all times. I found out my section sergeant had been ordered to help some other unit for a time so I've been "accidentally promoted" to his position. I'm now third squad leader and I think it's quite ironic that a guy who knows nothing about his job is now in charge.

I'm sitting in the hydraulic shop right now. I'm working the graveyard shift—2300 to 0700 hours and I just looked around and poked through the seemingly endless rows of drawers and shelving. Much to my dismay, I'm discovering that I don't know what any of this stuff is. It's been so long that I've done anything remotely close to aviation hydraulic work that all this equipment and parts are completely foreign to me. What have I gotten into here?

The shops are lined up next to the hangar, a long line of Component Repair facilities baking in the desert sun and a big ass Chinook helicopter right outside is being disassembled for a routine phase inspection—where they pore over every piece of it to ensure it is airworthy. Pete is in back of the shop cutting wood for the new shelving unit we are constructing for our room. And yet, even with him here I feel displaced again... or misplaced, as the case may be.

It's funny, you know? I felt so strongly that enlisting with the Army would bring a sense of satisfaction and purpose. I wanted to feel the honor of what it meant to serve my country, of joining my relatives who have served—as if it was my duty. But it's never seemed to materialize in a way that felt meaningful, and I find myself wishing that I'd never joined.

What was within me that *truly* compelled me to enlist with the military?

I could be home with you, Rita, and when I think of all these moments that we've been apart because of my mistake—lost forever now—I feel sorrow.

But this is my life right now, like it or not.

I can see how *some* would like it. Everything is rigidly structured and spelled out for you. On a daily basis, you end up having to do very little thinking of your own. In fact, independent thought and questioning authority are often discouraged. The military is its own society, a subculture that insists on obedience without question. That must be comforting to some people, but it feels like a prison to me. So... just how much independent thought is a soldier allowed anyway?

I don't know, but I'm continually drawn toward questioning and contemplating these ideas.

I know one thing for sure—I don't belong here.

I miss you... I miss you very much. I have homesickness. I've discovered it can be physically as well as emotionally powerful and it comes on when I least expect it. I feel as if I am slowly sliding into depression. I don't feel like eating or laughing. All I see around me is tedium, fear, anger, abuse, lack of cooperation or compassion, violence, resentment, and disillusionment—an environment polluting everything and every thought.

But as melancholy as I feel right now, there is a vibrant part of me that's still enthralled by the wonders of this world. Take, for instance, the stars at night. I admire how they are so far away, how they twinkle with their brilliant light. I gaze upon the vastness of the universe and think about how small our planet really is. I wonder what's up there, what's going on, and I stand in awe of that grand unknowable mystery.

Within the universe, I am a speck of sand on a vast beach. I'm fully aware my life doesn't mean much in the scheme of things and that's humbling, yet it invigorates me.

You are my beacon in the night.

I love you.

### April 18, 2004

Well… it's just another day in paradise.

I finished my night shift at 0700 and stopped off for breakfast at the mess hall before going back to what we call our "hootches"—or as I call them, our hovels. It was a meager breakfast since supply convoys are being ambushed all over the place down south. It consisted of an egg, some cold French toast, and wilted, soggy bacon. Then I walked over to the Internet tent for a second, hoping for a chance to email you.

But the connection was down (which is not unusual), and there was an exasperatingly long line of people waiting for it to come back online. So I went back to my hootch and lay down for a while—blessed solace. After a short nap, I ate an MRE, and then it hit… it was like a ton of bricks had been dumped on me.

I cried.

I don't know where it came from, but it just overwhelmed me, gushed out of me. It's kinda funny. I ended up chuckling to myself because I started thinking that in all the years we've been together, you've hardly ever seen me cry. I wish you could have seen this one and I've realized I wouldn't mind crying in front of you now. It's silly that I had still felt too self-conscious to cry in front of you after all these years together.

I've made up my mind that I'm not going to feel inhibited around you any more. Maybe it's a childhood thing, never feeling safe or secure enough to fully express myself. To be perfectly honest, I don't really care. All that matters is our future. You know what? From that perspective, this experience has been good for me. Being away from you is allowing me to grow enough to fully be me when we are reunited.

What a fool I have been all these years.

Sometimes it makes me laugh when you've mentioned how proud people are of me. They say we're fighting for America, fighting the war on terror, and defending our freedoms, eh? They say we are fighting for the Iraqis' freedom and for democracy? I know they mean well and I appreciate their support, but a lot of us here don't share those sentiments. Most soldiers I know agree that the justifications for this war were fabricated or at least exaggerated and that the Iraqi people don't give a shit about America.

Among the soldiers I've spoken with during this adventure, the typical responses are always something like "I really don't care. At least I'm getting a paycheck," "Well, I don't really have a choice, do I?" and "I'm just covering my own ass until I can get out of here."

How ironic, don't you think, baby? The people who want this war *aren't* here. The people who don't want this war *are* here. That keeps me up through the small hours of the night.

Why the hell *are* we here anyway? If it's mostly about big business and oil as I greatly suspect, then America has fallen ill.

Why do people put up with this? Why would anyone still feel what we're doing is right, even against overwhelming evidence to the contrary? Is it because if they lost that belief they would have nothing left to cling to? Something akin to religious fundamentalism? Is this another crusade? Is America the new Rome, as a buddy of mine thinks, an imperialistic state rather than a democracy? Am I contributing, even by just sitting here, to ideals that I detest? Should I hate myself for that? What will all this mean when I die? Is this merely yet another chapter in the long history of human violence?

I heard once that everything we do in life, whether it's negative or positive, no matter how small or large, affects the world in some way.

How far does warfare and its inherent ugliness ripple? By participating in war and blindly following orders, how are we helping or hurting our world? Or is it a combination of both?

I don't know, honey. But I love you.

You are in my dreams and my heart.

## April 19, 2004

I tried the coffeemaker you sent me today. I had a fabulous cup in one of the mugs you included. I love everything you've sent; it means the world to me. I don't know when I will get through all the junk food you sent. It's more than I usually eat in a year baby, but the coffee is a Godsend. I'm going to make some for the hell of it. It's a little taste of home.

I only have five or six months until I see you in Germany. That's not so bad, is it? I hope we can still plan that trip, that my leave comes through in a timely fashion and all the travel arrangements are smoothly coordinated. I do hope the time goes by quickly and I'm sure the closer the date gets, the more excruciating the wait will be.

I love you.

## April 21, 2004

Here's something to add to the hilarity (or hysteria, take your pick) of the situation here. When someone wants to use the port-a-john, they have to put on all their gear—ballistic vest, helmet, spare ammunition, and rifle. In fact, anytime you leave your shop, you have to wear all your gear. So say it's 105 degrees and you want to walk the 50 yards to take a leak or even go to the next shop, you have to put all this stuff on, then take it all off when you get back. The penalty for not doing this is menial work on your one day off. Kinda sounds like grade school, huh?

It's pointless. If you're in a port-a-john and this place gets mortared, the ballistic vest won't do you any good. You'll still be blown to bits, the juiced remains of you spread out over an area as large as 20 yards. The vest won't even stop an assault rifle bullet without the plates (which you're *not* required to wear). And what's the point of the rifle? Are we supposed to try hitting the mortar round, like skeet shooting only with a bullet? If we have to shoot the "bad guys" while we're taking a leak, then they are inside the perimeter of the camp. We'd have bigger problems to worry about.

Here's another one. Since I've been here, we've been mortared every day. A siren usually sounds to let us know we're on "red alert." When in our hovels, we're supposed to abandon them and take shelter in the concrete bunkers outside. But they can only hold 10 people at most and overcrowding quickly becomes a problem. The skittish start locking and loading their rifles, readying for the inevitable invasion.

Most have decided to stay in their hovels during an attack now, myself included. I have a couple of reasons for this. One, I don't want to be accidentally shot by a moron while crammed in a small concrete bunker. Two, if there are people crowded into a little concrete bunker and a mortar hits, there they go, all of them killed. But if a mortar hits in the middle of the hovels, it would maybe take out 20 people at most. Plus it plain doesn't matter where you are. If you're going to get killed… then you will. It's a fact of life here, something we are all beginning to get used to living with day in and day out.

There has also been a new rule mandating that we clear our rifle chambers when entering the mess hall. We've had a few incidents of "accidental discharge" because people were locking and loading during mortar attacks and then forgetting to unload their weapons afterward. One officer accidentally discharged his pistol in the mess hall and could have killed someone—the bullet ricocheting, everyone ducking for cover, spilling dinner plates, wide eyes wondering if we were under attack again. I was scared to death.

There was another mortar attack last night. It's really just luck of the dice whether one lands on your head or not. Sometimes they land over on the Air Force side of the base, sometimes they land here, sometimes they land all over the place and there's no telling where the next one will hit. It's really very random and I wonder who is giving these people their firing coordinates. Maybe they don't have any. Maybe they just lob them over here in the hopes of killing as many of us as they can.

It's about 0900 now and I just got word that a Blackhawk helicopter was shot down last night after the mortar attack. The two pilots were injured but rescued—they crashed right outside the base. Anyway, the two Iraqis who were mortaring us were captured, and one of them was discovered to have a "red tag" on his person. That has everyone on edge.

There are two kinds of "tags" for the Iraqi workers here— "red tags" and "green tags." They are required to wear them whenever they're on base. The "red tag" guys must be escorted by armed security at all times since they are suspected but unconfirmed insurgents. "Green tag" guys are allowed to work with no escort but… why are they letting these guys in here to begin with?

I guess it's because they'll do the menial chores the Army doesn't want us to bother with. The problem is they leave in the evening and promptly mortar the hell out of us. I've also heard they rummage through the trash looking for our addresses in order to spread havoc to our families back in the States. So we have to burn all the address labels on our mail when it arrives.

I'm tellin' ya, babe, this place is fucked up.

Mike looked at a work order this morning and said "This is screwed up" so flatly that it cracked me up. The tone of his voice was priceless.

I love you.


### April 23, 2004

Here are more camp uniform requirements for ya, honey. We strap an elastic band around our Kevlar helmets to secure the camouflage cover that goes on top. Both the bands and the covers come in green or tan. Well, if you have a tan cover with a green band (because you weren't issued a tan one) you will be punished, possibly with a formal write-up. They want you to wear the tan with the tan, you know, so that we are… color coordinated.

Please tell me, what difference does it make when you consider that the ballistic vest they issue is *green*? This is getting to the point of ridiculousness. Most people weren't issued the proper equipment when they left the U.S. anyway. There just wasn't enough. I bought myself a tan one at Ft. Knox.

My work hours have changed again. Now I am working from 1500 or 1600 to about 2300 or 0000 hours. I only get one day in seven off, and starting on May 1, I'll get one in 10 off. I wouldn't mind so much but all these hour changes are screwing with my sleep. What if I make a mistake while repairing a helicopter and cause an accident, perhaps injuring or killing someone? I couldn't live with myself.

Pete and I are getting along comfortably. We have our little hovel set up about how we like it now. Last night we sat in the camping chairs we "found" on base, watched a movie, and ate all the Easter candy you sent me. Well, not *all*, but I did significant damage to the M&Ms. Thank you so much, baby.

We were attacked again today.

I love you.


## April 24, 2004

I think it's really screwed up that I haven't done any real hydraulic work with the Army and in aviation for years and yet now I am here. People look at me dumbfounded when I say I don't know what they're talking about. Everything looks foreign to me. The only thing I clearly remember how to do is safety wire.

They changed the uniform rules again. Now in the

immediate area of your shop or the administrative office, you don't have to wear your ballistic vest and helmet, just the uniform top and soft cap. But if you go to the port-a-johns 50 yards away from the offices, you *do* have to wear them.

These folks are strange.

The wind blew like crazy today, and dust was everywhere. You could see about 40 feet in front of you at most. The flight line was one big, dusty haze. God, I'm all itchy tonight because of the dust in the air.

Pat Parsons came up to me tonight and said he has finally confirmed he hates it here.

I love you.

### April 27, 2004

Well, I'm at work and as usual, I'm thinking.

I am a useless part in the war engine. If I wasn't here things would go along just fine, maybe better because I wouldn't get in the way. So I've been wondering lately—if there is a God, why would he send me here? What exactly am I supposed to get out of this experience? What am I supposed to learn here? What am I supposed to *do* here? Am I meant to affect someone or something positively or negatively? Or is this experience random—like a roll of the dice? Is there a God? Is this destiny or just something that happened? I guess God and I are having a bit of a dispute… or at least a discussion.

If there is a God, is he laughing at me floundering or is he rubbing his bearded chin, thoughtfully wondering what I will do or where I will go next? Is he testing me? Is he trying to teach me something? I wonder if there is a divine plan, what some call fate or destiny, or if those are just human constructs we created to allow us to feel more secure on an all-too-insecure world. Are we trying to feel as if we're not merely animals scurrying about on a planet lost in an endless void of pitch-black, frigid night?

*I* feel as if I am a minute ant on an immense anthill.

What if all this really does mean nothing? What if there is no divinity at the end? What if there is no heaven? No hell? No purgatory? What if "ashes to ashes and dust to dust" happens to be the brutal reality we are all frightened of facing? Perhaps life does really wink out just like that. Our consciousness dissolves into oblivion, forever lost and soon to be forgotten.

Does that mean our lives are wasted? I don't think so, but it does teach you how to live if you look at it that way. It compels you to be acutely aware that the moments count—perhaps more than anything else.

Our very lives are a sum of moments.

Perhaps moments are all there are.

I love you.


## April 28, 2004

Well, it's yet another day in paradise here at good ole Camp Anaconda. Yesterday we had a platoon meeting, one of four scheduled for the week. Man, does Mike like meetings. All of them follow the same format—if you do these things, you have to do this additional thing. If you don't do this additional thing, this will happen and you will be spanked. So do this thing and by the way… you're all doing a great job. That's about it. Mike seems to volunteer our platoon for additional duties, all of them outside of work hours, which has pissed many people off.

But yesterday at our meeting, Mike told us the war is being escalated again. An entire infantry battalion is being moved to our base, which has also been assigned to conduct MedEvac operations. There will doubtless be many casualties on the U.S. side—hell, on both sides. I'm still not sure why we came here to begin with, but the immediate mission is to get rid of the people who want us out of their own country.

Here are some more thoughts to brood over, something I began thinking about while driving in the convoy:

How would you feel if you saw a convoy of Iraqis drive through downtown Boston and aimed rifles at you as they passed? Would you not take to the hills with your own rifle while proudly reciting the Second Amendment and defend your homeland? How far would you go to protect your home? Isn't that what these people are doing? Is that not the definition of insurgent? Would you become one? Would you begin adopting the ways of guerilla warfare? Would you plant a bomb? Would you strap a bomb to your chest and commit suicide in the name of your cause? Would you throw rocks at the Iraqi invaders? Would you toss grenades off a bridge to try to blow up their trucks? If you did, would you be labeled a terrorist by the occupying force?

What I'm getting at here is I think it's important to try and walk in another's shoes. There are always two sides to a story and ours might not always be right. Perhaps there would be a little less war if we empathized a little more.

I miss you very much today. Sometimes I get so lost in dreams of being home with you that the world around me disappears and all I can see is you. It's like you're so far away, but so close. My thoughts come alive. It's a form of teleportation, you know what I mean?

Do you think I ought to come home instead of meeting you in Germany for my leave? Maybe we can just spend time at the house. I miss our home so very much. I even miss watching those stupid tractor sprinklers we bought continually going off-track and getting stuck, their hoods butting into the fence and flooding the yard with their cold watery spray.

I guess I miss everything.

I love you.

### April 30, 2004

I'd like to describe Camp Anaconda—or "Mortaritaville," as they are calling it around here. It's the largest American air base in northern Iraq. Before we invaded, it was called Saddam International Airport. There is leftover abandoned equipment from Saddam's regime scattered everywhere, most of it stenciled with its former name in bright white lettering, forlorn epitaphs to a fallen dictator.

The U.S. has since moved into many of the old buildings—

what's left of them anyway. The northern side of the base has a small PX, a finance office, an air traffic control center, a movie tent, a barbershop, some Iraqi vendors who are allowed to conduct business on base, and all the other usual military stuff. That is where the Air Force is housed. I'm encamped on the Army side in the southwest corner of the base. All we have here are a couple of Internet tents, a couple of shower/latrine trailers, and housing. I've heard they are supposedly building more stuff but we'll see how long that takes.

We mainly have helicopters here except for the Air Force's few large airplanes—C-130s and C-5s—that they use to transport people on and off base. There are so many helicopters that the flight line literally took my breath away the first time I saw it. They're neatly parked in rows that seem to stretch to the horizon, each of them worth anywhere from nine million to 15 million dollars apiece depending on how they've been outfitted… kinda like options when you buy a car.

There is constant activity here. Helicopters fly over us all the time, sometimes so low you can clearly see the tread of the tires, the air from the rotor blades whipping up a furious dust storm, the whine of the jet engines piercing your ears.

There is one thin paved road stretching past my housing area. It leads to the main maintenance area where my unit has one hangar to work in. There are two things worth mentioning about our hangar: There is an unexploded mortar shell buried in a pile of rubble inside. It punched a hole through the ceiling at some point before I arrived and has never been dug out. The roof of the hangar still has a huge hole in it. The shell and the piles of wreckage around it have been roped off and we've been told to keep our distance.

Second, there is another roped-off section near the other entrance. Supposedly there's a bomb lodged in the wall there. Some say there is depleted uranium in the shell that's steadily leaking radiation. All we have for protection is the yellow "CAUTION" tape roping off the area, not very comforting to say the least. I always feel a little weird as I walk by.

We are mortared twice a day on average. Quite a few mortars have hit near us and I'm not entirely sure these pages do justice to how frighteningly close they can come. There were many loud explosions the other night. It makes my heart jump and my body clench.

Recently I sat against the side of my shop, smoked a cigarette, and listened to us getting shelled. Images of my life flashed before me as the night air rocked with explosions, my body and especially my eyes reflexively flinching each time a mortar landed.

Eventually it ended, and with drooped shoulders I went inside to write in this journal—another typical night at our camp. There's a lot going on at the Air Force side of the base as well. It seems the Iraqis know where the airplanes are. We've come to expect an explosion or alarm at any time during the day. I don't know how frazzled my mind will be after a whole year here.

We are about 35 miles north of Baghdad. All around the base is farmland, irrigation canals (I think fed by the Tigris

River) cutting through the landscape amid groves of beautiful green palm trees, maybe date palms. I was able to take in the scenery very well when I was coming in with the convoy.

The highest temperature I have seen so far has been about 102 degrees and the wind can really fucking blow through here. I have seen some nice dust storms—dust devils—spirals of swirling sand stretching up into the sky.

They are constantly burning every kind of trash imaginable at the dump here on base. It's a 24-hour, seven-day-a-week burn pit. Some people I've talked to are concerned about what we're breathing in on a daily basis, let alone what we're putting into the atmosphere.

Mostly the place is drab and brown, the lush green of the surrounding landscape abruptly ending at our single-strand, barbed-wire fence. Gravel is spread around the housing areas—or "trailer parks" as we have grown fond of calling them—in a vain effort to keep the dust down. There are rows and rows of these trailers. Some people still live in tents—I've heard they're trying to convert completely to trailers, but it will take some time—maybe after I leave here.

The convoys are still struggling to get through due to heavy insurgent activity down south. As a result the food is pretty shitty—when you can get it. Yesterday was a good day though. I stopped at the mess hall for lunch and had an overcooked breaded veal patty, soggy carrots, and instant mashed potatoes. That's a typical meal. You always, always, have to have those instant mashed potatoes.

They have a couple of shuttle buses that can take you to the other side of the base, complete with designated bus stops, one near my housing area. One bus runs north around the base to the PX, the other runs south around the base, coming back to the housing area. Sometimes you have to wait a long time, easily more than a half hour. I learned quickly to try to minimize the number of trips I make. There isn't much time in the day and efficiency is a must. Plus you have to wear all that combat gear and it's getting hotter by the day. Summer is going to be a nightmare.

Finally, it's really, *really* flat here, flatter than Kansas or Nebraska, if you can believe it.

That's Camp Anaconda in a nutshell—what a glorious place. I love you.

## May 1, 2004

I saw the most amazing lightning show in my life last night. We were right on the edge of a storm coming out of the west. Clouds were passing under a waxing moon and a tangibly chilly breeze was drifting through the trailer park.

I stood outside watching for about 20 minutes, in awe of nature and the weather here in Iraq once again. Lightning illuminated the sky and bolts shot out of nowhere—sometimes vertically, sometimes horizontally, and sometimes spreading their immense electric tendrils like a spider web. There was no thunder, only the bolts of lightning. They seemed to come from everywhere.

I enjoyed every moment of it until the rain finally came and drove me inside. It rained for just a short while, but it was enough to muddy things again, caking my boots and making it nearly impossible to keep my hovel clean. This morning there was a haze on the airfield and the sky was overcast.

Today I relearned how to bend hydraulic tubing and did fairly well practicing bending some lines. I must say I'm proud I was able to pick it up again without too much trouble. We've been issued a laptop that we're using to produce an inventory of parts, quite a task considering hydraulic work has a wide array of them. But I believe it will be infinitely helpful as we plod through the work we have here. All in all, the shop is finally becoming organized and I think we're actually becoming productive.

Lunch just plain sucked today. I swear that mess hall is the worst I have ever eaten in. I had some tough gristly "Swedish" meatballs, the usual soggy carrots and instant mashed potatoes. The salad bar is still lousy, consisting of canned cranberry sauce, beets, sliced cheese, and jalapenos. What an interesting salad you can build there. They did have little butter packets today, a novelty here, and they make the mashed potatoes a little easier to choke down. Instead of water, those almighty Kuwaitis bravely brought strawberry milk from the Danish Dairy Company. You know, eating an MRE is really no worse than the mess hall. Maybe I'll have one for dinner.

I love you, my dear.

### May 9, 2004

I've been put on day shift now. Here's the routine:

I get up around 0530 and if the power is on (it's very sporadic here) I get a shower; if not, I'll spend my spare time throughout the day picking sand out of my ears. Then I make coffee with the coffeemaker you sent me. I slurp it down, sometimes getting to enjoy the taste of it. I usually don't eat breakfast, but I didn't at home either so it's not that big of a deal. Normally I'm in the hangar by 0630.

At 0700 we have an accountability formation[25]and are given the morning's news—you know, like how many people were killed lately. That always starts the day off bright and cheery, smiles all around. After formation I go to my shop. Malcolm is back and I'm working with him now. He's still my section sergeant and head of the Hydraulics shop. If we don't have the necessary parts to do a job—as so often happens here—then we can't complete any of our work or we have to find some way to improvise. At 1100 I usually head to lunch at the mess hall— soggy carrots again, whoohoo. At about 1600, I am released. I find some dinner at some point, read, listen to mortars, and go to bed.

That's basically the day.

They are now doing what they call "Health and Welfare" inspections. A platoon sergeant from a different company is conducting them. When you're notified, you have to drop

---

25  To inspect the company and make sure that everyone is present

everything and go with them. They drive you to your room and poke through it with German shepherds, sometimes leaving the room in complete disarray while you stand outside waiting. I am of the personal opinion that it's an appalling invasion of privacy.

Three mortar attacks came in last night. We get attacked about once per night and there's really not much you can do except hope, pray, and go about doing what you're doing with tense shoulders and wide eyes.

Oh, one interesting note. They have now informed us we don't need to wear our equipment to the port-a-johns any more. That includes the small smoking area next to them that we've nicknamed "The Bombay Café."

I've been relearning how to overhaul Blackhawk brakes. Amazing isn't it?

Morale is low. People are depressed about being here.

I love you.


### May 12, 2004

There was an assault two nights ago. It happened about 100 feet from my hovel. Apparently at about 2100 hours, a guy was walking to the bathroom trailers when a KBR employee hit him with a brick and kicked the crap out of him. I didn't even know it happened until Pete went outside to go to the bathroom and saw the MPs, red and blue lights flashing like a crime scene in the States. They had closed off the entire area including the bathrooms to conduct an investigation. The victim is undergoing mental health counseling and will probably be sent home.

Today the major gave a speech about using the buddy system, to be careful of people who might want to hurt us. So I guess our situation is this: The Iraqis assault us daily, low morale and squabbling abound in my unit, and American civilian contractors attack us when we least expect it. Seems as though we are getting hit from all sides and no one knows who to trust at any given time. Suspicion is everywhere.

Since the assault, no one has cleaned the bathrooms and showers or filled the water tanks. It's as disgusting as you'd think and we have no water. The toilets are overflowing with unflushed shit. There was even some all over the outside of a toilet and smeared on the floor.

What an awful place this is.

I now know Blackhawk brakes like the back of my hand, and Malcolm and I are both learning a lot about tube bending. The shop is fairly productive and more so every day. I do a brake here and there, bend some line maybe get some parts. Work really isn't bad right now.

I love you.

## May 14, 2004

I was promoted to sergeant yesterday. To be honest, I'm not quite sure I really want it and part of me still doesn't believe it. I guess the real perk is a larger paycheck but it seems that when you are promoted, you are inundated with 10 times the responsibility for one percent in pay increase. I suppose it's still pretty neat though and I'll adjust.

It happened at the morning formation and they called me up to the front of the whole company. The major pinned the rank on me, giving me the traditional shove to stick me with the pins, and said he liked the sound of my new rank. That was it in a nutshell, except for the fact I was both excited and nervous. I felt that my legs were shaking and I hoped no one could see me trembling.

For the rest of the day, people kept coming up and congratulating me. It felt pretty weird—people shaking my hand, telling me it was long overdue… calling me "Sarge." It was a surreal feeling that I've felt only once before—at our wedding. I did enjoy the attention though and savored the moment because it will soon fade and I will be just one of the guys again.

I love you.

### May 15, 2004

We were attacked at least eight times today, volleys of countless mortars coming in with each attack. It went on for so long. The explosions started right across the runway at around 0700 and there was a helicopter taking off at the time. I bet they really shit their pants—it happened so close to them. It also makes me think the attack was planned that way. I think they've been watching the airstrip—watching us, our patterns.

At lunch, Ken, Derek, Jakob, and I talked about how weird it is to be getting used to being mortared. We joked about how we ought to make scorecards, like judges hold up in the Olympics, rating figure skaters or something. We could stand outside and hold them up in a line after the Iraqis are done with their routine. Today's was a 9 or a 10.

We also talked about how at night we gauge the distance of the explosions and only move if they come close enough to shake our trailers. That happened a couple days ago. My bed slid across the floor, concussions knocking everything to the floor and creating quite a mess to pick up. Debris clattered against the roof, sounding like rain. It was a real good bombardment.

I'm tired of war.

There was a full salad bar today, which made us look over our shoulders, suspicious about what was going on. It was the first real salad bar we had seen in a long time, and who knows how long it will last. Normally, we are still receiving meager provisions because the supply trucks are still getting attacked regularly on their way to us, some of them not making it all.

Even more unsettling, the ice cream man was absent today and a guy in line observed that we get mortared whenever he's gone. Maybe it's the ice cream man who's bombing us. Can you imagine what kind of epitaph that would make on my headstone?

*Killed by the ice cream man in Iraq.*

There's a morale meter in the hangar. What a joke that is. It's a half-circle with "Good" stenciled on the right in green, "Fair" stenciled at the top in yellow, and "Bad" stenciled on the left in red. Right now the arrow is deeply in the red.

Your recent email troubled me. I'm struggling to deal with

this whole guy issue you brought up. Are you partying with these guys you just met when I could be talking with you? How do you think this makes me feel? Do you care? What if something happened? What are they doing partying with my wife? I get up at 0400 in the morning to write you and would every day, but you can't fit me in just one day a week?

I don't hear from you much any more regardless of how many letters I write and I'm beginning to wonder what's going on. A vague feeling is creeping in that you're becoming distant. I don't know, maybe it's me. Maybe just being here makes me feel the distance more acutely but… no, my gut is telling me something. It makes me uneasy when I think of my wife spending time with guys from her gym while I'm over here immersed in this nastiness.

I know you hold things back. I've known you so long that I can tell pretty easily. You also said as much in your email and I *do* understand your reasoning. I know you don't want to hurt me but I can't help but question. Which hurt is worse? Not knowing but feeling your reticence or dealing with the fact of you spending time with guys while I'm here? I don't think you're being stupid for having feelings of guilt, for partying it up in the good ole United States while I'm away. Perhaps misery loves company and I want us both to be miserable while we're apart. Is that selfish of me? I don't know. I worry about the future too—every day in fact.

But you're right. Things are changing, aren't they? That

notion was driven home when you mentioned you couldn't read my thoughts and that my eyes looked vague and distant in the pictures I sent you. But *how* are things changing? How are we both changing? How will it affect our life together? Will we become closer? Will we drift apart? Will you fall for one of the guys you've recently met? So many questions and no answers. Just an unsettled feeling I can't quite pin down.

I feel angry. I feel hurt and I'm not sure what to do with that. I feel like I'm not really on solid ground any more. I've never had a scrap of doubt about us before. But here it is, I don't know what to make of it, and there is very little I can do except stew on it. What are you going to do when I come home? Do you honestly expect me to party with you and your guy friends, or are you going to leave me at home? How are you going to integrate this into our marriage?

I don't want to hang out with them. I can tell you that right now. They're on my turf and I resent it. I never thought I would have to deal with this. Do you mean to tell me I went through all this to come home to some guys partying with my wife?

I don't think you are a self-centered bitch for resenting people for asking about how I'm doing or bringing up all the bad news from over here. It would probably make me angry too, to have all the fear and worry thrown right back in your face when you thought you could have a normal, happy day. Just tell them I'm doing fine.

Perhaps that is all we can do.

**May 16, 2004**

Well, I think I'm over my anger. You have to understand, all this can be hard to swallow from so many miles away, but I trust you.

Maybe I'm just going crazy.

It's easy to do here.

And the craziness continues. In our morning formation today, we were told there was a chemical attack on a convoy recently. We've been instructed to be on the lookout for anything suspicious, whatever that means. Everything and everyone is suspicious now. Then it was quite casually put out, "But the softball game starts at 1900 hours." All of us derived some humor from that. It was so nonchalant, almost out of a standup comedy show.

Things heated up around our area again shortly after formation—more mortars.

Do they really have to attack us *every* day?

By the way, the ice cream man was in today and we didn't get mortared while he was on base. Interesting, huh?

I love you.

**May 17, 2004**

Well, I'm sitting here in my cell and it's growing hotter by the minute. The power went out again. It happens roughly twice a week now, sometimes more and always in the heat of the day. It usually lasts for at least a few hours, sometimes longer. I honestly couldn't say when it went out—I came home to it. Oh my, I can't believe I just called this place home.

Gary has found a friend. He was coming home from a shift the other day when a baby finch flew up and landed on his shoulder. He brought the little bird back to his room and is making a perch for it.

The weirdest things happen here.

I love you.

## May 19, 2004

So Gary's finch is now obsessively attached to him, almost as if it needs a parental figure. He named it Frederick—or if it's a girl, Francine; we don't know how to tell. He feeds it bread that he steals from the mess hall and Vienna sausages from a care package he got from home. The other day he built a perch out of some spare lumber and Frederick absolutely loves it. He sits on his perch and watches Gary attentively.

Sometimes it will fly to Gary, land on his shoulder, and peck at him until he feeds it. He bathes the little devil with drops of water and the bird will shake a little then groom himself. It's freakin' adorable. Yesterday Gary was outside with him before his shift and Frederick decided to fly off. Gary left for his shift thinking, "Well, that's it. He's gone." But when he came back from his shift, the little guy was waiting for him on the steps to his trailer.

That's amazing.

Frederick also loves Bob Graves, a friend of ours and Gary's roommate. He landed on Bob's face once, who got a little annoyed. But Gary will walk around with this damn bird on his shoulder, like a pirate; it's really hilarious. Everyone stares at them, but neither Frederick nor Gary seem to mind. The other night, Frederick curled up in the crook of his dad's shoulder and slept all night.

And check this out. Frederick was hanging out on his perch the other day and Gary said, "Come here, Frederick." The bird flew right over to him—smart little son-of-a-bitch. He can't fly very far yet and he really flaps and flaps to get anywhere, but he's trying. They do wing exercises in the morning before Gary goes to work. The bird sits on Gary's arm while Gary slowly moves his arm up and down. Each time his arm moves down, Frederick flaps like mad, hopefully building strong, healthy wings.

I got to hold him once, which was exciting. He perched on my finger for a while until he pecked at me—snack time. So we fed him and he was content again. Gary's plan is to take care of him for a few weeks then let him go. We all agree he needs a little upbringing before he heads out on his own. He seems very much at home and I couldn't help but marvel at this little miracle of life amid the ever-constant death, destruction, and chaos here.

It's beautiful, you know.

Beauty amid ugliness, so bizarre to see, but it keeps me going and gives me hope that there's more to this world than violence. How refreshing and inspiring. I hope Frederick stays for a while. He lifts my spirits and makes me laugh with hope for the world around me.

Do you suppose that's how God works?

We had no power until around 2300 hours last night. No running water for the showers or toilets, no air conditioning, no Internet, sometimes no power in the mess hall. It's like we're on one big camping trip in the desert.

I couldn't take a shower for more than 24 hours and let me tell ya, when you're in a room that's about 115 degrees and it's about 100 or so outside, you get rank pretty quick. All I could do was sweat it out. I got a bit of a heat rash too. What else can you do except mutter to yourself, "Who cares about being attacked? I'm dying of heat exhaustion."

The funny thing about it was just before the power came back, I took another bottle shower—hey, you gotta do what you gotta do. I grabbed four bottles of water, headed to the shower trailer, and did my best. It was a dismal sight, the whole trailer littered with bottles, toilet paper, shaving cream cans, some empty toothpaste tubes—everyone's trash. I found a relatively clean shower stall (sometimes they are hard to come by) and used two bottles to wash and two to rinse. I did it in the dark with nothing but the light from my flashlight coming through the shower curtain. I got fairly clean, felt a bit better… and as soon as I got back to my cell, the power came on again! The cheers resounded through the trailer park as if the war had ended. At least I was mostly clean for our nightly mortar attack.

I have to admit, I've never appreciated electricity so much. It has forced me to realize just how dependent humans are on power and how helpless we can feel during these blackouts. I will never take it for granted again. I don't want to take *any* creature comfort for granted again, but this has also taught me I can survive without.

I love you, baby.

### May 20, 2004

Happy anniversary, baby—just think, four years ago today we were married in front of our friends and family. God, I can close my eyes and still vividly see how beautiful you were in your wedding dress, how it flowed over your hips and clung to your shoulders and graceful neck.

I hope you got the flowers I sent. I wanted to at least do *something*. Not bad for a guy a mere few miles away, the Internet being such a useful tool… when it's available. I love you so much.

You're the best person I've ever known and I'm sad. Your latest emails seem so depressed and guilt-ridden. I wish I could tell you in person that you have nothing to feel guilty about. Someday I'll explain all this to you. I want to move on from this when I come home. We should free ourselves. I want you to be happy. Sometimes I wish you were as miserable as me, but that's selfish and I know it. You *deserve* to be happy. Slow down, take a deep breath, and appreciate the marvels of life. They're so beautiful if you allow them into your soul.

We lost power again today. It went out at about 0400 hours and my jail cell was really heating up when I left for my shift.

Pete got a box of goodies from the States and offered me one of his Twinkies. I couldn't resist. I haven't had a Twinkie in so long. One was accidentally smooshed flat with the wrapper intact so we tacked it to the wall. We're gonna put a sign next to it saying "Break seal in case of emergency."

I heard a lot of machine gun fire close to the perimeter this morning—lovely, huh? There's really nothing stopping them from coming into the base, just that thin stretch of barbed wire.

Also, half the Filipino workers quit yesterday so laundry service is now only available once a week. I don't even want to imagine that line, all those tense soldiers baking in the sun with laundry bags slung over their shoulders. That should be fun indeed. From what I've heard, the workers were tired of getting bombed. I guess a few of them got killed. It must be nice to be able to just walk away.

I love you, baby—happy anniversary.

## May 21, 2004

Well, here I am again. There were numerous explosions throughout the night and into this morning. I stopped counting them at around 2200 hours. Then this morning, more explosions a little farther away—seems like they're covering the area pretty well. Someday one of those things really *is* going to drop on my head. I'm learning how to turn my mind off as that's the only way to mentally survive this mess, but the day I don't have to listen to explosions any more will be a happy one. That day seems so far off, almost nonexistent. I can't even comprehend what it would feel like to be alive at the end of this deployment, to leave here and begin life again.

Your recent email disturbed me. I don't think you really get where I'm coming from, as I am sure you feel the same about me. I forget exactly what it was about, something about me stifling you, about how I am small and weak-minded for being jealous of your new friends. Quite frankly, I felt exasperated when I read it. I feel you have a lot of anger and resentment toward me and I am sorry for that, but I can't do anything about it, especially while I'm here. You gotta find yourself in your own way and you're obviously not understanding or really listening to my words.

Why does there seem to be a disconnect forming between us? It's strange—that feeling just kinda snuck up on me. I think right now you're too caught up in self-discovery, what seems to be the beginning of something new for you and you don't want to express love right now, so consumed with your own path. I feel sad about that.

If I had any advice that you were willing to take, it would be slow down. But you won't, I know that, and coming from me that advice would only push you further away. You're too hardheaded and there's a feeling developing in the pit of my stomach that I might have to deal with this deployment on my own. Of course there's always the distinct possibility that I'm way off-base, but that's the beauty of a journal. I can just write and try to sort out my feelings in the process.

I can't help feeling like you're way out there somewhere,

drifting out to sea in a small boat and all I can do is watch helplessly, my outstretched hand never reaching you.

It made for a gloomy anniversary in the end.

I love you.

## May 24, 2004

I am in a prison. It's confirmed. Today I got a knock on my door shortly after I came home from my shift and lo and behold, there were two sergeants informing me that they were conducting another "Health and Welfare" inspection with the MPs and some German shepherds. So I had to stand outside my cell again while the MPs went in and let a dog sniff around my room. They emptied my wall locker, poked through and overturned everything. I felt like an inmate, not an American soldier serving his country in the name of freedom—how ironic and disgraceful. They had a big set of keys and were opening rooms even if people were gone.

Is this really what being an American soldier is about?

I love you.

## May 28, 2004

I got your email about our cat. God, I just don't know what to say. He's our cat and I love him dearly. I know he's always had problems. He's always been very skittish, shy, and has had a peeing problem. But I guess it's gotten worse since I've been away. I understand why you want to drop him off at the Humane

Society and I'm trying to digest it. But you know what? I wouldn't have the heart to give him away as you are intending. I love him so very much. It's like giving away a child you've raised. These animals we decided to care for are *ours*. By inviting them into our home, we promised to nurture and take care of them. They are members of our family.

I can picture his fearful eyes when you drop him off, his legs trembling as they do. I'm sure he'll be wondering what's happening because he can't comprehend what he's done to deserve being abandoned. It's breaking my heart thinking about this. I've been brooding over this for days since I got your email and acquiesced to let him go. I can't imagine him not being there when I come home, that roar of a purr coming to life once he determines it's me again.

But I agreed for your sake. If you really can't deal with him, you have to do what you think is best. It's hard for me to be a part of that right now.

I wish with all my heart things didn't have to be this way. Sadness is beginning to creep its way into every aspect of my life. It's relentless.

I'm hoping you will change your mind. Maybe there's an alternative? Perhaps you'll decide to take him to the doctor and discover why he keeps behaving the way he does?

Do what you think is best.

I love you.

**May 30, 2004**

I've been neglecting my writing lately. No energy. I think I've been depressed because of what you've written lately—asking why I love you, how you're finding it hard to be a married woman, that you're getting rid of our cat. Your emails make me think we're losing the grasp of our relationship despite assurances from our friends there really is a life for me when I come home.

Why do I think I love you? Wow, do you really have to ask? And what on earth do you mean when you ask if perceptions alter our love, if it is the same for everyone, if it is tangible, fleeting, or everlasting? That doesn't sound like the same woman who was telling me we are soul mates, bound together, and meant to be with one another. Do you really think I am only saying I love you because I am over here in this hellhole, that I am simply missing the idea of you? My God, what is happening to you?

I know you analyze our relationship, I guess we all do, but I never question my love for you. I found it horribly depressing that you said it makes this experience worse when I say I am with you in spirit. Worse, my suspicions about your resentment that I joined the Army, that I have been away too much, that I have been deployed, have been confirmed. I wish you could read these journals and know that I've seen it progress and have become so very regretful about what I have done. Always waiting for me, huh? Wow, your words are sinking in and they are terrible to bear.

Is this the way it's supposed to be? Is it our destiny to be pulled apart? Are we victims of circumstance?

I don't know.

There is part of me that just won't accept the possibility of life without you. There is another part that does—not because I *want* to, but because I must acknowledge that the possibility exists. Perhaps this whole thing will ultimately make us stronger. I know you think your dominant personality and aggressive tendencies have hindered me from obtaining my own goals and dreams, that you've coerced me into directions *you* felt like taking. That may be true, but I have mired myself as well, mainly believing my sacrifices have been for us and our life together. I can't help but feel as if you're focusing too much on the negative. I know it's hard. It's hard for me too and I don't know what to do.

We *have* to survive this, baby. From the instant I met you I've wanted to be with you. I hope you can accept that. Sometimes I think you can't.

This is just something that happened. It will either rip us apart or make us stronger. If I had to vote on one, it would be stronger. I have always wished you the best in whatever your endeavor, like getting your master's degree. And like I said, there is a very strong part of me that has the utmost faith in us, in our bond. But I can't stop it if it's going to happen. I don't have control over anything in my life any more. I'm learning to accept that. It's kind of liberating in a way and it makes me feel as if I am riding the waves of fate right now. The trouble is I really don't want to be free—not of *you* at least. I want to be with you for the rest of my life. I just want to be free of society, the military, and the government.

I love you, my wife.

## May 31, 2004

I had the oddest feeling today I'll either look back on these journals and laugh or think I was full of shit—probably the latter. That's either an indication I'll feel ridiculous about how I felt and what I went through or incredulous at how my perspective has changed throughout this ordeal. It's always a crazy thing to go back and look at your thoughts. Sometimes they seem small or childishly blown out of proportion. So be it. It's a look at me.

Frederick died a few days ago. That was sad and his passing only amplified how depressed and possibly cynical I'm slowly becoming. "Good," I thought, "he doesn't have to be in this hell any more. Not even the beauty of nature can survive this place." I didn't ask Gary what he did with him, didn't want to know.

I've been very withdrawn lately. We're all very tired and angry. I have no urge to be around people. And I'm not the only one.

"What ya been up to?" Jakob asked me today. "Haven't seen you lately."

I told him I've been hibernating during my off time. He smiled and nodded his head knowingly.

I think you can only hang out with the same people for so long before you start burning out on them. Morale is really low and people are gravely discontent with the war, this base, the politics, the strife, the corruption, a seemingly apathetic America. It's evident the moment you start speaking with anyone. They are so sick of the bullshit around here that they isolate themselves and go into their own worlds, kind of like what I am doing now. It's a survival mechanism.

I have been pretty pissy lately and to be frank, I think some of it has to do with your emails. They have just seemed so out of whack. Not you. I looked at some of your previous emails and you seemed like the loving woman I am used to. The woman I talk to now is reluctant to even say "I love you." That sucks a whole big bunch. It's also hard because you've said you think I'm safe. Maybe you don't want to believe what is going on here. Admittedly I do hold back on some things. We're supposed to.

We're encouraged to lie to our families and loved ones for the sake of sparing them (at least so they tell us, although I have my doubts), but I find it hard to not tell you everything because I always have. I love you—you're my wife.

It occurred to me that it unnerves you to talk to me. But why would you feel that way?

Hell, I don't know anything any more. I just hope it all will get better. It's maddening to sit here and continually worry with no outlet, no answers, no resolution… no happiness, no support.

God, I can't wait until this is over.

I love you, baby.

### June 1, 2004

It was just damn blistering hot today. It's been in the hundreds for a while now and my uniform is utterly soaked after my shift every night. My pants are soaked. My socks are soaked. Everything's soaked except the sun and the sand. I can't do anything but sigh and go about my day. And the power is out again. It's so hot in the shop trailers it actually felt better outside. During a break, I sat on a stool for a while outside my shop, sweat endlessly streaming off me.

We were bombed a couple of times again today. Every day is the same. Mortars and sweat—that's my life. But I feel fairly mellow today for some reason I can't fathom. Maybe it was rebuilding a brake for a Blackhawk that took my mind off everything. Tonight Pete and I have plans to watch a Western on his computer. What the hell, it keeps our minds off everything for a while.

I got your email. I hope you're having a good time on your vacation. You deserve it. Go play—sounds like a good time, baby.

I love you, honey.

### June 4, 2004

I thought we had a good talk on the phone today. I'm glad you enjoyed your vacation. I know you get depressed when I call. I guess I do too to a certain extent but I just like hearing your voice. I begin to breathe easier and my shoulders relax a bit. It keeps me closer to you. I hope it does the same for you.

I thought a lot about our cat today. It still hurts he is gone. Images of him floated through my mind and made me cry. I hope they don't kill him. I hope he finds a good home. I want to hold him, tell him, "It's okay. Daddy loves you. You're going to be all right." I have such a soft heart for animals. Guess I picked that up from my mother.

I wanted him to have a good life with two people who would take care of him until his end days. And I feel as if we failed him. I remember when we picked him out at the shelter, how scared he was. It's like losing a member of the family. Who will take care of him?

I wish I could've said good-bye.

I understand why you did it. I'm not angry with you, although I thought I would be. I don't even feel a hint of it. Actually, I don't feel a thing.

My privacy has become imperative to me now, bordering on compulsive. Kind of ironic 'cause I used to really enjoy being around people. But here you have to actively find solitude and I get so little of it. I can't imagine being on a big ship in the Navy—they have my admiration for enduring that. It would drive me nuts.

I miss you. I want to be home so badly it hurts my very bones. I truly hope we don't have many problems when I come back. We both need to work on some things. We'll see. We have a little ways to go yet before they'll parole me. It will probably be one of those things that feels like it takes forever when it's happening, but looking back on it, it went by in a blur.

I love you.

### June 6, 2004

The power went off again today while it was 120 degrees outside. Summer is approaching very quickly—the rooms and tents are like ovens. I felt like a pot roast. You can almost feel your brain melting, it's so fuckin' hot. The wind kicked up later in the afternoon and dust was everywhere. It's hell on our equipment.

A couple of our guys came back from leave today. They were all smiles and talked about how the U.S. is everything we dreamed it could be.

I'm starting to cool down. Thank God for sunset. The power is back on again for a bit but now, we're getting mortared.

I love you so much.

### June 7, 2004

I'm not fond of the times when the stark reality of this situation becomes all too clear for me. At any given moment, you never know when your ticket will be up, when you'll be cast into the eternal dark within the tick of a clock.

It's the most frightening thing I've ever experienced.

It's a reality no one should have to live with day in and day out. In this sense at least, we're all the same here. Too rarely do any of us see this, let alone allow the notion to bring us together, perhaps even help each other get home alive. Instead our anger at our situation separates us with a chasm of hatred, of bitterness... and I am guilty of this as well.

Right now if I were told I'd never see another person, I would be a happy man. It's a dawning realization that people are nothing more than primates with technology—apes with cell phones, televisions, and fine silk suits. Or worse, with bombs and bullets. We may have evolved technologically but I can't help but wonder just how much we have evolved as a species. Not all that much, no matter how much better we look in suits than bearskins. The human race is rapidly becoming thoroughly unappealing to me.

I don't want to continue being sucked into anyone's dramas, my government's included. I never want to participate in anyone's violence, emotional or physical, ever again.

I love you.

### June 12, 2004

It's been a while since I've written anything. To be honest, I have never felt so burnt out and tired. The countdown until we get out of here marches to the beat of bombs.

I'm restless and edgy. There is nothing to look forward to at the end of the day—just the relentless mortars exploding all night while we try to sleep through the relative cool. I'm stuck in the doldrums like a boot in the mud here when it rains.

I get up and go to the shop. There may or may not be anything to repair or do. I come back to my hovel and dream of our life together, of a world that seems so far away from the chaos and madness of war. I dream of packing the truck with you, backpacking in the mountains for days. I dream of peace, friends, good food—those notions only apply in the United States, a place that has become sanctuary from the viciousness of the world.

I do have some news. It seems as though I will be able to fly directly out of here for Germany when my leave comes up. No passport required and the flight won't take up too much leave time, meaning more time to spend with you. Although hoping that the Army won't screw something up is actually more agonizing than being mortared.

I'm not sure how or why all this came about but I've heard the Army is worried about AWOLs. You can only go to two places for leave as of right now—Germany or the United States—and they don't want *anyone* leaving Germany for *any* reason. Maybe that's why they agreed to direct flights—it's easier to keep track of people. I guess not many of us believe in this war.

I took apart my first Blackhawk shock strut today. What a piece of work that part is. It went pretty smoothly. Malcolm and I are going to put it back together tomorrow.

But there is a bright side to everything in life: I had pizza for the first time in months today.

I love you, honey.

### June 14, 2004

Your last email really drove home to me just how distant you've become. It made my heart sink to read it, and now I have a sick feeling in my stomach that won't go away. At one time I thought you and I could share everything, but it seems that we're not on that wavelength any more. I'm beginning to feel as if I'm losing you.

I'm not trying to say you haven't been there for me. You send me care packages. They help keep me connected with a life thousands of miles away but I've gotten the feeling lately that you're just going through the motions or "doing your duty," so to speak.

I'm beginning to doubt that you want our life together. I honestly don't know any more and I feel disheartened. My feet feel like lead and it's all I can do to drag myself through the day, wondering if we are going to survive this trial. I wonder why this happened. I wonder if I will even make it home to know for certain. I wonder if this is just a dream that I'll wake up from, the sun shining cheerfully through the window of our bedroom as I turn over and see you sleeping next to me. I lay in bed and I can almost reach out and touch you but… you're not there.

You vaporize in my grasp.

Maybe I'm just projecting. I'm making assumptions, but they're all I have. My mind drifts with what could happen. I have no real answers and it's a horrible feeling. Not knowing compels me to think there's something very, very wrong.

Help me understand what you're going through. Let's work together to gain strength together. I know where I stand—I want *us*. I want to fight for our marriage but my confidence is dwindling and I don't know where to turn. The feeling of utter helplessness makes it worse.

At one point recently, I wondered what it would be like to let you go. I'm sure you would be happy with your dog, your life with your friends—our friends—making money, seeing your folks. I'm sure you'd move on. You don't really need me, you never have. You always speak of what an independent woman you are, but you know what? That makes me feel insignificant, as if I have been a convenience, as if our relationship was never anything more to you than just an episode in your life that you were always going to move on from.

Have I been living in a fantasy?

If you don't want to be with me, I'm not going to argue. I refuse to grovel, to beg for a life with you. That's beneath both of us. I'm tired of trying to draw you out, to get some sort of affection, some tenderness I crave. It seems like it's a monstrous effort for you to even attempt to show some semblance of love for me. You haven't written any kind of loving letter in ages, never talk about your feelings for me, never helped me to help you, to help us get through this seemingly infinite span of time apart.

I suppose I could find my own way if need be. I did before you entered my life and I could again. I'm in the background of your life now. I don't like or deserve that. I'm beginning to feel frightened that I'm going to have to find my own way home. I'm sure you'll be fine and I don't plan on telling you any of this right now. I don't need any more boats rocked at this point. Maybe you're feeling the same way.

I honestly never thought this would happen, but I have to

accept this. I wonder what September will be like. Are you flying to Germany for me or because you want to see Germany? I'd like to think that you're coming to see your husband.

Give me a sign.

I suspect you're going to tell me that you want to separate when I see you. It's a specter that is becoming less transparent by the day.

I hate this feeling of helpless speculation but I'm readying myself for what might be.

We've been together for almost 10 years now and you have to wonder what we've been doing all that time.

What's it all been for?

### June 17, 2004

We were attacked again yesterday—it actually made the news back home from what I heard through the grapevine. They hit the PX with a few mortars, taking out a good portion of the building, killing two or three people, and wounding several others. Sometimes those fuckers don't hit anything, but they really got it this time.

I'm scared.

I guess I'd been conveniently becoming complacent to the peril we face here every day—I mean, we've been bombed so many times, some of them so very close, some of them pretty damn scary. Fatalism has begun to creep in, an apathetic feeling that nothing will happen.

Every night I roll over and close my eyes and my mind keeps trying to convince me that the mortars will go away, that they're unreal in some sense, specters I must have conjured up. I fall to sleep until the next attack, maybe even make it through the night without hearing them again.

That's all I have to do.

All I have to do is shut them out of my mind and the movie will be over. The tape will stop.

Then I realize the tape hasn't stopped and I become numb again, my old friends apathy and resignation greeting me once more. It is then that I find the energy and strength to make it through another day.

Isn't it strange? I just wrote that and it still really doesn't feel like it happened. I can remember feeling so jittery the rest of the day, my mind swirling because I had just been to the PX.

What if I had gone just a little later?

In my head, I see you driving down the highway, watering the lawn, taking our dog for a walk, watching you glide ahead of me as we went cross-country skiing, playing cards with your folks… so many images have flashed through me as I've reflected on this latest event.

Maybe someday you can read this but I don't want to tell you about this latest tragedy now. I don't want you to worry. Actually, I worry that if you knew what is really going on here, it would only push you away even more. Maybe it would scare you, overload you so much you wouldn't be able to take it. Maybe you'll leave me for some other guy who you don't have to worry about dying in a war.

It was 120 degrees today. I can't believe how hot it is here.

## June 18, 2004

I had the day off today. I truly adore my days off and the time I get to spend alone. But inevitably my mind will wander and if my thoughts turn toward home the desire to fast-forward the coming months can be quite unbearable.

I got a lot of emails today from my concerned parents and our friends. It's almost grimly humorous how concerned they are. They're just now barely beginning to perceive that I might be in some sort of danger. There is a pleasant ignorance of living in the United States.

This is not their fault of course and I'm not being entirely fair. I haven't told anyone about the bare reality of my situation, so their naiveté is only to be expected. Maybe I should simply be grateful that people care. I wonder how you and others will feel when I come home and I have the chance to explain this hell.

I do hope that won't make you angry because I'm truly doing what I feel is best for everyone at this time. There is no need to worry anyone right now. I would only add that I've noticed how it keeps everyone at home from taking seriously my meditations on life and the continual change of a personal ideology that's slowly coalescing in my muddled, overheated brain.

Reading what I just wrote, I admit that it sounds pompous.

I don't really care. I feel completely powerless to do anything about these changes that are happening to me, but I don't know whether this experience is making me wiser and more insightful or just more sarcastic and jaded. Am I becoming more aware of the world, more in touch with myself or more bitter? I guess only time will tell. I already know I'll never forget this war and it will certainly always be an emotional topic for me. I can feel that. It's creeping into the pores of my skin and becoming part of me. I know because I've already begun to look back on memories and they have evoked a tear, a laugh, sometimes a grimace or scowl.

I am on a personal odyssey.

We were attacked again today—several times. I heard some F-16s taking off to patrol the area.

It's so freakin' hot.

I love you.

## June 19, 2004

I found out today that an American was killed in Saudi Arabia. Apparently some al-Qaeda militants had kidnapped him a few days ago and threatened to kill the poor devil—a civilian helicopter mechanic or engineer, I can't remember which— unless America and the Saudis freed some prisoners. I don't know who they are, but they weren't freed.

There were some downright ghastly, horrifically graphic scenes of the execution—some of us caught it on the Internet. I watched them take this guy's head off because both the U.S. and

Saudi Arabia didn't comply with their demands and this latest event has generated a fair amount of fear in all of us. What if one of us were kidnapped or caught outside the wire for some reason? How can any of us sleep at night knowing that could happen to any one of us at any time? And what about that guy's family? I can't imagine how they must feel.

I felt like throwing up while I watched the execution. I have no words to describe what it's like when someone is being killed so brutally and I am seldom speechless. What struck me was the horror of how despicable *all* humans are. We really are just animals squabbling over our natural resources, even fighting for no good reason other than some sorry excuse like it's "God's will." I feel disgusted being a human.

I can't tell you how sick to my stomach I am of all this. I don't think I will ever forget those images, so brightly are they burned into my memory. I can see them when I close my eyes and even now when I think about them, I still feel queasy.

Here at good ole Camp Anaconda, we were attacked again. Three nice mortar attacks to liven up your day, keep you on your toes, and remind you of where you are. As if we could forget.

There were no helicopters to work on today. We are between phases on the helicopters right now and most of us are sitting around in the heat, wringing out our uniforms.

So here I am, writing in my journal. Our good friend Paula (we've been writing as of late) sent me some booze that arrived in today's mail. I love it. Since alcohol is forbidden by the military here, we've had to resort to smuggling. We've come up with a surprisingly simple idea. She empties a Listerine bottle and washes it out thoroughly. (Well, mostly—I can still taste some of it in the booze. The mouthwash adds a cool minty taste.) Then she fills the empty bottle with vodka and adds green food coloring.

She told me she even keeps a full bottle of Listerine handy to make sure she gets the colors right. I chuckle when I think of her as Doctor Frankenstein in the kitchen mixing up a brew, exclaiming with arms raised to heaven "It's alive" when the bottle is full. And I've been wondering what else we can smuggle in. I must admit, part of me is reveling in these shenanigans. I love the feeling of pulling a fast one over the powers that be. It eases the helplessness I feel. I still have *some* power over my life.

I've had several sips and am quite pleasantly buzzed, a welcome relief from my thoughts and the mortars I'm listening to. I'll write more tomorrow. My enthusiasm is low right now, probably partly due to the heat.

Please remember that I love you, baby.

### June 20, 2004

Last night I had a very interesting talk with a buddy of mine. We agreed that trying not to care is about all you can realistically do here to keep sane. You *have* to become apathetic to everything. As meaningless as this deployment is, apathy is the only saving grace.

With the exception of Mike, everyone else I have talked with believes this mission is a waste of lives, resources, time—you name it. Iraq was never a threat to U.S. security. It's well known that nothing has been found here. The WMD scare was just propaganda to seduce Americans into this invasion. *Most* feel this war is nothing but a money-making machine for a far-away businessman or politician. I also understand gas prices are rising in the United States. I believe that would make any oilman happy.

It's interesting, the connections you can draw. Sure, it's speculation, but I smell corruption. It makes me wonder what else my government or some large corporation is up to. I wonder sometimes if the attacks on the World Trade Center were at all linked to this stupid war—and not in the way most people think. I guess we'll never know, but my mind wanders there from time to time and I can't help but feel there is more going on behind the scenes than we will ever be privy to.

We had a thought last night. Why don't we send those motherfuckers in Washington over here since they are the ones who want this place so bad—let *them* fight it out. I suggested we construct a "Leaders of the World Boxing Ring" where any leaders from any country could enter with another and have it out. Whoever comes out on top is the winner of the war. It makes sense to me. They're the ones who feel so compelled to fight all the time. Wouldn't that save a lot of money, lives, energy, and resources? But people climb to power to make someone else fight their battles for them.

And I have a few questions I'd like answered: Will the American people ever realize what their government is doing to young Americans and the populace at large? Will they stand up? Or will they blindly accept what is going on over here? Is it easier for Americans to turn a blind eye and go to a football game than attempt some sort of change?

The few who try to make a stand against our government's hypocrisy would probably be laughed at or squashed by those who stand to lose by such an outburst. They might be labeled as radicals and unpatriotic. It worked for the Nazis didn't it?

These ideas could get *me* labeled a radical or freak, perhaps even a traitor. I could become an outcast, ostracized by the people who live with blinders on. If you took their blinders away, they would have nothing else. Their entire illusion could come crashing down like a ton of bricks and I'm sure anyone would fight to maintain that. And those with power will do anything, absolutely anything, to protect that power.

I guarantee that if you walked the shops and talked to the soldiers flipping magazines, playing chess, smokin' and jokin', any one of them would tell you exactly what I just said. They're pissed that they're wasting their time here, putting their lives on the line, all for self-serving politicians or the CEO of some corporation whose mouth is watering for another beach house.

The disillusionment and senseless dying here is breeding an incredible amount of discontent and anger. The lying and profiteering in the name of freedom—at the *expense* of freedom—is blasphemy and hypocrisy at its worst.

And what about the American families who are told their son or daughter died over here? Will they desperately cling to the notion that their child died honorably serving their country? And why don't you ever hear about the bodies, the coffins, the draped flags, as the dead must come into the U.S. at some point? Isn't that censorship?

Perhaps if the honorable notion I just mentioned disintegrated, people would be forced to realize their child's life was wasted by people who profit from war. The notion of honor and serving my country is fading from my psyche. Reality is driving in a convoy through downtown Baghdad and seeing a group of Iraqis smiling and waving amiably while waiting for you to plow right into an ambush.

I feel sad that I don't believe in American politics any more but I don't see why I should. The underprivileged continually get stepped on while we idolize the rich. And why do we live vicariously through them instead of concentrating on our own moments and lives? Does wealth and power really mean you've succeeded in life? Isn't there something more?

Celebrities and politicians have become the American aristocracy. So many people suffer in this world and yet all celebrities do is talk about themselves and their fame and their fancy cars or whatever. Would they be willing to make a sacrifice, like being here? I know there are all sorts who have served in the military and I'm sure there are wealthy who have served in wars but it seems that they're mostly fought by the poor.

This place is having quite an impact on me. I now see things in a somewhat clearer light—at least a different light. Remember how I used to speculate about this stuff? I was never really sure if I was right. I only had some instinct that what I was seeing on television or in the media was a manipulation, that there was something wrong I couldn't quite pinpoint. But my desire to give people the benefit of the doubt was reinforced by others telling me I was being too harsh or critical.

Now I have no doubt I was correct. I know our government is corrupt. I know I am a conscientious objector. I know people with power will do virtually anything to protect it. I know it would make me sick to watch late-night talk shows and see the same people pat each other over and over on the back, congratulating themselves on how brilliant they are and how hard they worked on some movie. What about the guy working for the welfare of people—curing a disease or trying to help the starving or impoverished? America is infatuated with the superficial, not substance.

The truth is often too brutal for most people to stomach. Perhaps that's why they'd prefer to live in a distorted, myopic world. But when you're sitting in the middle of this shithole, your blinders are removed whether you like it or not. You can choose to face the truth, digest it, wonder what you can do about it—or you can choose to buy a reinforced set of blinders. The latter doesn't work for me. Those who choose the latter may have been programmed beyond repair.

Will the blinders ever be taken off? How many young sons and daughters must die in the name of hypocrisy and greed? When will people stop living vicariously through those with fame, money, and power and concentrate on themselves? When will the rich and powerful make the same sacrifices as those who've been providing them with their comforts?

I can't see it happening. We are *all* prisoners of war. We are all prisoners of *someone else's* war.

I would like to think these ramblings are profound and have enough merit to shed some light on how we could change our lives in a positive way. I would like my thoughts to come through clearly, but I'm afraid I don't have the eloquence to express them. I feel I am speaking the truth, no matter how cynical my ideas may seem.

I just read back through some of my journals and saw how my impressions of people, attitudes, and beliefs have changed. And this is just in a few short months? How will they change the longer I'm here? I must be more careful about how I judge character. I've found I'm becoming increasingly wary of perceiving goodness in people.

I love you, but I don't love mortars. We're being attacked again.

### June 22, 2004

It was around 120 degrees again today and the wind blew so much dust I felt like I was back in Kuwait for convoy training. I came home with my hair encrusted with dust, dust in my ears, dust stinging my eyes despite my sunglasses. There is absolutely no place dust can't get into.

I had a conversation with Mike today and he told me I'm

an excellent mechanic, a free thinker, and a free soul. That was nice to hear. "If it makes you feel any better," he said, "I think being here is unnecessary, a waste of time, of our lives, and all I'm doing is just trying to live through it without changing too much of what I am inside and what I stand for."

I guess I was wrong about how he feels. He's really a good guy.

I love you.

### June 23, 2004

Today it was announced by our fearless leaders that we can't wear civilian clothes while we're off duty, only PT clothing. Guess another chance to rebel has come my way. God, I'm such a willful prick. When I am off duty, I'll wear what I want. Fuck them. I think Mike is right—maybe I never belonged in the military. Or maybe I'm just another spoiled American brat. The bottom line is that my ability to care about what people think I *should do* is rapidly disintegrating.

This morning I decided to go to the Internet tent to make a phone call to my folks. It went pretty well, but it's been so long since I've seen them that I could barely picture their faces, and their voices sounded strangely unfamiliar to me. It's an unsettling feeling, as if the intimate connection with the people who brought me into this world has been dismantled in some way.

The day went by smoothly and I left at 1400 after I finished rebuilding a brake for a Blackhawk.

We were attacked again today, same thing—sirens and mortars, explosions and fear—bring your change of underwear.

That was the day.

Where's the fast-forward button again?

I love you.

### June 24, 2004

I feel like a great weight has been lifted from my shoulders. I loved getting your email and was relieved that we've begun speaking of the difficulties plaguing our minds as of late. I feel we're finally being honest with each other about what we're experiencing and how we're dealing with it. Many people have told me to only speak of light things, casual things, and not to get too deep about what constitutes reality here. I have complied with that to some extent but I don't want to do that any more. We've always been honest with each other, and keeping up a façade made me feel as if I was betraying our relationship and contributing to the distance between us. That, coupled with the distance you have been imposing, has been terribly difficult for me.

Since yesterday, however, I feel lightened. We actually wrote of the deep matters troubling our hearts—matters that up until now, for whatever reason, we didn't have the tools to begin mending. I think we might have taken at least a small step toward that. At least I can only hope so. I really do want to right my wrongs that have caused you pain.

I have taken responsibility for them and own them in my heart, please know that. I have been unfair and selfish and I fear that I've taken the precious bonds we formed so long ago for granted. It's horrible to admit but I must own up to it. It's only fair to you.

I'm sorry, my love. I'm sorry for being so lost and directionless with my career goals, for leaning so heavily on you for support and guidance. I'm sorry for taking advantage of your good nature as I tried and failed to find my path so many times. I hope I can make it up to you someday. I trust we are strong enough to endure these trials. My dream and hope is to find a solid direction and perhaps, over time, once again be the man you fell in love with so long ago.

It felt good to be able to express these feelings in my email and explain that I feel a certain reawakening to a portion of myself that existed before we met—my free spirit, my independence. This reawakening is mainly due to just being here, apart from you, having to fend for myself and take on responsibilities I never really wanted. Being promoted to sergeant was an important step because now I'm accountable for not only myself but for those under me.

I am relearning how to think on my own, not as two, but as one. I am more confident in myself than I have been in years. All the dangers, traveling, close calls, and stress have also contributed greatly to this new feeling.

I don't know, my dear, but I'm hoping we have nudged open a door between us and at least peeked through. I love you so very much and I really want us to be happy, personally and together. I think we can get there. It might be rough with a lot of speed bumps, but I think we'll be okay. Either way I'm sure that this is only the beginning of a profound metamorphosis for each of us and our relationship.

It was quite a relief to hear that you didn't want a divorce. For quite some time now I had braced myself for what I thought was an inevitability. I thought you were only going through the motions of communication and support because I'm trapped over here and you felt a sense of obligation.

I have hope.

I miss you and love you.

### June 26, 2004

Yesterday was scary. I got up at 0400 and after relaxing with a cup of java, breathing in the morning air, walked to the hangar for my shift. As I was passing the mess hall, a strange whistle shattered the stillness that often encompasses that time of day. The sun was just topping the horizon—I couldn't see very well, but it seemed to pass just over my head and I flinched. It scared the shit out of me, but for reasons I can't explain I kept walking, shrugging my shoulders after a moment and dismissing the incident. Maybe it was because my shift was coming up and I was focusing on that. Maybe I'm just getting used to the strange experiences over here. Maybe it was my old pal apathy asserting itself again, compelling me to plod on with the day.

A few minutes later, just before I got to the hangar, the mortars started coming in—a whole bunch of them. I stopped counting after 10 had exploded. They kept coming and coming, explosions here and there, the alarm sirens going off. Those of us at the hangar took cover as usual and waited it out. Shortly thereafter, I was told that a mortar had soft-landed—meaning it hadn't exploded—right next to the mess hall.

Well, that was what I'd heard on the way to the hangar—that was the whistle over my head. "CAUTION" tape was still around the area after my shift and I realized it had landed not more than 20 yards from where I was walking. It must have been the grace of God it didn't explode or I would've been severely injured, if not killed. I think I'll wait to tell you about this one. I feel so strange about it, as if I need more time to allow my mind to process this latest brush with death. I'm constantly thinking about how close to death or injury I've come on this adventure—on the convoy or at the PX, now the mess hall. And I hadn't written about this before but we narrowly avoided an attack in Baghdad. A convoy was ambushed in IED Alley not 10 minutes after we passed through.

Maybe I have a guardian angel after all.

There are a great many concerns within my company that the implementation of the new government here in Iraq that's supposed to be taking place soon will create a great deal of civil unrest. Everyone seems to be more on edge.

I've heard gas prices are soaring in the United States. How interesting, considering there's no shortage of oil or gasoline. Do you suppose the rise in gasoline prices was part of the plan when this invasion was conceived? That perhaps the powers that be are more interested in their profits than anything else? I wonder.

Today as I was finishing a brake job, CW2[26]Brown came into the shop and dragged me out to the flight line to look at a busted hydraulic line on a Blackhawk. The pilots said it was flying that evening so I had to stay for the repair. Two hours later, the line arrived at my shop and by the time I fixed it, I had worked a solid 12-hour shift. But I can feel good that I did my part by getting the helicopter flying on time.

Other than that, the day was calm except for getting mortared again in the evening—whoohoo. They had gristly meatballs and soggy broccoli at the mess hall. That's it—nothing else. Can you believe it?

I love you.

### June 27, 2004

Top told me the leave date I signed up for is looking pretty good, no hitches or problems as of yet. I put down September 26 as my departure date. Here's the plan for Germany, the way they're working it right now at least. I leave here early in the morning, the actual time yet to be determined. I fly into Ali Al

---

26  Chief Warrant Officer 2

Salem Air Base in Kuwait then I am to be bused to Camp Doha to check in with someone, God only knows who. Then I am to fly out of Ali Al Salem sometime that evening. I'm not sure why I have to go to Doha—maybe it has to do with the plane I'm flying on.

So what I want you to do is fly into Germany on the 24th. This way you can check into the hotel, get settled, and relax for a while. My plane flies into Rhein-Main Air Base and I can take a cab to meet you. I just hope it all goes according to plan. It would really be a bite in the ass if it didn't, but Top told me to start working things out. I can't wait. I have to give them the address of the hotel we're staying in, but I think we can still go somewhere else if we want to.

I found out that the helicopter I fixed yesterday, the one with the busted hydraulic line had an incident on its flight, news that made the bottom of my heart drop out when I heard it. Apparently they were flying a night support mission for a group of infantry guys who are in the area rooting out "insurgents" hiding in small houses near here. Turns out there was also a family living in one of them. In the mayhem of the firefight, the helicopter crew accidentally gunned down the entire family—12 of them—men, women, and children.

When I heard this, I felt like throwing up. The world faded from my eyes for a few moments while the news sunk into me with its awful weight. I desperately wish I had never fixed that line. What if I hadn't? Would those people still be alive? Would my conscience not now be stained by what I consider to be a crime, even if it was accidental? I'm at least partially responsible for this latest tragedy and I can't describe the guilt I feel. Either directly or indirectly we are *all* responsible and I feel dirty. I feel... guilty.

Oh honey, I can't believe this place. It's just one thing after another over here. It's systematically dismantling who I am and what I've grown up believing. This is one more thing to throw on the pile of memories that will never leave me.

I heard the pilot was devastated when he discovered what they had done.

And yet the day goes on. The lines form at the mess hall, the helicopters still fly, we still brush our teeth in the morning, and still watch as the sun goes down. We all hope and pray that soon we'll see our last sunset in this godforsaken land.

We had no food service because of a busted main water line in the mess hall. I might end up scavenging. Maybe I can scrounge up a case of MREs or something. Maybe I'll just wait until they open again. I can't write very well right now. I'm hungry and my brain feels foggy. I can't seem to clear it. It's been that way all day.

I love you.

### June 28, 2004

I got your email. All I can say is... wow. You expressed a lot for which I am grateful... but my head is spinning. It seems both you and I are doing a tremendous amount of thinking and analyzing. I think that's good in a way. Perhaps every couple has to evaluate their lives from time to time—both individually *and* together—but I still have this nagging sense that we're not on the same page.

For instance, you mentioned that you have been with someone for your whole life, never having the chance to truly be free, independent, and on your own. Now you have that chance and are discovering your passion again. I didn't realize you had lost it, that you were just plodding through the days, doing what needed to be done merely for the sake of "us." I didn't realize you felt as if you were "sitting on something," some undeveloped potential and that our relationship was holding you back.

I always thought we encouraged each other to fulfill our dreams and it was distressing to hear you needed to be on your own to achieve what you want in life. I've never wanted to hold you back from anything. Haven't I always told you to find things that moved you, encouraged you to branch out and live to the fullest? I've certainly never felt being in a relationship meant that a person couldn't realize their passions.

Perhaps you're right. Perhaps I don't understand your train of thought. You feel I "idealize" our relationship over here. Maybe that's true to a certain extent, but I don't feel that you appreciate the profound changes taking place within me as well. It's not merely idealization. Although I am all too aware every couple has their troubles and we are no exception, I feel a new sense of appreciation for what we *do* have. I've moved beyond the petty things in life that always seemed to distract from enjoying the gifts that we have been given… and that includes our relationship.

Working through issues is part of the game, but we can't get so caught up that we forget to love and be grateful for the person we're with. Together we can do anything if we keep an uncluttered vision. I don't know if that makes sense and I'm not at all convinced you understood me when I tried to explain.

You asked what I would do if we parted ways and I put my answer in the front of this journal. It's like that same old question people always ask—"If you didn't have to worry about time, money, and all that jazz, what would you do?" I know the answer and apparently so do you. I would live in that cabin in the woods like you said, writing my stories and enjoying that simpler, less materialistic life with no credit cards, phone, or cable bills, even piles of stuff I don't know why I have.

I feel like I've covered this topic so many times with you and it's never ended well. You have been so focused on materialism and attaining as much wealth as you can. I think both you and I have realized long ago but were hesitant to admit, in our heart of hearts, your notions of achievement have never really been my game, that I've never really paid attention to what you call success in life. Perhaps that has caused a tremendous chasm between us.

Anyway, I must admit sometimes it's felt like your ambition has been off the charts. Maybe that's why I'm confused about your introspective thoughts about losing your passion. If anything, I would have guessed you were the most passionate person I've ever known.

I also feel like I'm caught between fantasy and reality. It's fun to fantasize about living in the woods writing my stories, but the stark reality of my situation has me somewhat fatalistic. What does it really matter now? I might not even come home to realize those dreams anyway. I'm caught in a place where only the moments matter and in any moment I could die.

I can only say that I can't imagine life without you. If we parted ways, I would be utterly crushed and heartbroken. I just don't understand why we couldn't fulfill our dreams together like we've always done. At least that's what I *thought* we were doing. Am I blind? Am I idealizing our relationship like you say?

I feel so confused.

They are making us carry our gas masks everywhere now because it's been rumored that there will be a chemical attack soon—lovely, a nice chemical attack to liven up your day.

I love you.

### June 29, 2004

My feet hurt. The boots I've been given are really starting to hurt. The bruises on the top of my feet are large, spreading, and Supply says they have no other boots to issue. I can feel my shoulders aching all the time now, tight with tension. My right eye is twitching again. It's a bother since it makes it difficult to concentrate let alone see what I'm working on.

I've been jumpier since the mortar flew over my head the

other morning. I'm pretty sure it's just paranoia taking root and will fade over time. I hope so.

Today is Day Two of the new government here in Iraq. Nothing much has changed. We are still getting shelled. We were mortared eight times last night, the sirens constantly wailing— hard to sleep through it all. I've also heard that the convoys are still regularly attacked on their way north and many died last night. I don't know who or how many. It may take a while for the new government to put things in order.

After rebuilding a brake, Malcolm cut me loose early but not before I was required to read a three-page memo regarding the proper wearing of military clothing. It seems we are back to wearing our uniform tops everywhere again, even in our shops. It was also reiterated that everyone wear PT uniforms when off duty. Additionally, if you are out of the immediate vicinity of your hovel you're supposed to wear your combat vest and carry your gas mask although they didn't specify the distance. This all came down the chain of command from a sergeant major, I have no idea which one. His memo undoubtedly took very deep thought and intricate planning. So here I sit in civilian clothes, blatantly defying authority once again.

It's my humble opinion that these people are insane, not just the ones in Washington but everyone participating in this, maybe even the whole human race. You would think a sergeant major would have more on his plate to worry about. Maybe he's really uptight, a real stickler… or bored. Who knows? It all seems so silly. Mortars are landing everywhere and what I'm wearing wouldn't make a difference if I were hit.

Just for wearing these civilian clothes, I could be brought up on charges for disobeying a lawful order. Can you imagine? My perfect military record blemished for wearing a T-shirt and shorts in a combat zone or taking off my uniform top while working in the shop.

I'm resolved to carry on the way I have. If I get into trouble then it will just give me more to write about. If I survive this madness, I'm sure it won't matter much. If I die over here, it won't matter much. So who really cares one way or the other?

I got your email. So you want to sell the house. I could easily say, "It's just a building. Sell it. It's us that matters more than anything else and we can take ourselves anywhere we want to." And to be debt free does sound awfully enticing. Sell it. What do I care? I may not even see it again anyway. But I must admit, part of me is reluctant. I'm tired of not having a home and I would like something to come home to. But it would be enough to come home to your heart and warmth.

Perhaps it's my destiny to be constantly on the move. It certainly has felt that way sometimes. I remember all the road trips around the country I took when I was younger as I worked from place to place, even for a day like I did in Utah once, picking raspberries with migrant workers for a tank of gasoline. Even after meeting you, I was always on the move. We bounced from place to place to pursue dreams like a college education or a better career. My life seems to keep pulling me down the road, sometimes even against my will.

I guess it's that "adventurous spirit" in me you mentioned in your letter. I thought it was interesting how you mentioned you were angry with me for that—angry because you believed my adventurous spirit drove me to enlist in the Army. I've always known you were angry about that, but I'm glad you're trying to come to terms with that. And you're right, we would fail if we tried to pick up where we left off when I come home. Things are changing, baby, I hope for the better, but you and I are going to have to adapt and begin a new life together if we survive this trial.

I've known for a long time you have been trying to mold me into some image you had of me, not what I had for myself. I've known you were trying to control me and I have tried to resist that. Perhaps I haven't always been successful but it made me cry when you said you were sorry that you were trying to make me into someone other than the man you fell in love with. I could feel my heart beating for you so very strongly while reading that.

But hey, sell the damn house. If that's what you want, how can I argue with you from so many thousands of miles away?

I love you.

### June 30, 2004

This morning at formation Top informed us the attacks are only going to get worse. That only confirmed my suspicions. Last night Pete and I were hanging out when we heard a tremendous explosion. It felt like it was right next door and it turns out a mortar detonated right behind the mess hall, perhaps about 30 or 40 yards from my hovel. It damaged two trucks parked nearby and took out part of the wall. Pretty close, enough to make your heart jump for sure.

Can I go home now?

After formation, Top and I chatted for a couple of free minutes. I asked him what was up with the new uniform policy and why it was being so obsessively enforced. He told me that the sergeant major who implemented it is regular Army, then smiled and said, "He's also a fucking idiot."

Top truly does have his moments. I've found there is a distinct difference between regular Army and the National Guard. Reconciling the two can be difficult. It's my belief that the National Guard was originally designed for domestic missions. It was never intended for this type of foreign duty and that's one reason it's harder for people like me to be here. People in the National Guard are not used to being deployed like this. We're "weekend warriors." But since we're stuck here we're all becoming regular Army regardless of whether we want that or not.

My feet hurt all the time now, even when I take my boots off for the day. I have a real nasty blister on the inside of my right foot to go with the bruises. I'm often limping. I thought regular black combat boots were bad, but these are definitely the shittiest boots I have ever been issued.

The mess hall has gotten better as of late but since it isn't always the most reliable when it comes to food (it's closed right now due to the mortar strike), Pete and I have decided to fend for ourselves with regard to creature comforts such as eating. He just came back from the Internet tent and said he ordered some food: mac & cheese, Spam, and Twinkies. What the hell *is* Spam anyway?

I think I'll end up laughing my ass off if he comes back with groceries one of these days. Life is pretty strange over here. I wish I could have a cheeseburger, a real thick one with cheddar, lettuce, tomato, and onion. Oh hell, put everything on it, load it up. Throw on some guacamole.

God, what I wouldn't give to be sitting on a beach right now. I can just about feel the ocean breeze.

Not much else happened today. I took a brief nap this afternoon and when I woke up my head was filled with visions of Germany and being at peace, just a bystander for once. I think you coming in a day later is a good idea. I can spend one night just looking at the streets of Frankfurt from my hotel window—anonymous.

I love you.

## July 2, 2004

I am once again confused about where you're at and what is going on with us. It's like our marriage is a gigantic seesaw and neither one of us knows how to balance it. The instability is adding intense unwanted pressure to my situation here, ever nudging me beyond the maximum amount of stress I can take.

I keep trying to be an understanding person, husband, and

lover. I am trying to find a balance between understanding what you are going through—the stress of being apart and handling everything in our life alone in the States, the worry of whether your husband will even come home, the stress of figuring out who you are and what you want—and my own selfish needs. That coupled with trying to do my job and stay alive is wearing me down.

It's difficult for me when I hear of other soldier's spouses or significant others getting webcams, flashing them when they talk, sending them dirty pictures, writing love letters, telling them they love them, being emotionally supportive, wanting them to call, to write, giving them updates on how life is going in the States—all the things husbands and wives do. We haven't done anything like that.

There have been a couple of times when I have felt as if we connected but our relationship feels too erratic and I desperately want some love. Then I think about you saying "I want to sell the house," "I want to get rid of one of the cats," "I want to sell one of the cars," "I don't want to talk," you having fun being independent and meeting new men, and I don't know what to think any more.

I'm trying. I really am. I'm trying to understand and have faith. Either that or I am very good at being a fool. I'm trying and getting nothing back. It's frustrating and I am beginning to feel lonely and unloved—unloved by the one person in the world I need to love me, the woman I thought would love me forever. I know you love me in the bottom of your heart and I'm not trying to be accusatory. I'm just a guy who wants some positive reinforcement. I need more inspiration, love, and desire from the woman I married.

However, I realize that's not going to happen. I know that from the bottom of *my* heart. I am beginning to feel withdrawn from you. If you are unable to give me what I need, (especially during this time of such intense stress) we have no choice—we must part. I'm not willing to give my life to a woman who I'm constantly coaxing out of her emotional shell.

You've always felt removed from me in some form, never fully letting me in or expressing what's in your heart—always holding back something. We both know this and have talked about it for quite a while.

God knows there's passion inside you. I know it. Every once in a while you've let it out but mostly you've kept yourself locked up tightly. Perhaps I just never found the right way to draw you out. Perhaps that is my failing as a man, husband, and partner. I've never wanted to admit that possibility.

How do we repair the damage we've done to ourselves and our relationship?

We were attacked a few times today. The alarm went off at least twice and one explosion around 1130 or so was pretty close.

If I leave here alive that will be the happiest day of my life, regardless of what happens between us.

I love you.

**July 4, 2004**

Independence Day.

How ironic.

It's too bad I'm not independent of the Army, although the option of giving up a foot or a hand to achieve that is definitely not off the table.

Today I was required to attend some mandatory classes: "Detecting IEDs," "Equal Opportunity Employment," "Electrical Safety," "Safe Driving Techniques," and "Suicide Prevention." They were incredibly mundane, but a good method for suicide prevention did occur to me—send us home. I nodded off at one point, which reminded me of when I fell asleep in basic training. Gosh, it seems like a whole lifetime has passed since then and I smiled somewhat cynically as I recalled the memory. I had gone under during a class on proper rifle cleaning and maintenance. The drill sergeants, with their ever sharp, keen eyes were all over me in a heartbeat, leading me outside, yelling, making me do pushups until I was practically puking all over the lawn.

Falling asleep was not an option after that experience.

And I smiled even more broadly—and less cynically—as my mind turned to other memories of those long nine weeks at Ft. Leonard Wood. I recollected being chosen for the Drill and Ceremony team. We practiced for hours upon hours getting every move in exacting, precise order until we were completely synchronized with one another. During the end of the last week we had a competition with the other platoons in the company.

We won.

I remember being so proud of myself that day, to be wearing the uniform, of having accomplished something I thought was very military, very soldier like—that I was part of something larger than myself. What happened to those days? Have I merely forgotten the honor and dignity I felt for serving my country? Or have I become jaded by this senseless war? Have I lost something or gained something? What am I becoming?

I feel liberated inside somehow, unafraid of facing the world alone—a sense I haven't had in ages. It's as if my inner strength, a force that has lain dormant for so long, is rising up again. At least that's what I'm trying to tell myself because I have to admit that no matter how liberated I feel, I'm aware of how terribly sad my heart has become. Maybe I've just been busy trying to lock my sorrow deep inside some compartment of my heart that I'm afraid to open and I'm deluding myself, distracting myself with the belief in this rediscovered feeling. No… it's both.

Part of this renewed strength might derive from bracing against what seems to be the impending and inevitable loss of my marriage. My gut is informing me that she's leaning that way more and more. I haven't heard from her in a few days now… and the silence is deafening.

Rita has been changing things so radically of late and I seem to be inconsequential to her plans. Her decision to sell the house seems long decided *before* she deemed it necessary to loop me in. It's as if telling me was merely a simple courtesy and I'm just now absorbing the realization that I might not have a home to go back to.

No candle in the window.

I have no idea why I agreed so easily. Perhaps it's because I am so overloaded with stress here that one more thing would truly throw me over the edge into insanity.

My God, what the hell is happening over there? The more we've emailed, the more I get the sinking feeling that she no longer feels married to me… or even attached to me in any way. Recently, she's closed our two joint savings accounts without consulting me. I found that out right on the heels of her letter that had made me feel we actually made a little progress.

I wish I had never signed that Power of Attorney. But I guess I can't blame myself too much. At the time it never dawned on me that all of this would ever take place. It had never, *ever* occurred to me that she and I would ever be separated by more than just miles.

And I honestly thought I was getting my life back on track before they alerted me to this deployment. I had a decent job. I was making money. I had a home, Rita, a dog and two cats… even a lawnmower. I felt as if I could finally turn my full attention toward settling down once and for all and living a loving life with Rita. Now I'm not sure of anything any more.

It's funny. I've noticed how everyone else seems to have a tangible track they're on, some sort of solid ground in life, whether it's with their spouse or a career or with family. How is it that I've never been able to seize what they have? Maybe it's because I've always grown restless so quickly. Have I taken life too whimsically? Have I, consciously or subconsciously, doomed myself?

The weird thing is that I *do* want to settle down and have children. It's just never happened for me. I guess I always thought that would come after I had chosen a solid direction for myself.

Maybe others are content with the life they've chosen, maybe not. Perhaps I need more than just being content. But more of what? Something inside has propelled me, but I'm not sure why or where it's leading me. Maybe it all comes down to having some semblance of faith in a higher power that might be looking out for me from time to time.

Always questions, never any answers.

We can now wear PT clothing to the mess hall (it's been repaired and reopened), but only for breakfast and only to get a to-go plate. The catch is we can only wear them on Sunday. And we no longer have to carry our gas masks everywhere. Honestly, can't these people make up their minds?

## July 7, 2004

It's about 120 degrees today, sunny, a slight breeze, and not too much dust—all in all a fine summer day in the desert. When I got back to my hovel, I felt a bit dizzy and discovered I have what we call here, the "salt crusties"—fine grains of salt clinging to the eyebrows—a sure sign I am dehydrated. All my gear and my uniform were soaked with my sweat.

I must be especially careful today. If the power goes out, that could make for a long miserable afternoon and night in the heat.

It can get insanely hot, about 130 or so in the tents and trailers. Even the floors and sheets on my bed get hot to the touch. There is just no way to escape it and it gets even worse at night, when the flies and bugs come out from their daylong slumber.

I wonder if my body will adapt if I stay here long enough. How will my body react the first time I encounter *real* cold again? Just the thought brings a nostalgic smile to my face.

We've taken quite a few bottle showers. Creativity and improvisation are a must around here because most of us have learned you can't depend on anything working the way it's supposed to—or working at all for that matter.

And again, I can't help but be provoked to thought. We take so much for granted in our daily lives it's really quite astonishing. Having running water whenever we want, being able to flip a light switch and have power at our command, being able to take a shower without shower shoes (without a time limit or line), or even being able to run down to a convenience store and buy a soda or a hot dog on a whim. Or how about being able to go to a fast food restaurant wherever you want to? Or having your own car to take you where you want, whenever you want? Or being able to sleep at night without getting shelled or shot at? Or being able to choose what you want to wear on any given day?

The freedoms and means I took for granted in my old life seem like a distant memory now. Now, they are a reminder to me of how precious *everything* really is, of how many gifts have been bestowed upon me (and all of us for that matter) without my even realizing it. I am going to try to make it a point to never overlook those things again. From here on, I want to be fully appreciative of what has been given me, that I grew up in suburban America with a home, two dogs, a family, friends, video games, dinner every night, and the luxury of being able to choose how I want to live my life, where I want to go, or who I want to be with.

I guess what I'm trying to say is, I used to think of these gifts almost as if they were rights. I was accustomed to believing they were a given, that I would never be deprived of the electricity, water, food, shelter, and freedom that are actually privileges meant to be cherished, loved, and not squandered by complacency. I realize now just how good I've had it living in the United States. More than that, I have been blessed with benefits I seldom gave a thought to and that those things I've been so comfortable with may be taken away all too easily.

I will never forget this lesson.

I wish more people could see this. It saddens me to think of how we fritter away our resources and lives as we sit in the complacency of our homes flipping TV channels until we saunter off to bed. It saddens me to think that we've become so self-righteous with the basics of life that we overlook how lucky we are to have them at our disposal in the first place.

I must say, however, the creativity here is impressive. Some, like me, take a couple of bottles of water with them to the showers. We tape a half bottle that's been cut, with holes poked into it, to the showerhead and pour water through for a makeshift running shower. It's better than nothing, although the water doesn't last long and you usually end up sponge bathing, wiping off as much grime as you can before you are sweating again in the heat of the trailer.

You don't really cool off and sometimes I'm not sure if it's worth it. Maybe it is for the psychological effect of having a creature comfort. I usually end up saving some of the water so I can brush my teeth and wipe my face. Deodorant is a blessing. It saves us from having to smell each other day in and day out.

When we don't have power for an extended time, it gets pretty nasty. One time when I went to the latrine, I was almost knocked over by the stench. Standing in the doorway, I saw piles of empty water bottles strewn over the floor, an overflowing trash bin, and trash littered all over the sinks—empty dental floss containers, toothbrushes, even shaving cream cans. Flies were everywhere, landing on my nose, buzzing in my ears. Toilet paper was scattered all over the place, some in damp piles, others just stray sheets that happened to land where they may.

The smell was coming from the toilets. They hadn't been flushed in days and the odor of human feces and urine was overwhelming. They were literally overflowing with waste, yellow pools baking next to the toilet. Next to my left boot was a brown smear from another boot and as my eyes backtracked where it had come from, I realized someone had had an accident and had smeared crap on the floor from the toilet stall to the doorway. It was foul beyond anything I had encountered before. But that's life at Camp Anaconda.

So the power is out again. Last night after the power came back on, my trailer was rocked with an explosion and the alarm sirens went off. Just a few mortars this time, but the one that landed close to my trailer was especially unnerving, the concussion from it shoving my bunk about four inches across the room. I believe that makes a couple of times this has happened.

The power outages the last couple of days have also kept me from getting online. It couldn't be more perfect timing, of course, since Rita and I had been attempting to communicate some feelings toward each other. I guess that will have to wait. Conversations with her are sporadic and unstable. She still seems distant and I don't know what's going to happen next.

The mornings are usually pretty good for me. I feel alert, it's cooler, and I'm ready to work. But after lunch, I sure go downhill.

The breeze around here (when there is one) is like a hair dryer thrust into your face and usually kicks up a fair amount of dust until the evening, when it settles again.

I hope the power comes on soon. It's rapidly getting hot in here.

I love you.


**July 9, 2004**

I feel a bit better today regarding my situation at home. Rita and I recently emailed a bit and I was encouraged by the direction of our conversation. Only two things concerned me. One is I feel a bit worried she will go so enthusiastically overboard with her recent personal discoveries and explorations in life that she'll push people away—namely me. Second, there is still a distinct lack of affection coming from her, an ever-present distance that's crept into every aspect of our communication. It's irritating because she's supposed to be my wife. Perhaps she doesn't feel passion for our relationship any more. She said as much but also expressed desire to feel that way for me again. Maybe that will come in time. Maybe she needs time to settle into her new self, integrating her discoveries before she is able to express affection toward our relationship again. Who knows, but I want to be patient.

I am trying to go with the flow, to be as easygoing, understanding, and as supportive as I can. Maybe we'll come together. Maybe our marriage will collapse. Whatever happens, we have a little ways to go yet before we can understand each other.

We have less than 70 days until we meet in Germany. It should be fun regardless of what happens and I can't help wondering what will happen when we see each other. Will we feel awkward? Will we leap into each other's arms? That would be nice and a welcome surprise. Maybe we'll have mad, crazy sex. Maybe we can ignite some romance between us again.

I'm committed to her and will continue to listen to her, to help if she wants me to. I love and respect her. Life can always be worse. It can be very exciting and refreshing if you look at it like that. Maybe, like she said in her email, we can wipe the slate clean, start fresh, and come out stronger than ever.

I've heard rumors that Congress wants to cut veterans' benefits. I'm sure that will help the military fulfill their retaining and enlistment quotas. I think it's even more interesting that politicians who are more than willing to start a war and send people into harm's way give so little support to the veterans who manage to come home and have to deal with their physical or mental injuries.

I love you, Rita.

## July 10, 2004

I got up this morning and since the power was on I eagerly jumped in the shower. It's so wonderful to be clean again. I'm treasuring every moment of it. When things go well over here, life can almost be tolerable.

On my way to the shower trailer today I was surprised to see it was overcast. I hadn't seen a cloud in the sky for weeks. I wonder how long the clouds will stay with us.

I didn't get an email from Rita yesterday and I must admit I don't like that. It's unnerving.

It's as if I have two sides that are always in conflict. One part of me really doesn't want to lose her. We have had such a good relationship for so long and when things work well we connect so naturally. I think both of us have felt that from the moment we met. The other part is firmly stating that I'm not taking any more shit from her... or anyone else for that matter. That part of me feels like a defiant child in the face of hurt and pain. I know I am capable of taking care of myself, but it would be such a shame to throw away what we have built together. I probably won't know which side of me will win until I see her.

A thought just occurred to me. I would really love some shrimp and scallops with linguini, smothered in a portobello/ red pepper/onion/garlic cream sauce and topped with Parmesan cheese right now.

God, I miss seafood. I really do.

### July 12, 2004

I haven't heard from Rita in days now. I'm frightened and have a lousy, nauseous feeling like I can't wake up from a nightmare. My mind turns and turns—what's she feeling, what's she doing, how her day has gone? Is she out with our friends or making new friends? More and more, that civilian life—my old life—seems like a dream I once had.

There's not much I can do. Words seem empty, gestures hollow. Kind, loving gestures have only a veneer of what they used to have. They are too few and apart. She's in control of the situation. The little child in me is screaming to not let her have that control, but I am helpless. So I sit and wait.

It's agonizing.

Things have been rather quiet here lately. Although I did just hear the "all clear" siren so there must have been a mortar attack I wasn't aware of.

Who can keep track of them all? The longer you stay here, the better the odds of being killed—it's just a matter of time.

The days tick by and I'm getting anxious. I've been having some pangs of homesickness and I wish I could be left alone. I just don't want to see anyone's faces any more.

I miss the feeling of carefree exploring and glassy reflection that always comes over me when I drive somewhere. I've always returned from road trips feeling clear-headed, more sensible in a way. Perhaps I should have been a trucker. Nah, road trips should never involve work. They should remain sidelong pleasures that are treats for the soul.

Doomed to be restless, I guess.

Not a blessed thing has come into our shop lately. Many of the helicopters are sitting on the ground, dormant beasts panting in the heat for their next kill. I must say that it's nice to leave that sweaty combat vest behind. I brought it up to the hangar and left it there.

And whattya know, the power hasn't gone off in two days.

### July 13, 2004

My house has been sold.

Rita sent an email simply stating the facts and said she is using the profits to allow us to become debt free. That's the most I've heard from her in days. I didn't like that she was so short— no "I love you," no words of affection or comfort at all.

The power is still on and I haven't heard any mortar attacks today. I wonder why it's gotten so quiet all of a sudden. Was it the bomb the Air Force dropped a while ago? Some planes flew over us and dropped some sort of bombs in the area. I've had no intel from anyone.

I think I'll have a shot of the whiskey my friend Tim so graciously mailed me. He's learned how to smuggle just as well as Paula.

I love him for the relief.

### July 16, 2004

I can't feel my life in the States any more. And I can't feel my body—I'm detached from it.

I feel more than ever that I'm losing you. It makes me want to cry from the depths of my soul. It would take just a breath for the tears to come. It makes my heart ache and pound with nauseous tension. I don't want to lose you. You said in an email once that you felt your heart break when I left for Iraq. Right now mine is being broken into razor-thin shards, tinkling away as they fall onto a cold, icy floor.

I know we have so much to deal with, the nagging haunting of wrongs we've done to each other. Our relationship hasn't been perfect, but shouldn't we also look at what's been good? All the joys we've shared that meant so much? Shouldn't we scrutinize the right as much as the wrong and perhaps glean a glimmer of hope and love?

The past 10 years can't have been all *that* bad, right?

They can't have been so completely miserable as to not allow us strength to still believe in the bond we have formed, the connection we have always relied on. I can't accept that we should walk away after having come so far. But all my reconciliations and banal talk won't make a difference if you aren't willing to participate.

I am so lonely now that you are not with me in spirit as well as in body. I'm so sorry, so sorry for the way things have turned out between us.

What can I do? What inspiration can I offer? What piece of my heart can I give to you that will turn back the tide? I think it is utterly crazy that you can drive me so bonkers.

What is wrong with me?

Do you know that we've spoken just twice in the past two weeks and neither time you gave me a single sign to let me know which road to travel? Is a husband supposed to be this disconnected from his wife while he is at war?

I wish I knew what to do. There's nothing to do but wait for some absolution from this hell. In a few months my prison sentence will come to an end, but then what? How do I pick up the pieces? Will you want to pick them up with me and make a better life?

It makes me nauseous to think of you with someone else. I remember you saying once that you're a fighter, you don't give up. Well, is that still true of us? Are you still fighting?

I remember looking into your eyes at our wedding and thinking what a beautiful woman you are and how much I love you. I vowed to spend my life with you that day.

Maybe I *should* die here—then I'll have at least kept my promise.

You've been so stinging in your recent emails—how I haven't been home enough the last two years, how you feel I don't want to have sex with you, how you have felt neglected.

I would take it all back if I could. I fear you have too much anger and that you'll harbor it until you feel I've paid enough of a price to atone for what I have done.

I've saved many of your emails. I reread them a couple of days ago and noticed how they became less and less affectionate over time. It was slow at first, almost imperceptible, but your discontent had been building, gaining more speed every day.

I wonder what Germany will bring. Will it help us or will it confirm the division between us once and for all?

You say you want to live for the moment. You say you want passion. You say you want to be swept off your feet. Well, here I am. I am ready and I love how you scorned me when I wrote that I could give that to you. You said I was too far away. My only response is that we should take advantage of what we *do* have, what we feel in our hearts. Maybe right now that's not enough for you but it's enough for me and it has to be a two-way street between us.

I feel loneliness so profoundly over here as I lie in my bunk at night it almost drives me insane. I am stuck with the long nights that seem to stretch into lonely eternity, worse now that you are pulling away from me.

I am alone and the war just keeps rollin' along, oblivious to human troubles.

I love you.

### July 17, 2004

Last night I was reading Dante's *The Divine Comedy*, my latest and greatest literary endeavor, when an explosion shook my hovel. It was incredibly close. I felt the floor and my bed vibrate as chunks of rock and debris peppered the roof and walls.

It always scares the shit out of me. I feel butterflies leap into my stomach, a lump forming in my throat. And what did I think about? I thought about you, my wife—my girl. Your picture is tacked to the wall next to my bunk and I just looked at you for a while, vainly attempting to calm my nerves.

A two-star general came by to tour our hangar and repair shops the other day. I wasn't there. It was my day off but apparently he was very quick about it and didn't really talk to anyone. Mike had told me about the inspection but I had forgotten. It sounded like the usual dog and pony show for the bigwigs and I don't care for those sorts of things.

It's as if they are not interested in the real story. I've been ordered to look busy anytime they come around for inspections. *Look busy*? Why? Are they not interested in what we really do? The reality is we *do* smoke in back of the shops, we *aren't* all that busy, we *are* all scared and miserable. We don't want to fight in a war. We want to go home.

So the question becomes: Why do we feel compelled to put up a false front just to impress somebody we don't know? It's amazing to me because it happens everywhere... the business world, the dating world, even when someone asks us how we're doing. What are we afraid of? Are we more infatuated with image than truth?

Perhaps things could change if we stopped feeding them the image of what they would like to see. Perhaps the world would be a better place if we, as people, were more honest in general. Or is filing a "sweep it under the carpet" report more important in Washington? I have no appetite for being a puppet in their show, but I've been ordered to play my part.

I think that if you allow yourself to participate in the show, they go back to their offices content with the knowledge that things are going just fine over here in the desert. In other words, they buy into a fabricated spectacle we present for them and the most ironic part of all this is I don't think they are really fooled. So does that mean *both* parties are willing participants in a façade? It just doesn't make any sense to me.

I scribbled some thoughts I wouldn't mind imparting if a general asked my opinion:

1. My wife is lonely, sad, and uncertain about our future. I fear I may be losing her.

2. I've lost my cat.

3. I've lost my house.

4. I've lost my car.

5. I don't have a job if or when I get home, whenever and wherever that is going to be.

6. I don't believe in war, especially this one.

7. My feet are bruised, sore, and blistered thanks to the cheap boots I've been issued.

8. I'm tired of the constantly changing uniform directives.

9. I don't like camel spiders. They creep me out.

10. I don't like being bombed every day and wondering if I'm going to die.

11. I don't like that I drove through Baghdad without any armor for my truck.

12. We can barely perform the necessary helicopter maintenance due to lack of parts.

13. The desert heat is incredible. It blows my mind how hot it is here.

14. I don't like being in a position where I might have to kill someone.

15. I'm scared for my life.

16. My body aches.

17. My mind aches.

18. I don't know who I am half the time.

There you have it. But in all likelihood no one would speak with me. After all, I'm just a lowly sergeant.

So yesterday, my dear, I sent you a gift box from that chocolate company you like so much—dark of course, your favorite. I wanted to be spontaneous and romantic. I hope you'll like it. I never hear from you any more. You are so distant now. It's been so long since I've gotten a letter.

I wish I had just kept walking when I saw the recruitment table at our college so long ago. The worst mistake I ever made was joining the Army. It has been confirmed more with each passing day.

I guess I really only have myself to blame. You never deserved this and I don't deserve you. You have put up with me for way too long. There is nothing to do here except ponder my mistakes, going over and over them until it feels like my head is going to burst.

In *Inferno*, Dante wrote that the seventh circle of Hell consisted of flaming hot sand with little sparks, like burning bits of coals, falling from above onto the condemned. Perhaps I am in that circle. Perhaps this is my penance for the hurt I have unwittingly inflicted on you, on the people around me, on nature and humanity due to my own selfishness and participation in this war. Perhaps I am doing my time right now, on these searing desert sands.

All I can do is wait—wait and learn what I can. Wait until my time is up one way or another, either dead or alive. I still have hope that I might carry something positive out of this place. Regardless of what happens with us, I don't want all of this to be for nothing. That would be truly horrifying. To go home and forget all I have been through over here would be a waste.

Shouldn't we do this with every experience in life? Maybe that's the ultimate lesson—learning how to truly live each day, bettering ourselves as we move forward. Maybe that's the highest truth you can achieve over here. I think if I can manage to sustain that notion and resist how society dulls you with its mundane worries, then perhaps I can ultimately make sense of my life. Perhaps I will be able to enjoy every moment, *be* in every moment, savor every breath until my eyes finally close, my soul slipping into the dark of eternal night.

The power is out again. It's been out for hours now. I'm glad I had the chance to order that chocolate for you first.

### July 20, 2004

Yesterday Top came up to me after morning formation and told me to meet him in the Administration office in 10 minutes— the major wanted to see me. I reported as ordered and was led into his office. Apparently word had gotten out that I have a bachelor's degree in Professional Communication and the major had selected me to design and write a monthly newsletter to be mailed to each family.

He explained the premise was to keep them informed of our activities and introduce them to various members of our unit. The newsletter was to be a link between us and the families back home so they could feel comforted that we are safe, that we're performing our mission—a communication they could take pride and comfort from. Apparently it had been on the major's mind for quite a while but he hadn't found the right soldier to complete his idea. I don't know how Top knew I had a degree, or even that I was a writer, but he told the major "Sir, I've got your man. He's the best writer here."

Perhaps it's because everyone here knows that I'm keeping a journal of our experiences. Obviously I couldn't say no—this was not a request.

By late that afternoon I was interviewing soldiers from our unit, specifically each platoon sergeant for an article to include in the first issue. As soon as I got to my hovel, I dug into my half-forgotten desktop publishing skills and promptly began planning the layout and content of the newsletter. It came out to be four pages long. Here's a quick breakdown:

The front page will contain a title, the date, and graphics. It will also include a table of contents, a "Did You Know?" trivia column, and a main article.

A section for both birthdays and promotions and a "Question of the Month" will take up the second page. I plan on interviewing five soldiers each month and I'll post their responses next to a "mug shot" of each person.

The third page will primarily be a "Letter to Home" and a "Special Activities" section. Members from our company will write about special missions that they've taken part in—sort of an editorial in a sense.

Finally, the fourth page will include "Notices," the "Monthly Weather Report," and a letter from the major to the families updating them on our progress. It will also include any credits that might be appropriate.

Talk about a fair amount of work on top of my other duties.

Most of it came bubbling off the top of my head, almost boiling over—the ideas kept cookin'. I just have to finish it and see if the major likes the layout. Both the major and Top were smiling at me though. I think they were pleased with themselves because they knew I was having fun and this is more along the lines of what I do. They had indeed found the right man for the job.

So I'm going to finish it and bring it to the major by this Saturday. That's my own personal deadline; they didn't really set one. Printing this little project will be a separate challenge. That will have to be worked out later as I have no printer, only a minimally powered laptop with a basic office package.

We agreed that each member of the company should receive a copy—sort of our own company newspaper—and each family should be mailed a copy too. I have no idea how that's going to work. Supplies are at a minimum, postage needs to be paid for, and someone will have to deliver more than 200 copies of this newsletter to the APO[27]here on base. Perhaps the major will come up with a brilliant solution. I have to say, I'm excited about the prospect of seeing my work in print again. I used to work for a local newspaper as a copyeditor. I also worked as a reporter

---

27　Army Post Office

for my college newspaper—two of the best jobs I have ever had.

Those were good days for me and wow did I have fun. I was also incredibly busy. I remember it clear as day. I was taking a full course load, reporting for the college, and working at night for the newspaper—often past midnight. I was responsible for the weather page, several news pages, and the Saturday morning insert that contained special articles and a TV schedule. As busy and tired as I often was, I was always elated when I saw my work in print.

I would buy a newspaper and grin so broadly I thought the top half of my head would fall off when I opened to the pages I had worked on, seeing them actually in my hands, knowing that everyone in town who bought one would see them too.

I miss those days.

I got an email from Rita for the first time in what seems like weeks. How long *has* it been now? The days are blending together. Anyway, her message was a barrage of anger, pessimism, and resentment. She really had nothing productive or loving to say. I'm mystified by why she was so angry. I'm almost wishing that she hadn't bothered writing me at all.

The Bahamas are sounding better and better in my mind. I wish the Star Trek people would invent that transporter already. It would make all our lives much easier.

Ahhh fuck.

I don't even want to think or write about the troubles at home right now.

I'm tired and she just pissed on my evening in Hell.

**July 21, 2004**

I finished the lead story for the newsletter while at the shop today. I think it came out pretty well, but I'm sure the major will have something to say before it prints. He mentioned he would like to see a copy before it gets mailed out. I don't really have much of a voice when it comes to that. I am, after all, in prison and operating under my warden's orders. Freedom of expression may be censored at any time. That has been made very clear to me.

My feet hurt. The bruises are still there, a nice deep purple.

I haven't heard from Rita other than the nasty email she sent.

Mike put me on two shifts at the hangar again—so much for days off.

Who am I to argue any more?

I'm so tired.

**July 22, 2004**

We have a saying here—"What are they going to do… send us to Iraq?"

It's an attitude.

We all share it here.

It's the soldier's way.

It's *our* way.

It's the way of a soldier with full knowledge that what he's fighting for doesn't mean anything in the grand scheme of things, that the politicians will keep making imbecilic policies and retiring to the comfort of their homes, detached from the consequences of their actions while we are here spilling blood in the sand, that they can't do anything worse to us than what they've already done. So we have nothing to lose—nothing left to hope for.

It might be too late for Rita and me at this point. In her last email, she said she was tired of waiting for me to come home, that she needed to begin living her life and was moving on. Yet I hope. I will always hope. She is my wife, my best friend, my love, my soul mate.

It's hazy today—clouds hovering overhead, ominous but without action. It seems like there is some humidity in the air but it's hard to tell for sure. The heat is unrelenting.

There were eight mortar attacks today.

Will it never end?

I love you.

## July 24, 2004

I have been working on the assignment the major has given me. It came out pretty decent. I've rediscovered that feeling of pride in my work and I'm luxuriating in that as much as possible. There's not much to be proud of here.

Creative pursuits are what stimulate me. They fulfill me; they're where my interests ultimately lie. There's really no point in pretending otherwise. Perhaps I'm just not a very good soldier.

I felt profoundly sad and homesick yesterday. Images of

places I've been literally popped into my vision and I once again felt as if I was watching a movie.

I relived driving to the Grand Canyon while on spring break, taking an epic road trip with Rita from Montana through Las Vegas and into Los Angeles via the Hoover Dam, Death Valley, and Joshua Tree National Parks, then driving the entire stretch of the Pacific Coast Highway into Portland, stopping along the way at a Bigfoot museum and Alcatraz in San Francisco. I relived standing in awe of Mount Rushmore and the Devil's Tower, hiking Capitol Reef and Arches National Parks, and flying to Disney World, spending a week frolicking in as many rides as I could while eating my way through Epcot Center.

I relived watching deer grazing the front yard of my apartment while I was in college and browsing the aisles of the local video store on a Friday night. I relived camping in the mountains, sitting by my campfire, going snowshoeing for the first time, jumping into a mountain lake for a swim, seeing my very first wild bear, the moose I accidentally stumbled across, and the porcupine who studied me for a few minutes before lumbering on his way through the woods.

I relived working with fellow students at my college on a paper we wrote, trying to figure out calculus, and giving a 20-minute presentation on a novel I studied for a class about the history and philosophy of society and technology that was taught by one of my favorite professors. I relived writing for the school newspaper while taking classes full-time, barbecuing a salmon fillet in the summer rain one evening, reading a book on the lawn of my campus in the afternoon before class began—all the little, tiny fragments of my life.

Sometimes I can feel home so strongly. My mind is already halfway there. It probably never left home in the first place. But part of me is no longer here *or* there.

I feel surreal, out of joint, not myself... as if I'm metamorphosing into something new.

Will the time go by fast enough? Do I have yet more to learn over here before I can continue with my life?

I haven't heard from Rita.

She's a distant shadow now.

## July 25, 2004

Pete and I are trying to become more self-sufficient since we never know if the mess hall will have food or power. We've stolen plastic spoons, knives, forks, and Styrofoam bowls out of the mess hall. We've cut the tops off water bottles to hold our plastic ware. We've stolen boxes of Tech Wipes[28] to wipe out our saucepan and clean the hot plate he found, sometimes soaking baby wipes in isopropyl alcohol that we steal from the maintenance shops. We also steal naphtha[29] from the aircraft hangar to use in our Zippos. We've made late-night raids on the palettes of water, stockpiling the treasure next to our bunks. We

---

28  Like napkins, but for extremely delicate tasks
29  A liquid mixture of hydrocarbons used to make high-octane gasoline

have a stack of MRE boxes piled up as well. We steal just about anything we can. We're learning to fend for ourselves since our government won't properly provide for us.

Everyone is counting the days now until we can go home. People are starting to burn out—you can see it in their eyes, their mannerisms, the shortness of their conversations, and the tones of their voices—their tired faces hot and itchy with the desire to go home.

I finished the first issue of the newsletter today. I'll print it out in a couple of days and we'll see whether the major likes it. I really hope the company likes it—not that it would devastate me if they didn't, but I do have my creative pride and I feel it turned out well.

Not much else to write right now—I'm weary. We got attacked again but I'm starting to feel like a broken record on that point.

I have no more enthusiasm or energy, yet I must go on.

I miss everyone at home very much. They are always in my thoughts.

I haven't heard from Rita.

I love her.

### July 26, 2004

I turned in the final copy for the first newsletter to the major today. He added some things I don't like but I don't really have a say in the matter. We certainly can't send our families the real story of what we're going through. It must be positive, upbeat, even inspirational. They deserve the truth, but that will have to wait until we're home, far away from the censorship taking place simply for the sake of morale. So his corrections are going to stay.

Sometimes I feel so isolated, stuck without freedom and nowhere to turn or no one to talk to. I've come to realize that you can only truly count on yourself. It's an almost enlightening thought but it's a hard truth too. The liberty it gives you comes with the grim reality of being alone.

There are no free rides in life and whatever you might think is free will, eventually catches up with you. I know that now. It may take years... but it will.

### July 27, 2004

My mind constantly wanders to thoughts of home, my wife, my friends, my family. Images of all the places I have been as well as incessant questions about what my new life is going to be like continually batter my brain. They bump off each other like virtual particles in a quantum flux, or balls on a pool table and the world around me often disappears as my head swims through them all.

I haven't done a single bit of hydraulic work in quite a while now—not one ounce. I am starting to feel useless again and the newsletter is my only saving grace, the only thing that can distract my mind.

I had a talk with Mike yesterday. He honestly still expects to be home by mid-February, so from now on we are going to try to get rid of as much equipment as we can by signing it off to other units. The more we leave behind, the sooner we will leave. It's amazing the creative things people can come up with when they really want out of a place.

He also told me that the maintenance shops are staying in theater, which is great news. (The shops are portable, so they could have had us pack them up and take them with us when we leave.) According to rumor, our replacement unit's advance party is still coming here in November. If that comes to pass, we should be packing and leaving here by December, or January at the latest. God, I can't tell you how exciting that sounds. It's all anyone can talk about.

The major altered my newsletter again and I don't like what he did. He edited some of my writing and added some graphics. The graphics are pretty good but, gosh, he's not the best writer in the world. I don't like having my name on his writing but for obvious reasons I'm reluctant to edit my commanding officer. Caught between a creative rock and a hard place I guess. But it was printed and distributed to the company after I had left the hangar and it seems as though people enjoyed it—at least that's what Pete told me. I have to keep working on the next one. I have some interviews to do but this is all just mundane news.

I wonder what Germany will be like. She hasn't cancelled yet. I wonder if we will like who the other has become and accept the changes we have both undergone.

Is this the calm before the storm or is it a lull between storms?

We were attacked three times today.

**July 28, 2004**

I don't remember the last time Rita wrote to me—we've just left each other to our own devices.

There are days when I feel besieged by this life. I feel completely overwhelmed by what I've experienced and my concerns about my future but, there is always a flipside to everything in life. Admittedly, some might think that this experience would be very exciting. They would argue that my odyssey has opened a door and given me a chance to start anew.

I would agree with that. How can you not? It's rational, sensible, and positive. But even if this may very well be my chance to be reborn, there are days when I feel horribly depressed and scared. It's quite a shock to the system when you have to take it all in one shot to the head.

KABOOM!!!

Congratulations… you've been reborn.

It's like a mini-Big Bang inside me.

I am a new universe beginning to expand.

Sometimes I ask myself why I couldn't have just been one of those guys who followed that normal, everyday routine. You know the type. He goes to college, gets the steady job, meets a woman, gets married, buys the house with the white picket fence, has 2.1 kids, even mows his lawn every weekend while chatting with the neighbors about the crazy people down the street who don't clean their yard.

But I don't think that's in the cards for me. All I can do is play the hand I was dealt and make the best of it, live to the best of my ability wherever the wind takes me.

Who really cares anyway? When I'm dead and buried, what would happen to that white picket fence? Would there be someone to not only care for it like I did, but to remember who put it up in the first place? What does staying within the lines of society really do for you anyway? How much do you lose by caging yourself within the confines of what someone else says you must or should do? How much of your life is pissed away by doing that? How much of life is wasted by living in fear of how others might judge us or love us?

And what makes them so right anyway? What makes them so omniscient that they have the power to tell you how to live your life? What makes my viewpoint any less valid than theirs?

It seems to me now that we spend our lives compelled to do what someone else feels is the correct path. Go to college. Get a job. Build for retirement. Buy things you don't really need or want. Stay within the lines.

It's beginning to solidify in my mind that I have never truly believed in the rules that we have been programmed to believe in. Since we were old enough to speak, we have been encouraged not just to compete but to push and shove against each other as if we're opponents, separate entities who are only out for ourselves. We're taught that the acquisition of material wealth signifies how much we've achieved in life, that there is only one way to get ahead and create meaning in our lives.

Living here in this hell, I've realized that *things* don't give you meaning, they merely temporarily fill a void within us and ultimately leave us to wonder why we still feel so empty. Money only allows you to buy more things to keep dumping into that bottomless inner void. Sleepwalking our way between the lines that others have drawn for us never allows a true chance to become who we want to be.

So where is true meaning? I'm still working on that but I'm suspecting it must come from within. Internal reflection seems much more gratifying to me than external rewards. If nothing else, this deployment has been a pure existential experience that has shattered every mundane ideal I have been programmed with like a wrecking ball pulverizing a brick wall. I am coming to terms with all sorts of hard truths that I had known in my gut but had never allowed myself to voice.

Living through this madness here has allowed my eyes to focus differently. And yet, everything I just wrote sounds absurd, silly, and perhaps even pointless. I am all too aware of how fleeting life is, how delicately balanced it is with death.

God, I really hope that I'll be able to put all this together someday.

I want my life to make sense.

### July 31, 2004

Yesterday I emailed Rita, gave her some news about Germany and asked if she was excited to see me. Her reply did nothing to comfort my lonely heart. She did say our remaining pets would be okay while she's in California for a week and that she'll only be able to stay in Germany for 10 days. I can't get through to her. She just won't let me in.

We've had several attacks in the last few days. No matter how hard I try, I still can't shake the jittery feeling that overcomes me when it happens.

There have been many jets flying around lately.

Counting the days…

### August 1, 2004

Today Mike told me the best thing I can do right now is to just ride the tide for a little while and see where my life leads. He's right of course.

His advice sounds kind of exciting, but I am so confused.

On the war side there is nothing new to report except no aviation work, lots of heat, and lots of mortars. The power has been working for two straight days now.

The latest rumor floating around the company is that November and December will definitely be the months when we will be preparing to go home. It's very exciting to hear. I keep having visions of the mountains, the cool breeze—the freedom to do what I want.

I can't fucking wait.

### August 2, 2004

Top told us this morning while we were at formation that more than 23 mortar rounds came into the camp last night.

That's quite a bit for one sortie but it didn't seem different from any other day. I'm not sure where most of them hit, but I do know there were a number of explosions close to me and a few landed in the field next to us. One went right over Malcolm. It freaked him out pretty good.

Today has been quiet so far, but rumor has it that an attack is impending. It's sure to get worse before we leave. And those fuckers are getting more accurate. The longer I stay, the more I'm pushing my luck. Maybe someday soon my ticket will be up and I'll win the "lucky lottery" and go home in a plastic bag. It makes me feel sick to my stomach to think that all I have to do is take a leak at the latrine and BAM—that's it, lights out, my thoughts and memories scattered like leaves in the wind.

Maybe a mortar will just land on me while I'm smoking a cigarette or working on a helicopter.

Maybe I won't even know it.

Maybe I won't feel it.

Or maybe I will.

"This place sets you on edge all the time," a buddy once told me. "It's the all-encompassing underlying stress of potential death, day in and day out, that I'm completely fatigued by."

And he's right. The incessant, unrelenting fear of *when*, not if, you are going to die is what wears you utterly to the bone.

I'm finding that my entire mindset here has become etched with mortar attacks and the threat of death. In other words, what I used to think of as normal moments and activities are now slowly being interpreted by my brain as nothing more than *abnormalities.* It's a strange feeling and my mind wants to grasp at any tiny moment to provide me with a sense of security— going to the hangar, drinking coffee in the morning, thinking that it might be fun to build another shelf for my hovel. It's become critical to have these fleeting moments of not being afraid and I seem to be helpless against the mortars who are steadily insisting on establishing themselves as the new normal of my life.

But a feeling of resignation has also crept into me and taken root. I shrug my shoulders when an attack happens now—why bother worrying about it? If it's my destiny to die over here, then so be it. The sadness will be over and I won't have to worry about a life in the States that could have been. I won't have to worry about career choices and life insurance and what to have for dinner or whether I will have a wife to come home to.

I just need my luck to hold out.

That's all it is—survival.

I worked on the next newsletter today. I interviewed some guys from the unit and took a few photos. I've resolved myself to getting as much done as quickly as I can. It keeps me focused on something other than death.

What's going on at home is still constantly on my mind. I haven't heard from her. I have no idea what's going on with her.

Well, you know what, I love her.

No matter what happens, I always will.

**August 3, 2004**

Mike made an interesting observation today. He was saying how he can't wait to get home just to hear the serenity of quiet. It made me realize just how bombarded we are by noise here, everything from mortars to helicopters to gunfire to trucks to the pathetic generators that quit when we least want them to. Maybe that's why I get so frightened when everything becomes quiet. I've found myself listening more now that he has said that, trying not to let my mind filter out what I might need to pay attention to.

I've gotten mixed comments about the newsletter. Some think it was very well done while others think the article I wrote was unrealistic. I had only one thing to say: "If I wrote the complete truth about this place, how would that make your relatives feel?"

Small consolation, I know—that no one back home knows what we're going through causes some in my company a fair amount of anguish. But it was the best response I could come up with at the time. And who ever sees the full picture anyway?

We're limited by our own knowledge and perception of the world around us. In other words, we all see what we want to see. I certainly have been guilty of that—I make no excuses for myself. But awareness is a huge step in growing and learning. Without it, how *can* you grow? Without awareness, what steps can anyone realistically take? The ability to apply greater awareness in a more positive light feels like *significant* growth to me. I think it's a worthy goal for any person.

That's what I ultimately want. Through experience, observation, and a willingness to compassionately consider any angle of any situation, perhaps I may be guided to some sort of enlightenment. Ignorance is easy; a broadened mind hard work.

I don't think that most people worry about these things. Or if they do, only as a passing thought, everyday distractions becoming more prominent. Perhaps they are content to be wrapped up in the bubble of their own world. Not everyone is like that to be sure, but I bet there are a lot.

It's got to be easier. Who can really blame any of us? Perhaps, no matter what we do, no matter how much work we put in, no matter how hard we strive for enlightenment, we will always be wrapped up in some kind of bubble. Maybe the bubble just takes on different forms as we age and mature.

Can any of us honestly say that one bubble is better than another?

Americans, and I guess humans in general, love the easy way. We're always looking for a shortcut—the closest spot in the parking lot. It seems natural. From electrons to water to a bee searching for pollen to a planet orbiting a star—everything takes the path of least resistance whenever it can.

For that matter, it's easier to go to war and kill people than it is to begin to learn about the culture and nation you're disagreeing with, negotiate, to have compassion, tolerance, even grace. Over here the only thing we care about is to survive and get home as fast as possible.

I've never been with a more frustrated, disillusioned group

of people. Everyone I've talked with keeps saying the same thing. We can't voice our opinions. Our government wouldn't listen anyway, even if we had bullhorns.

As Mike likes to say, "We are just pawns in the great chess game."

It's true over here and it's true back in the States as well. It's just that we soldiers trapped on this base are merely much more acutely *aware* that our lives don't really matter. We are only numbers on a balance sheet to people who are far away and couldn't care less about us, people who have no knowledge of the combined experience of the lives they have sent to a possible empty death.

It's the difference between playing chess and being a piece on the game table.

I've come to think that there's a vast ideological chasm between the people of this world who view war as a giant chess game, moving pieces around in some absurd callous manner, and those who can understand that the human beings who fight or are helpless victims of war are *not* chess pieces.

For me, I am well aware that I am being pushed around the board and that awareness has seeded a significant amount of resentment deep within me. A rage is building within me, directed at the extreme injustice in this world.

What do I do with that? I have no idea yet, but the feeling cannot be denied.

It seems to me there are a few select people who hold all the power. They call the shots and we beg for the scraps after they've wiped their greasy mouths and pushed back from the table.

This is not a new concept to any student of history.

But it's the truth of a soldier and a harsh reality of America that most don't want to hear about. It's much more comforting to think this has all been for a "good cause," that we are fighting for the freedom of America and the world.

It's a notion that has very little meaning for most of us here.

### August 4, 2004

I'm so tense right now that my shoulders ache. It feels like a sharp knife has been driven between my shoulder blades. No matter how I sit, stand, or lie there is no relief.

Rita is drifting away and I am powerless to prevent it. She once said in an email that she wonders how we're going to relate when I get home. Well, she's not helping the matter by being silent. And I am really fucking hating being strung along like a docile little puppy. She doesn't like to be pushed, but she seems to be pushing me hard.

I'm not perfect. I don't deny that. But I have always been there to support the people in my life through whatever trial, like when I had to call 9-1-1 when my mother collapsed one morning and had to be hospitalized. I stayed with her all night, reading and sitting by her bed while she struggled to breathe.

I don't know what to do but try to keep at least half my sanity. I might end up leaving here with mush for a brain, but if I can be content with something, *anything* in my life, then hey, what's a little insanity right? Maybe it'll just spice life up. It's hard to put this out of my head and try to focus on the tasks at hand but that's the only way I'm going to live through this.

### August 7, 2004

I feel so strange, really out of joint. I'm homesick and tired. I was going to read but my book looked foreign to me, almost unreal as if I wasn't really holding it.

So I've been sitting here and just... staring blankly at nothing. You know how sometimes your eyes get out of focus and you feel like you're going inside yourself? It's as if nothing at all interests you and the world disappears. I feel bland, odd, like I'm in a waking dream. I'm finding myself sitting and staring more often. My mind just spontaneously blanks out and becomes numb. Sometimes I feel myself rocking back and forth, unable to stop, staring at the floor, the world fading into a grey fog, everything around me unreal and blurry.

It feels like I really *am* going insane.

### August 8, 2004

Rumor has it that there's a good possibility we will be turning over everything (including equipment and supplies) to the incoming unit or the other maintenance company that operates closely with us. I'm keeping my fingers crossed. If we do, it would mean a flight directly out of here and no convoy through Iraq. Best of all, we wouldn't have to wash our equipment when we get to Camp Doha for the return trip to the States. But we probably won't know for sure until a couple of months from now.

Things haven't changed much here in the last few days. As Mike likes to say, "Welcome to Groundhog Day."

I have to overhaul a couple of Blackhawk brakes tomorrow. That's about it for maintenance.

Rita and I haven't talked for weeks now. Yesterday I sent an email asking why we never seem to talk like husband and wife any more, ending it with an "I love you" and an "I miss you." Her response was that she really enjoyed going out for the day with our dog. She said she was enjoying living on her own and being independent. She also said I shouldn't push her.

There's not much consolation and comfort I can take from that.

Nothing seems real any more.

### August 9, 2004

It's so hot here.

The thermostat next to the hangar pegged out at 143 degrees today, although I could hardly believe it. Somebody scrawled "Dude, it's too f-in' hott" next to it in stark black, scraggly lettering. It can't be that hot, no place on earth could be *that* hot.

We were attacked today.

Some people are so used to the bombings, they complain about having to go to the hangar for shelter now. It's becoming routine for me too. I hardly acknowledge the alarm sirens any more. If a mortar is going to kill me, let it.

It's agonizing... tantalizing. It almost draws you into its lunacy. You begin to dare it to kill you, part of you wishing it would happen.

There must be some stress in me right now although I am numb to it. I can't feel a thing, only the pen in my fingers, the paper beneath my hand, and the unbearable heat of the desert.

The tic in my right eye is back and worse than ever. My hand sometimes trembles when I write. It comes and goes. It's worrisome, but I suppose it could be worse.

Yep, I keep hanging on.

Today there is hardly any hope. Rita's recent email provided a glimmer that I'm trying to cling to, a faint hope that we might yet find a way to reconcile our differences. Perhaps I'm a fool. I'm beginning to think so.

She says she feels horrible about what is going on and has never meant to hurt me, especially when I'm so far away from home. She went on to say that this situation is not all about me, however. She said that when I first left, it was horrible for her too but as the weeks went by she began to move on, began to learn new things about herself, and in the process discovered just how unhappy living with me had made her. She realized that she had been putting on a happy face for quite some time. She had internalized everything and swept her unhappiness under the carpet.

Apparently when I left it gave her the chance to realize that she does pretty well on her own and is happy with that discovery. I always knew that; we both did. She has always been fiercely independent. What *did* surprise me was that she said she felt drained by our relationship, both emotionally and physically, and asked why she would want to go back to that. She said I haven't given her much reason to.

That hurt. It hurt because it became readily clear to me just how stark our differences are. I've always been the dreamer, the romantic. Rita lives in a pragmatic world even when it comes to relationships. Perhaps I never wanted to recognize that in her.

I guess she was upset because in a recent email I asked her not to touch the money in our joint bank account (where my Army pay goes) and that proved to her I haven't changed as much as I think. Truthfully, I don't know why I did that.

I think it was because I feel panicked.

I feel panicked by the silence, the dreary emails that only come through every once in a while. I feel panicked when I see her emptying bank accounts, selling our things, dismantling the life we had built together. It was a kneejerk reaction.

She thinks I've left our entire marriage in her hands, that I'm lazy. I think she even feels that I want her to pay for her trip to Germany so she can fly herself there and do all the work of repairing our relationship. She doesn't think we have a partnership and that we've been immersed in co-dependence for too long. She also said she felt neglected because I was always trying to figure myself out.

Perhaps she's right; I really don't know any more.

My brain is so tired and overloaded.

She says she's not lonely, not unhappy, perfectly content to be by herself, and given that she has no reason to go back to our marriage. Finally, her parting words were that she loves me but she has to live for herself and no one else. She comes first no matter what. She doesn't want to be angry any more and doesn't want to lose me from her life.

I feel like softly crying for the past. Eternal memories of a mortal mind tattered by experience. I guess it's the drama of the human spirit.

*A dance with death*
*Amid the bittersweet breath of life;*
*The breath of joy, of sorrow, of love, of strife;*

*A beating heart today, perhaps tomorrow*
*A beating heart... of place... of time*
*Will atonement be mine?*

*Boom, boom... the war drums march;*
*Never far, always near... in this burning desert shrine.*
*I've come to drink the sacred wine.*

*Trapped within a tangled net of souls*
*Only fleeting moments matter,*
*Amid the violent clatter.*

*A burnt, curled fragment of photo paper;*
*A snapshot of time*
*Worn with grime.*

*Smudged and blurred,*
*Stained with the tears of past.*
*Yet I love her steadfast.*

I don't know why I just wrote that, it came right off the top of my head. I've never been much of a poet.

I don't want to go to Germany any more. I just want to go home.

### September 26, 2004

All I can say is "Whoa."

I didn't realize it had been so long since I had written in my journal. It's like a lifetime has passed—this is not good. I feel so guilty, but I'll do my best to try to catch up.

It's official… we are getting a divorce.

My mind feels foggy right now but I seem to remember writing about how she had begun to systematically dismantle everything we had built together. Anyway, here's the story from the beginning.

Top arranged my leave and scheduled me to fly out of Camp Anaconda on September 2. I can remember August—in fact the majority of the summer—being filled with anxiety and depression about my domestic problems as well as the tremendous pressure here in Iraq. By the time I left this miserable place, Rita had closed every joint bank account except for our account where my Army paychecks were deposited. She had sold the house, sold one of two cars we owned, dumped our little cat at the Humane Society, and had rejected any form of communication I suggested other than the occasional email, those becoming increasingly distant. When she did email, her words mainly consisted of anger, berating me for mistakes that I'd made and blaming me for ruining our marriage.

Every resentment she had stockpiled came gushing out of her like some scalding geyser. I felt so tense, so worried, so upset I didn't know what was going on half the time. I felt as if I was swimming in murky water vainly trying to find the shoreline. There were quite a few days when I thought I really was going crazy, the feeling of it almost bubbling over, making a mess of whatever I had left for a brain. Several times I considered seeing the psychologists stationed on the Air Force side of the base, but instead I preferred to endure the pain on my own.

On a few occasions Mike threatened to send me over to the other side of the base for a psychiatric evaluation. He seemed very worried about the flimsy balancing act I was performing between my duties and my troubles at home. I don't know how I made it through that time without just shooting something or someone, or stripping off all my clothes with some wild, out-of-control look in my eyes, streaking through the camp like some mad gorilla, screaming incoherently. But I *have* survived.

However, at one point I *did* go to the JAG office and

completed a Power of Attorney Revocation, which gave me some meager sense of security. It was a horrible time clouded by an unrelenting emotional fog. My head was as fucked up as it could ever be.

At some point (I don't remember when) I canceled the trip to Germany. It seemed futile for us to meet there and I felt an overwhelming need to go home instead. Perhaps survival was my modus operandi; I don't really know but at the time I felt it was the right thing to do. Maybe it was because I saw everything—financially, mentally—slipping away. I felt as though I had no control whatsoever and that it was imperative to go home to survey the damage. Rita's response was less than encouraging.

She exploded in an email, her vicious resentment bursting forth like a supernova. I could hardly breathe. It felt as if a knife was piercing me to the core. She accused me of being a worthless, spoiled brat who had been mooching off her for years and that there was nothing she hadn't given me. She worked her ass off while I did nothing to contribute. Her parting words were not to come home, that there was no home—it was all gone.

I didn't hear from her again.

So I made it through August, carefully balancing on my emotional tightrope. Top was resolute in his assurances that he would get me out of Iraq and back to the U.S. as soon as possible. I don't even remember doing any hydraulic work whatsoever although I'm sure I did. Yes, I think it would be safe to say my heart was broken. The one person I have ever considered to be my soul mate was leaving me. It leaves a void in the frayed remains of your heart. And the wounds of the past few months haven't yet begun to heal. I can hardly fathom what reaction all this will bring forth from me.

Yep, it's safe to say Rita almost broke me.

But on August 30, Top told me I was flying out on September 2. I packed up all my movies, books, spare clothes—everything I had discovered I really didn't need over here—and at 0600 on the second I was at the KBR trailer waiting for the bus to take me to the Air Force side of the base to catch my plane. At about 0630 the bus arrived and seven of us piled in.

We sat through some briefings, checked in with our identification, and waited some more. At about 1230 a big ole C-130 came barreling in, flying what they call a "combat landing approach." We were in a "holding area" tent lying on cots, reading books, dozing, when some civilian guy came in and told us our plane had arrived. The 40 of us were led to a bus waiting outside the tent and were driven to the flight line and the waiting plane. Our big baggage was being strapped down on a palette. We got off the bus, lined up, and boarded through the rear, the engines of the plane still running, the force of the propellers blowing hot air in our faces as we awaited our turn.

We strapped in and our palette was loaded with a forklift. C-130s are extremely raucous—the whine of the propellers and engines is incredible, almost deafening. Earplugs are definitely a good idea. The seating is as follows—four rows of seats, two outboard that face inward, two inboard that face outward. They have just a few tiny windows but I'm not sure you'd really want to look anyway—some things are better left to chance. The pilots are skilled but rough—they take sharp turns and steep descents, the plane shakes. They're trained to fly this way when landing at or taking off from a "hot" landing site. It's not the most comfortable way to fly but it beats getting shot out of the sky.

About two hours later, we landed at Ali Al Salem Air Base in Kuwait. Buses were waiting to drive us south to Camp Doha, where we sat through more briefings and were in due course assigned a warehouse to spend the night. I slept in my clothes, using my backpack as a pillow—they don't provide sheets or anything at all while you're at the base waiting to go on leave. The next morning we were on our own for a little while so I wandered around the base, visited the PX, and browsed the shop vendors who were selling all sorts of trinkets from hookahs to "Co-ed Naked Camel Watching" T-shirts to "Operation Iraqi Freedom" coffee mugs and grand American flags. I even went to Starbucks for a vanilla latte—what a treat.

I signed up for a few minutes on the Internet, emailed my parents, and talked with people who were wandering around. Around 1300, we were made to assemble again and told we were now on "lockdown"—meaning they wanted everyone in uniform and ready to go because our plane was due to arrive shortly. A good 300 of us were there waiting. They issued us travel itineraries and ticket stubs, prepaid for all our travels to and from the States, and we assembled in a huge auditorium to endure more briefings. The bottom line was everyone who was going to the eastern side of the United States were getting on a plane bound for Germany then Atlanta, and everyone going to the western side of the U.S. were getting on a plane for Ireland, then Dallas/Ft. Worth.

They then began to call us out in groups to go through the customs process. We marched to a giant building and were told to stand in four rows. There were amnesty boxes placed here and there and we were told to dump anything illegal—pornography, weapons, artifacts, flammable liquids—in them before we were searched. Hell, we couldn't even bring photos of our spouses back into the United States.

Then we were ushered into another room filled with wide, open tables and instructed to completely empty our bags and pockets. An Air Force sergeant came around and poked through our stuff, confiscating anything illegal that might have been overlooked. They took the one pornographic DVD I had. Just like everyone else, I claimed that I had honestly "forgotten" it was in there but I didn't really care what he thought.

Night had fallen by the time we were done performing this bureaucratic ballet and sent to a secure holding area. We were issued MREs and we waited again. At about 2130 hours or so buses arrived and we boarded for a 45-minute drive to Kuwait International Airport. We waited at the secure U.S. military side of the airport for a bit, enjoying the night air and smoking cigarettes. Then we were bused to the terminal where our airplane was waiting, several maintenance and service trucks surrounding it.

There was my plane, a sight to behold—a big ole Boeing 767.

They let us board immediately. It was around midnight and we were scheduled to leave at 0030.

We took off and I felt such relief as I watched the lights of Kuwait City recede in the distance as we flew over the Persian Gulf. I settled back in my seat and did what I always do on a plane—I slept, wrapped cozily in a blanket, leaning against the wall of the plane, my head resting on a small commercial airplane pillow. I don't know how long I slept but I remember being awakened for a meal, promptly falling asleep again, then waking up when the sun began to stream through the windows, its tender golden rays warming my face.

For hours it was a never-ending cycle of falling asleep and waking up to eat, the minutes slowly drifting by, bringing me closer and closer to the United States. It takes roughly seven or eight hours to fly to Ireland from Kuwait equaling two meals, three movies, and a snack. It's like you live on the damn thing. It was a quiet ride though, no turbulence that I can recall.

We landed in Shannon, Ireland. There was a 90-minute layover while they refueled the plane but we were restricted to a small waiting area with no place to smoke, just a small shop selling cheap souvenirs—capitalism at its best. I looked, somewhat out of curiosity but mainly out of boredom. I must admit that I mulled over buying something for Rita, but reconsidered.

We boarded again and began the longer trip to the U.S. It takes nine hours to fly from Shannon to Dallas—a miasma of sleeping, eating, watching whatever happened to be on the airplane's movie screen, cramped legs, and anxiety, waiting for the trip to be over so you can limp into the real world, a world without bombs, mortars, gunfire, heat, sand, insects, anger, frustration, and dismay—a golden world of opportunity called the United States of America. A place filled with people bustling to and fro, each involved in their own little enveloped world. A place green beyond my wildest imagination, of mountains thrusting themselves into the air with an awesome silent pride—a place of freedom.

When the wheels finally touched down, the rubber screeching in a brief puff of smoke, my shoulders drooped. I was in the United States again. I could let my guard down. I could smile and walk lightly.

It felt like a miracle.

We disembarked and were immediately bombarded by a veritable throng of people at the end of the connecting ramp. They stood in two groups on either side of a narrow walkway made for us—the returning soldiers. There were grandmothers, mothers, grandfathers, fathers, and children all waving colorful patriotic banners, pompoms, and signs stating "We Support Our Troops." Old men with VFW hats perched precariously on their grey, wrinkled heads were clapping furiously. Women with USO[30]pamphlets were waving with an almost hysterical mania, eagerly beckoning us to let them clench us in support.

It was overwhelming.

---

30   United Service Organization, a nonprofit dedicated to lifting the spirits of troops and their families

I was stopped by one elderly man who had to be a World War II veteran, his VFW cap cocked in a proud manner. He enthusiastically yet somberly shook my hand and penetrated me with his aged green eyes.

"I understand," he said, then turned away.

I'll never forget that as long as I live.

He knew—he had been to war. There was an immediate connection. He had seen my eyes and understood how I felt being barraged by something I couldn't even quite comprehend at that point, the feeling of returning to a world now seen with new eyes.

A small elderly lady grabbed and hugged me with a strength I would never have expected. "Welcome home," was all she said.

It brought a tear to my eye. I recalled the pleasant embrace and smell of my grandmother the last time I saw her alive. I was speechless but I think she understood.

My throat choking, I moved on and made my way through the crowd. My heart felt so sad and happy, all at the same time. Emotions were welling up in me that I never even knew existed. It was ironic to be surrounded by people who seemed more proud of me than I was.

I made my way to the relative quiet of the baggage claim. It was too sudden, too much at once—too sharp, too pounding, too resonating, the depth of my profound sadness and happiness penetrating to the very core of my existence.

It made my head whirl. I felt dizzy. I hardly knew how to stand.

I stared numbly, my knees wobbly, not even thinking of my bags for a good 10 minutes. After collecting my luggage, I went outside the terminal and deeply inhaled the first breath of real American air to grace my lungs in at least six months.

It was amazing.

I have never felt so taken care of; it's humbling. There were people bustling us to different buses to catch our last remaining flights. Civilians on vacation or taking a business trip stared blankly at all the uniforms. I got on a bus and headed to Terminal B. I was supposed to fly to Denver and then to Montana, so my trip was far from over and I was tired despite the sleep I had gotten on the plane.

I remember thinking how humid it was in Dallas, how curious that felt after the dryness of Iraq. I could almost feel the water in the air clinging to my skin, making me feel slightly slimy—very reminiscent of the first time I set foot at Ft. Knox at the beginning of this odyssey. I felt slightly uncomfortable and found myself wishing for dry air—a very distressing thing to realize. What was becoming of me? What adjustments would I have to make to enjoy this easy, carefree way of life that had been gifted to me for 15 days?

I changed into civilian clothes (partly in an effort to remain anonymous, partly to wear something different) and sat down at my gate (32, if I remember right). The wait for the plane to Denver was a short one, only about 40 minutes or so. I had no conception of what day it was and frankly I didn't really care. The only date that matters to a soldier on leave is the day they have to go back to Iraq. The sheer exhilaration of "being"—being able to breathe easy for once, to not hear explosions or gunfire, to know without a doubt that you're safe—makes everything else irrelevant. The troubles in America seem almost meaningless compared to the reality and horror of war.

I had a fairly long layover in Denver. I watched the people go by, immersed in their own lives and complications. I found an airport bar, drank a couple of beers, and eventually the plane arrived. It was so tremendously exciting to be on my own, no one breathing down my neck, no pressure to act a certain way, no bosses, no responsibilities, nowhere to go except to catch a plane bound for the great white north of Montana.

It was a somewhat crowded flight that took about two hours. It was kind of a bumpy ride with some turbulence. It's to be expected—flying over the mountains always does that. I can't remember a flight into Montana that wasn't at least a little bumpy. Butte is especially bad. You fly right over a mountain range called the East Ridge that always disrupts the airflow and shakes you like you're in a washing machine.

So I landed in Bozeman… with no one there to meet me. I had called Rita when I landed in Dallas and told her I was on the way, but she was visiting our friends, Paula and Rod. I must admit it really hurt that she couldn't make the effort to come meet me after so many months apart, but I guess it was only to be expected. At this point I'm pretty sure she had already moved on, removed herself from our commitment, our years together, but I would have thought that common decency would require you to meet your husband who had just come home from Iraq.

There was only empty silence when I walked into the Gallatin Field terminal in Bozeman—a sharp contrast to the greeting I received in Dallas. So with a heavy heart I rented a Ford Excursion, a large monstrosity of an SUV, but all they had available on such short notice; I christened it the "Big White Bastard." I resolved to get any lingering belongings Rita felt were mine and had saved for me then go to Colorado. What was there for me in Montana?

I was steeling myself against the inevitable storm I felt coming, like a breeze thrashing through the trees before it rains.

I drove the Big White Bastard to a hotel, checked in, and called Rita. We spoke for just a couple of minutes, mainly for me to let her know I was coming to see her in the morning. Then with a hurt heart and numb head, I watched HBO and fell asleep to unsettling dreams.

The next day I left to meet Rita at around 10 in the morning after luxuriating in a hot shower (without shower shoes or a line waiting to use it) and indulging in a continental breakfast. I almost felt human again. With a bellyful of Frosted Flakes and my body feeling fresh and alive, I hit the road. It was so pleasant to be driving, on the road, self-sufficient, beautiful scenery zipping by, mountains looming on the horizon, their peaks wrapped with low-lying clouds, kids in passing cars peering out the window, pressing their noses against the glass, drink boxes clutched in their small hands, parents talking or staring blankly at the road in front of them. I stopped for a soda at a small country convenience store and it was the best one I had ever had, every bubble from the carbonation tingling on my tongue, the sugar dazzling my mouth. I felt *alive*, a feeling of deep satisfaction washing over me like the surf on the sand of some pristine Caribbean bay at high tide.

When I crested the pass that leads to Whitehall on I-90W, the gold mine gouged into the side of the mountains reared its ugly head. It didn't bother me. The scene was stunning. Everything I saw, smelled, and heard was beautifully alive with vibrant color and sensation—the sun gracing the valley with a warm smile, the broccoli heads of trees dotting the terrain where water was most prevalent, the roofs of a few small buildings squatting between the trees, the hawk, regal wings spread, gliding on the wind.

I did 85 mph the whole way.

The road has always given me a great sense of freedom. Some people think only of Point A and Point B, how many stops to make after leaving Point A in order to minimize the time to get to Point B—logistical tedium consuming their every thought. But I've always enjoyed the beauty of everything along the way, right down to the grasshopper that sloppily flattens himself against the windshield of my car.

For me—it's the *experience.*

"A long drive is not so much about the destination as it is about the journey," a friend of mine once told me. Because not only is it a physical journey, it's a spiritual one that has always allowed me time to reflect on my life—lost loves, regrets, inspirations, turning points, laughs, tears, friends, and family. Then I shake my head out of my reverie and look around, taking it all in—all of life, the scenery—the exquisiteness of just breathing.

Some time later, I came upon a mountain pass and with a broad grin gunned it to the top, whizzing by fully loaded semis struggling at 25 mph, gravity trying to drag them back down to the valley below. Then as I rounded a corner of the highway, there it was—the town where I was supposed to meet Rita. A mass of square buildings nestled in the mountains.

Rita. My heart jumped with a sudden panic—what would I do, what would I say? I fantasized that perhaps the last months had been a dream, some horrid nightmare I was just waking from, that today would be like any other day with my wife. We'd go to a friend's for dinner or perhaps just grab lunch before we had to go back to work.

Perhaps we would plunge into each other's arms, eyes locking, memories of a life together flooding both our minds, two soul mates who had been forcefully separated for far too long. Then… reality set in and I realized it wouldn't be that way. Our souls had separated. She was no longer in love with me. She was no longer my girl, the girl I met in college—the girl I had built a life with.

Then I didn't know what to expect and felt peculiar, almost nauseated. I felt awkward, unsure, nervous. Why the hell should I feel awkward coming home to my wife? Because she didn't want me any more, that's why.

I had called her before I left the hotel and she was meeting me at the grocery store just off the highway. I parked and soon thereafter she was there, pulling into the space next to me. My heart missed a beat when I saw her face smiling through the glass. My throat clenched and I couldn't swallow. We hugged when we saw each other but the affection didn't last. It really was over between us, the feeling was different. She had pulled away from me... really... truly.

The one woman in my life I had truly loved and devoted myself to was gone.

We went back to our friends' place, Paula and Rod's, each of us driving our own cars. I must say I felt numb. I wasn't quite sure how to act, how to react, what to do with her and this situation. As usual it was hard to read Rita, hard to ascertain what was going on in her head. She has always been very good at putting up a front.

When we got to Paula and Rod's, I began to feel relatively good. The familiar sights were there, the mountains in the distance overlooking us, the quiet of midday. But when I walked into the house, I felt as though I was being stared at, as if a spotlight was suddenly turned on me and my eyes were squinting under the glare. They welcomed me warmly, don't get me wrong, it just felt as if I was an exotic traveler and they gazed at me with wide curious eyes. Perhaps it was all in my head (a very real possibility) but it was how I felt at the time. Cathy was there but her husband, Jan, was attending to some business in town. Rod had been ill as of late and was in bed.

So I sat on the most comfortable couch I could remember for a good hour and a half, happily sipping beer and munching on chips and spinach-artichoke dip as I answered Cathy and Paula's questions about my experiences in Iraq. Rita sat on the other side of the room, mostly quiet except for a few simple comments. I couldn't be sure what she was thinking, which was very unsettling.

Eventually Jan arrived, Rod managed to pull himself out of bed, and we ate a fabulous steak dinner prepared by Paula. It was exquisite, a feast piled with fresh asparagus, a perfectly grilled New York steak, buttery mashed potatoes, and all the beer we could care to drink—all of my favorites. This was undoubtedly due to Rita; she is well acquainted with my favorite foods and I must give her credit for that.

Shortly after dinner, Rita asked if it would be a good time to leave. The dinner was excellent but the mood had been tinged with a quiet, tense feeling. It crept about like a shadow you can't quite ignore but disappears when you try to look directly at it. I began to question whether I belonged in this house any more, in the presence of these people. I felt as though I had been gone too long, that they had moved on without me, and I think that's what Rita was feeling too. It was sad and I don't believe I'll have the same relationship with any of them as I did before. It was as if I had passed on, was not really there.

I can't really remember what happened after Rita and I left.

I must be getting senile. Either that or the emotions are too powerful. I believe I spent the night alone at the hotel. In the end, Rita and I parted ways and… that was that.

There was no Hollywood romance, no lingering kisses, dramatic redemptions or sudden revelations, none of the things romance writers live for or what we secretly dream of in the depths of our hearts.

It was simple, dry, and completely anticlimactic.

I don't remember the next day all that well either. From that point on, I was resolute to be drunk out of my gourd for the rest of my leave. I believe it was not just a reaction to the deep pain I was feeling but also a way to cope with my inability to handle American culture. Outside the confines of Camp Anaconda, I felt lost, confused, isolated, afraid, alienated. It was as if I had become institutionalized. What they say is true—after a time you adjust to a new environment, you become accepting of it and eventually come to see it as natural, as your whole world.

I don't expect anyone who has not had the experience to understand but it's a very real feeling and alcohol was my only solace. It wipes the mind clean of worry. Yes, I drank and drank, methodically deadening my pain.

If I remember right, Rita and I met for lunch the following day and had the big talk, a talk that had obviously been coming for a long time. It was time to face the inevitable, time to get it all out in the open, to show our hands. Oh hell, I had discovered I actually *wanted* the damn divorce. I was sick and tired of being berated for my mistakes and there was nothing I could do to quell the anger that had welled up in both of us.

In reality, the only holdup was my disinclination to leave the safety of a relationship I had come to rely on all too much. In actuality, that safety was long gone—it was just a matter of admitting it. With a moment's courage, it would be done. I was ready.

"I want a divorce," she said flatly.

When the words were spoken, painful as they were, it actually felt like a relief. We had acknowledged the truth. Perhaps now I could move on. Perhaps now I could face a new dawn and a new day.

A day or so later, I was on the move again. I had planned on going to Colorado to visit Tim and Veronica, friends of mine since before I had met Rita. Rita had asked if it would be a good idea to go with me, but I was insistent on going alone. In retrospect, I wonder if I should have let her come. Perhaps we could have reconciled, rediscovered what we had lost. But that's not the way it turned out and there's no going back now. It was too late by then anyway. We had given in to a momentum that seemed to be dragging us along in spite of any reluctance we might have felt.

We went to the storage unit where Rita had temporarily stashed our belongings and I loaded up the Big White Bastard with as much as I could carry. I was planning on going to Colorado to stay when I came home for good and Tim and Veronica had already offered to put me up for as long as it took for me to get back on my feet. That moved me greatly for I was homeless now—a nomad with a load of books, movies, and assorted odds and ends in a rental car—a superb homecoming, let me tell ya.

So I trucked on down south. Leaving was difficult but not as difficult as I had expected or imagined it to be. Like I said, we had already moved on anyway. But I'll always wonder if things could have been different. Hopefully those reflections will make me stronger. *Learn from the past, live for the present, and look to the future*—that's the adage I'm going to live by now.

I mean, what else could I realistically do? This was what Rita wanted—what she had asked for outright as I numbly stared at the floor, studying the patterns on the carpet. It really didn't matter what I wanted.

Besides, Lord knows she has enough anger and resentment for both of us to chew on for the next 50 years, and what's the point of living with that type of agony? It's like jumping into a cold pool—you know you don't really want to, it's gonna suck, but you know you'll get used to it and that everything will be all right in the long run. You'll swim again after you get your breath back.

About 10 hours later I was in Colorado and by 2100 hours, I was parking next to Tim's house, the weary traveler able to rest again, able to soothe bloodshot eyes. They welcomed me with open arms. I had a fabulous chicken dinner with real—yes *real*, not instant—mashed potatoes. Veronica is a wonderful cook and they gave me beer after beer after beer and we talked into the night.

I spent the majority of my leave at Tim and Veronica's. We spent every day talking and eating fabulous food. We went to our favorite Indian restaurant on 6th and Grant three times. It felt so good to just veg out for a while—nothing to do but let the brain dump, empty itself of all its concerns.

Before I had left for Colorado, Rita had asked if I was coming back for any of the remaining time on my leave. I was hesitant to answer because I didn't know if I'd be comfortable with that or even why she would bother asking that question. But as the remaining days wore on, I decided to call her and told her I was coming up for the last two days.

So I hit the road again, another 10 hours in the Big White Bastard, bidding fond farewells to my dear friends who didn't treat me as if I was an alien just landed from Mars bent on a mission to infiltrate the world with my insidious plans of destruction. They are true friends. I would like to find a way to adequately pay them back for their generosity and kindness, but I just don't know how to yet.

I called Paula along the way and stayed with her for a night. It seemed like the best thing to do since Rita had not yet moved into her new condo, nor had she invited me to stay with her. And I wasn't sure if I would have liked to stay with her or not.

Paula was up when I came rambling in around 2200 hours. Rod was out of town on business, having recovered from his sickness. But we stayed up for a good hour or so, relaxing, bullshitting over mundane events. She's a good friend as well. She will always be Rita's friend first, but she does make a valiant effort to remain neutral.

The next day I was on the road yet again, this time to meet Rita. We fought about nonsense and I remember feeling strange, even idiotic. *Why had I driven all this way on leave to go through this?* I wondered. It all seemed so silly and ridiculous.

That feeling was intensified the next day when I helped her brother move her into her new condo. There right in front of me was all of the stuff we had accumulated together throughout the years—what I had considered to be *our* stuff, stuff she felt was rightfully *her* stuff. That was a very difficult thing for me to do, helping to move boxes from the rental truck up a flight of stairs to the new condominium, knowing that with every step my memories were being abducted by my now-estranged wife.

Words cannot express that heartache, yet I helped anyway because in the bottom of my heart I still loved her. She was having fun, decorating, scratching her chin as she pondered where to hang things, how to unpack the dishes, where to position the entertainment center. She acted as though the whole thing never affected her—oblivious to the person who was despondently slouched on the couch staring into space and wondering how his life had gotten so far out of control.

I was allowed a few things—my Army clothes, the silverware (which she planned to replace anyway), the tent we had slept in on innumerable camping trips, one painting, and a few other miscellaneous items of very little importance—everything else was apparently hers.

Our old neighbors Roy and Sasha came over to check out the

new place. I asked them if I might stay with them for a night or two until my plane left. Later I found out that Rita had already planned for this and had asked them while they were touring the upstairs. Apparently my somber mood was depressing for her.

I guess I should've been as happy as she was.

Roy and Sasha told me it was completely cool with them and that I was welcome anytime. I remember telling them that I'd be okay staying at my hotel, that they didn't have to put themselves out on my account. But they insisted that it was no problem and they would be glad to have me.

So I stayed with Roy and Sasha for two nights. I believe it was a Thursday and Friday because I was scheduled to fly to Iraq Saturday morning. We had a wonderful two days. I hung out, they went to work, and we chatted in the evening, watching television until we drifted off to sleep. They said they sympathized with what I was going through, that what Rita had done was really "shitty" because I was overseas fighting in Iraq. Roy especially just kept shaking his head, saying he wondered what had gotten into her head and didn't understand it all.

Rita did stop by Roy and Sasha's the night before I left. It was for about 15 minutes and it was far from an emotional good-bye. I think she felt obligated and wanted to get it over with as quickly as possible.

Saturday morning I dropped off the Big White Bastard and got on the plane to Dallas. Alone again—alone when I arrived, alone when I left—no hugs or tears this time. I began the long ordeal of getting back to Iraq. I don't remember much of it, but

I do remember when I finally arrived in Kuwait. I was flown out that night, around 0100 hours or so. I remember getting into Camp Anaconda in the early morning hours. There was no one from my company to greet me or pick me up, so I ended up hitching a ride with some people from a neighboring company to the other side of the base.

I was back—back in Iraq.

My leave had all been a blur—a jumbled haze I really didn't understand. It was strange, surreal, almost as if it didn't happen. When I glance at Rita's picture I still have hanging on my hovel's wall, my mind cannot reconcile the woman in the picture and the woman I encountered on leave. It's as if I've known two different people. I still can't quite pinpoint how all this came about.

A few days after I was back in Iraq, I received an angry email from Rita. "Don't drag our friends into our personal business," she wrote, and attached a message from Sasha. Sasha had complained to Rita that they didn't like how I was "pushed" on them and never had wanted me in their home to begin with. When I read this my stomach dropped and my throat caught with a stifled cry. It was all too much, this was the clincher. It was probably the cruelest hurt I had experienced so far—in some ways even more so than my impending divorce.

I don't think I've ever had someone I trusted so openly do this to me. I replied to Rita and told her to forward my message to Roy and Sasha since I didn't have their email address. I explained my hurt, how I felt betrayed, and how it would be the last I would ever speak with them. Perhaps a bit harsh, but that is how I felt and still feel. They never wrote back.

I *have* heard from Rita, however. She wants to speed up the divorce proceedings so she can buy some rental property. She's sending the divorce paperwork to Iraq for me to look over and sign. I'll be glad to do it. The sooner I get her and all those other motherfuckers out of my life, the better.

I asked if she had met someone in my last email to her, if that was the reason for her decision. Her response was very defensive saying she resented the question and that her life didn't revolve around men. Gary thinks she has been seeing someone based on her defensive response—who knows. And at this point, who cares? I always knew how cold-hearted she was but I thought I could live with it. Well, I won't settle any longer. Good riddance. She can be as "money hungry," as she puts it, as she wants. I don't think she has a clue as to what life is really about.

She hasn't emailed me in quite some time and I don't expect to hear from her.

I'm not at all fond of people any more.

That was my 15-day leave from Iraq.

# PART FOUR

# ENEMY WITHIN

*Before freedom is achieved, before one arrives home, first you
must be lost, wandering, devoid of hope; first you have to
traverse the abyss.*

—Dante Alighieri, *The Divine Comedy*

**September 29, 2004**

NOT MUCH HAD REALLY CHANGED around the camp when I got back from leave—mortar rounds were still coming in, gunfire still crackled on the perimeter, and the occasional suicide bomber was still trying to get through the front gate—typical times at Camp Anaconda.

The hangar and the shops were still doing the same thing—either sitting on their asses bored to tears or cranking out phase inspections and daily maintenance for the never-ending demand of flight operations. Guard duty was still being rotated through. The mess hall was still serving the same wilted lettuce and soggy carrots. The heat was a bit better, down to around 100 or so. The power was still unreliable, the Internet lines still obnoxiously long, and sullen soldiers were still gutting out the day's duties.

Nothing had changed.

I guess I shouldn't have been surprised, but I was. Maybe I was expecting something different. Maybe I was *hoping* for something different. I can't quite put my finger on it… but something that would have allowed me to feel as if I hadn't stepped off the edge of the planet and into Hell again. Perhaps I was even hoping our politicians had finally gotten their heads out of their asses and ended the war. That we would suddenly be notified we were all going home and this despicable business had been condemned for what it was.

Alas, my dreams hadn't come true.

It was fairly easy to fall into the routine again, although I loathed it right from the starting gate. My 15-day leave had amounted to a brief taste of liberty, a tease, like a piece of candy dangled in front of a child then abruptly snatched away.

I've been working hard since I've come home from the States but not at the hangar. Instead I've been producing another newsletter for the major. There is a lot of work to do to finish the issue and I am behind schedule. I've been interviewing soldiers, writing the lead article, taking pictures, and searching for a member of my unit willing to write the Special Activities section.

I haven't heard from Rita, although I am sure I will at some point. She is sure to be finalizing the divorce paperwork that she promised to send to Iraq as soon as possible.

And… my mind feels anesthetized—it's simply telling me that I've been abandoned and betrayed, nothing more. I am simply aware of the *presence* of those feelings, that they just exist, and how deeply infused I am with this way of thinking, I have no idea.

That's scary in itself.

I see so much that has gone wrong with my life, how hollowed out I have become. Perhaps I am realizing that I'm not a good person after all, that I've betrayed every value I had since setting foot on this forsaken ground. Perhaps I really have fallen into a pit and there is no way out for me. Perhaps I am merely waiting for someone above to start shoveling in the dirt.

We were attacked today. Several mortars landed quite close to my hovel.

My eye twitch is constant now. I wince every time I hear a loud noise.

My feet still hurt.

There is no power.

Welcome back to Camp Anaconda.

### October 3, 2004

I'm angry today... so very angry.

I'm angry at the world, our utterly insane world of violence, betrayal, and absurdity. Hatred and blind rage are bubbling over in me. The cauldron containing these feelings has been simmering for a long time, but now it's come to a boil. If I don't express it, at least in these pages, I'll flip out.

We were mortared again today as always.

Who gives a shit?

I wish they would just kill me already. Let it end.

I feel ashamed to be involved in this despicable affair, this completely senseless war that should never have begun. I just can't turn a blind eye and hope that someone will have wisdom and power enough to bring a halt to this insanity. They will never stop it.

I remember when the question of whether to start this war was being debated back in the States. Our top leaders in Washington assured the American public it would be over quickly, that it wouldn't cost very much, that the Iraqi people would view us as liberators as we set up a democratic state. I remember all the talk that Iraq had developed weapons of mass destruction and harbored terrorists. Well, I was right from the beginning—*none* of that was true.

The entire justification for this business was fabricated. It blows my fucking mind to finally come to that conclusion beyond a shadow of a doubt. But I cannot deny it even to the slightest degree any more.

And you know what? Those bastards can all fuck themselves if they think I will ever put my life on the line for them again.

It turns my stomach when I think of the money that's been made here by an oligarchy that never shared the risk. That was money stolen through the blood spilled in these desert sands, the blood of people just as confused about why we are here as I am. We are the passive cogs in some demented killing apparatus. When will people wake the fuck up and realize their sons and daughters, fathers and mothers are dying over here for nothing?

No matter how long we stay here, even if we pull out in one year, two years, or three, however long it takes for the politicians to finally get their act together... or for however long it takes for the American public to realize they have been duped and do something about it... we will come back.

I've realized that this whole mess was not only ill conceived, it never began because of terrorism or some vile plot of Saddam's to end the world with his arsenal of weapons. Those threats were *used against us*, the American people, as an *excuse* to wage war. And with energy interests controlling our government, it's inevitable—if we ever leave this godforsaken place to begin with—that we'll get sucked back in.

I've always found it interesting that we initially supported Saddam, helped him rise to power. Now we have displaced him and try as I may, I find it hard to believe that some sort of democratic state here in Iraq will be possible to achieve. There are too many irreconcilable differences among the different sects and I'm sure corruption will always play a hand. Our actions are going to end up *promoting* rather than reducing the terrorist threat facing the United States by creating avenues for terrorists to infiltrate Iraq.

The hawks of the U.S. wanted this war. They wanted this because it's profitable for them. They make money off people dying over here and anyone who stands in the way of that is merely an expendable piece on the game board.

God, it tears me up inside thinking about this.

Those fucking assholes.

I am not a chess piece. I am a *person* and I should have just as much say as someone with money or power.

If I had one thing to say to my politicians it would be, "You don't get to walk away clean. You have just as much blood on your hands as a terrorist, or those of us who are sitting here sweating and dying in the desert, getting shelled by a people who don't want us here. You've ruined hundreds of lives. How many more before this is over? How and when will you atone for your sins?"

And I'm angry at all the motherfuckers who have fucked me over in the States, all my supposed friends who smiled while they sharpened their knives. You can all go fuck yourselves too. I'm especially angry at you, Rita. You rotten little bitch. How dare you pull what you pulled while I'm here in this shithole wondering if I'm even going to live! After all these years, you couldn't find an ounce of compassion for a guy you claimed was your soul mate?

Maybe I was blind. Maybe you are just now showing the true self that you had carefully hidden deep within you. You know what? I hate you too!!

There, I've said it. I've said what I've wanted to say for a long time now.

You pulled the ultimate betrayal so… FUCK YOU BITCH!!!

## October 5, 2004

The power is out again today—business as usual. It's been out for quite a while now. It's out in the latrine as well and there's no water yet again. Pete and I have been scavenging for bottles of water to get us through.

The good news is it's only 108 degrees, not the usual 120 or 125 and the insurgents went easy on us—only a few mortars came whistling in.

Thank God for small miracles.

Divorce is like a plague around here. I've heard so much talk about it, so-and-so getting a divorce, so-and-so having marital problems, so-and-so fighting with his wife.

People are on the edge, fried... burned out.

This place is an insane asylum.

### October 6, 2004

Rumor has it that the aircraft undergoing a phase inspection in the hangar now will either be the last or the next to last one we'll be working on. We are getting so close to leaving this desolate place. We're still so far away but it is encouraging.

The temperature today was down to the low hundreds, almost bearable.

### October 7, 2004

There's a dog here on base, his name is Sippy. I'm not sure where he came from or who is taking care of him but apparently the MPs here are most upset.

When this base was first taken over by the U.S. there were stray dogs and cats everywhere. They're feral, so the Army MPs decided to exterminate them all. But someone took in little Sippy, a total mutt with white and tan fur decorating his lean haunches and always begging for scraps. The MPs were champing at the bit to get rid of him but he was too quick for them and had too many hiding spots. Eventually a soldier took him in. He wants to send him to a decent home in the States, perhaps to the Humane Society, where he will at least be taken care of.

Apparently it's much more complicated and costly

than anyone could have anticipated. Sippy would need a comprehensive list of shots, to go through customs, be fed, transported, have an owner… and the list goes on.

Well, the person taking care of him doesn't have the money, so there is now a "Save Sippy" program spreading around the base. They've asked for donations and it's got the MPs all disgruntled. It's like our own private war and Sippy's well-being hangs in the balance. I find the whole thing rather amusing.

Here's another one. Apparently another stray dog stowed away on a Chinook helicopter the other day—no one realized it until after they took off. Well, the dog panicked in midflight and jumped out the open back hatch before anyone could stop him.

Can you imagine the flight crew vainly scrambling to catch the dog before it jumped out of the helicopter? Or the dog's fear as it realized it was flying for the first time, hardly comprehending what was happening—the unimaginable panic? Trying to envisage that is horrifying. I feel so badly for the animal—yet another innocent in the theater of war. I don't know how far the pitiable dog fell, but the consensus here is it didn't survive.

They named that one Snoopy.

Snoopy's dead.

### October 8, 2004

We were attacked mercilessly today, the worst being a barrage of more than 20 shells. There is just no way to express how frightening it is to be constantly bombed day in and day out.

I cannot find the words.

The power is out. Morale is low, people are miserable. I am miserable.

## October 10, 2004

We were attacked again.

There is so much fatalism here, a nagging instinct to keep gutting it out although it feels futile. I seem to be fighting the desire to live... or die... I don't know which any more; mainly I'm resisting the compulsion to go insane. Every day—every minute—is a struggle to keep my wits.

The power is out. We are all weary beyond imagining.

Reality is not an issue any more.

The only reality I know of is the threat of death.

No one has saved Sippy yet.

## October 20, 2004

The power is still out.

Although it's only in the low hundreds now, it still gets very hot in my hovel.

Yesterday they tore down my company's office tents to replace them with some new trailers that were just delivered. So now the phones and the Internet at the hangar are shut down. The only surviving phone/Internet tent is only open during certain hours of the day and so crowded it's nearly impossible to get any time online.

It might be a few days before the power is restored. I took a bottle shower today and will again tomorrow. I am so utterly and completely tired of this place. Tired is not a strong enough word.

We're almost completely cut off from the outside world now. It's like one big hellish camping trip. Some have taken to lighting small fires at night to sit around, but that draws mortar fire. Still people do it, if for nothing else than the comfort of crackling, burning wood. At least someone did a little cleaning in the latrines so they're not as monstrous as they were.

We have renamed our dwellings as cellblocks. I live in Block 15, Cell C-69. Perhaps that should be stenciled on my uniform nametag instead—I don't even feel human any more.

We're supposedly rounding the 100-day mark before we get out of here now. That's not too bad, but can I remain sane for that long? What if we're extended?

Sippy has disappeared. I guess he decided to save himself.

### October 31, 2004

I would like to hike way up in the mountains with nothing but a couple of cans of beans, a backpack, and a flask of whiskey. I'd build a campfire and gaze into the curling flames, wood crackling and hissing as the moisture is burned out. Nothing but the wind, the trees, the stars—just me and the wilderness.

Solitude… peace and quiet.

No people, no civilization… no war.

I would like a real outdoor experience, a spiritual getaway. I would like to deeply breathe the fresh clean air, to rediscover an inner spiritual balance, to reflect on this whole rotten year and find some meaning in my life. I'd find a cozy place under a grove of trees with a view of the snow-covered peaks, pitch the tent, cook some beans, sip heartily from the flask, and sleep. I might just sleep under the stars. They are so brilliant, so striking—so clear you can see the Milky Way.

They twinkle, you know?

They wink at you with their eternal eyes. When you look at the stars, you are really looking into the past. The light takes so long to travel to Earth that by the time it gets here, the star may have disappeared, perhaps exploded, creating new life from its remains—renewing the cycle of life and death. I read somewhere that we are made of stars, the material they throw out across the universe when they explode.

Amazing isn't it?

God, I really enjoyed taking physics classes in college. I always thought if you blended astronomy or physics with philosophy, it would be a perfect combination. That begs me to ponder. Why didn't I listen to my heart when I was in college? Why did I let Rita pressure me to change my course? She wanted me to pursue a degree that she felt would nurture a more solid career path. Why? To make more money. Looking back on it, I allowed her to have too much influence over me. I was wrong to abandon my dreams and goals simply for the sake of making money.

I strayed too far from my original course when I met her. I

wish I never had. Perhaps I wish I'd had the strength back then to pursue my desires no matter what. I always wanted to graduate from the university I began attending. Instead I moved with her when she went to graduate school.

I moved because of her.

I moved because I felt our relationship was *that* important to me.

Was I wrong?

I don't know. But in the process I sacrificed too much of myself, my goals. I settled for an engineering major I never really wanted from a school I never really wanted to attend. I ended up switching majors a bunch of times out of restlessness, ultimately graduating with a degree in Communication—again something I never wanted. It just seemed to be the best fit and compromise given the situation. And look where those sacrifices ultimately got me—divorced and on the brink of starting all over again.

What the fuck was I thinking? I hate engineering.

Why didn't I have the strength to complete my goals back then? Is it too late now? I don't think so, but so much grief could have been avoided if I'd had the courage back then.

I became so confused, so lost that I was never fulfilled no matter what I tried and the immensity of that dissatisfaction eventually led to desperation.

Ultimately, desperation compelled me to enlist in the Army. The rationale was that I could find some semblance of direction and fulfillment. I hoped the military would open new doors for me, be something concrete instead of groping in the dark.

I began to think that as an American citizen I owed it to my country to enlist. It was my duty, my obligation, a way to be proud of what I stand for… and here I am… in Iraq. So much for idealistic dreaming.

What a strange twisted path. It should never have been this way but as they say, hindsight is 20/20. The real question now is—do I have the strength and courage to begin a new path for myself after all the shit I messed up and managed to put us through?

Is it too late?

Am I too old?

Truthfully, I don't think so. It's time for me again. I remember how fresh I felt when I first moved to the university I wanted to attend after working my ass off in Colorado for a year to earn enough money.

I knew where I was going. I knew what I wanted. The whole world was open to me. All I had was a sleeping bag, some clothes, and a crappy four-door sedan. I was happy. I didn't need more. I didn't *want* more. How fresh and alive I felt.

I didn't have all the stuff you eventually accumulate, all the shit that begins to weigh you down. I had pen and paper. I had solid dreams, solid goals—how free, how alive, how light. I must seize this opportunity to do it right this time. I have been blessed with a second chance to truly live the way I want to.

I don't like failure and I don't like to lose. And I lost in these past years. I lost sight of my goals, then my ambition, then my self-esteem and with that, my marriage. It's time to begin the long painful process of becoming who I should have been all along.

My sight is different now. I'm older now, hopefully wiser, definitely more experienced and perhaps even more cynical. But I'm still me.

Hello me.

I've missed you all these years.

## November 1, 2004

I feel an intense fury building within me. I know the caring compassionate person who wants to be loved and live a peaceful life is still inside me but a colder, angrier side of me is developing now. It comes out every now and again whether I like it or not and it's virtually unmanageable.

Will that side come back to the U.S. with me?

This experience will undoubtedly leave scars here and there, but just how deeply this place is infusing me with negativity, I don't know. I can't let this place fundamentally change who I am. It's frightening when I find myself acting out in strange, unfamiliar, angry ways, sometimes almost uncontrollably.

To let it change you is to let it beat you. I can't let this cock sucking war do that.

I have no choice but to deal with my anger. It should, at the very least, be directed at the fuckers who deserve it, not the people I love.

Now that I've gotten that out of my system, I feel much

better—calm. All I really want in life is to be happy, peaceful, to love and be loved. The world can have the rest. I have no desire to be some ruthless millionaire wondering if tomorrow will be the day when I can't stand to look myself in the mirror.

### November 3, 2004

Yesterday was quite an eventful day.

I went up to the hangar as usual for morning formation at 0700, and one of our mechanics came into the shop with a conked-out SAS[31] actuator from a Blackhawk. This was an important repair because a SAS actuator essentially comprises the entire flight control module that controls the roll, yaw, and pitch of the aircraft. It can be broken into three separate components—the servo valve, the actuator, and the base of the component. The servo valve is electrical in nature, transmitting small voltage signals to the hydraulic component, the actuator. The base is just that, a base that attaches to the flight control module on the helicopter. They all work in unison to help maintain level flight. They're expensive, intricate little buggers that cost thousands of dollars.

Well, each component has to be zeroed, or "nulled," before installation so the actuator reads level flight as actually level (think of how a scale should be reading zero before you step on it). It's standard procedure that after my shop has completed any necessary repairs, we turn over the part in a nulled condition.

---

31 Stability Augmentation System

Some can be a real pain in the ass to null out.

It turns out this helicopter was having a flight problem no one could figure out. It stumped the best we have here; no one could understand why and they wanted this SAS actuator nulled to make sure this part wasn't causing the problem.

Griffin shrugged. "Hey, no problem, we do that all the time. We'll have it for you as soon as we can."

So, we nulled it. It took a couple of hours. We completed the paperwork and figured we were through with it. Every test we conducted was within the specifications outlined in the procedures from the technical manual. We wrote up the work order, submitted it, and everyone went on their merry way.

The pilots took the helicopter on a test flight and quickly realized it was still virtually uncontrollable. They came back to our shop and suggested that we replace the servo valve and null the actuator again.

This kind of caught us off guard. If we had nulled the actuator and it was within specifications then why begin changing parts on it? It seemed as if the methodology was essentially shooting in the dark hoping to find a target. But the pilots were adamant, insisting that the SAS actuator was causing the problem.

When pilots begin telling mechanics what's wrong with a helicopter, the conversation is never going in the right direction. A lot of them don't know shit about the actual mechanical operations of the aircraft. After a somewhat heated debate with the pilots and an officer from Production Control, we acquired a new servo valve for the actuator and replaced the old one. We connected the component to the test stand, only this time it wouldn't null to save our lives. The officer was watching the whole procedure and finally suggested that we change out the actuator component.

Dumbfounded but undaunted, Griffin and I acquired a new actuator and tried to null the whole thing again. It was a "no go," meaning it wouldn't respond to the test stand at all. The officer pondered a minute, scratched his head, and shrugged. "Let's try another servo valve," he said.

With eyes growing wider by the minute, we installed a new servo valve and tried to null the whole actuator again. It was a no go—same as before.

Yet again, the officer pondered and scratched his head. Then to our complete and utter disbelief he said, "Let's try one more actuator."

So we acquired yet another actuator for the SAS and installed it. Again it wouldn't null no matter what we tried. Throughout all this, the pilots were constantly badgering us, asking if the part was ready yet, exclaiming that they needed to fly, a mission was at stake.

Now we were putting our feet down. We defiantly informed everyone that we took a perfectly functioning part by all the standards outlined to us, dismantled it, and now it was all fucked up. It would have been amusing if the situation wasn't so tense.

Then one of our mechanics from the Avionics department came into the shop and told us that they hadn't finished troubleshooting the electrical wiring on the other end of the SAS and the problem might be there instead. She suggested we wait until her work was completed before doing any more of our own. The pilots were certainly not happy about this bit of news.

It turned out after all that hassle, the entire problem was a gyro instrument in the cockpit. The repair was as simple as taking four screws out of the instrument panel, unplugging the gyro, and replacing it. But at least the helicopter now has a brand-new nulled SAS actuator on board.

Oh, one other thing. I ruined a shirt that day because hydraulic fluid operating at 6,000 psi[32] sprayed all over both Griffin and me when we were bleeding the air out of the system for the umpteenth time. I narrowly avoided getting some in my eyes.

We got attacked again like always. My tic is as strong as ever, my eye constantly fluttering throughout the day.

A command directive has been issued requiring female soldiers to be escorted by an armed male soldier everywhere on base. A $50,000 dollar reward has been promised to any Iraqi who captures an American female soldier and turns her over to the insurgents outside the base.

They really are a sick bunch of assholes.

I don't know what's going on with the presidential election— we're cut off with no power. America is a distant land that I can hardly remember. What they do over there barely seems to matter any more.

---

32  Pounds per square inch

### November 6, 2004

We just got word that George W. Bush has won—he'll be in office for another four years.

Now *that* is fucked up.

Last night I was startled awake by a dream. When I woke up I was sitting straight up and yelling "No." I don't know what *that* was about—this place is really getting to me.

I received an email from my soon-to-be ex-wife. She apparently took a few hundred dollars from the account where my Army pay is being deposited and won't answer my email asking why.

### November 9, 2004

I received the divorce paperwork from Rita yesterday. It came in the mail in a neat, tidy manila envelope that looked very official. I borrowed the platoon's Humvee, had it notarized by the JAG office here on base, and signed it today with the officer on duty as witness. Then I promptly mailed it to the States and emailed Rita's attorneys to let them know.

I just couldn't stand to have it in my hands for too long—it felt like it was burning my fingers.

It should be there in about three weeks if all goes smoothly. Rita's attorneys emailed me back to say that they're going to appear before the judge to legally ratify it. Soon thereafter, it will be a done deal. As far as I am concerned it's done already.

It seems so surreal that when I left she was kissing me and

crying and now… she hates me.

I just don't know how to process these things sometimes and I have to take it in small chunks because the entire picture is too overwhelming.

Where did everything go that I had worked so hard to build?

How could a person change so much? Or was she that same person the whole time?

I guess everyone *does* change. The forces of nature drive that.

When I was at the JAG office I asked the duty sergeant about the divorces that come through their office, mostly out of curiosity, and I was surprised to learn they see at least three divorces per day. That's rather alarming.

It compels me to wonder just how happy people really are in their relationships. Just how stable and strong are they? And what does it take to make such a fragile foundation crumble? Is it the deployment or is the deployment just a test? Is it a test of wills against the government, fighting to keep what we've built? Or is it more personal? Is it the ultimate test of commitment or a test of character?

The stress of a deployment will drive people to do crazy things, things they wouldn't ordinarily have had the time, inclination, or drive to do otherwise. But perhaps it not only brings out the worst in people but the best in people as well. Perhaps it allows people to make better, healthier decisions they wouldn't have made otherwise. Perhaps how we choose to handle stress is entirely up to us. All I know for sure is that eventually, at some time, it's inevitable that people will break down emotionally and *everyone* has their *own* breaking point.

War is an insane engine of torment on every front.

## November 11, 2004

It seems as though the major likes my work on the newsletters so much that I have been assigned more extra duties—a digital company yearbook. I am now the "official" liaison sergeant for the company and the families back home.

I drafted a friend of mine here to work on the yearbook project with me. He has a better laptop and software that I'll need. We've decided to format it on a CD complete with a photo archive, a movie archive, written history, graphics, and thumbnail galleries—all the trimmings. Considering our limited equipment and working conditions, it's going to be a work of art.

Also, we recently produced a video for the major. His orders were that he wanted something to send home to the families for Christmas. So we labored over what turned out to be a nine-minute video/slideshow for him.

Thanks to the improvisational inspiration and hard work of my friend, it opens with a truly artistic graphic of our company's logo. It's a stop-frame animation and quite a wonder we pulled it off. It took hours of editing to get it correct with a helicopter fading in, bullets puncturing holes in the screen.

Then up comes the music. It covers our time from Ft. Knox to Kuwait and Iraq, photos dissolving into one another with some fancy graphics to boot—really quite striking. We pushed the software to the limit with our feeble hard drives. I'm very proud of it.

Presently I am in the process of burning more than 200 copies onto CDs. In the meantime, I still have to finish this month's newsletter, complete my shifts at the hangar, go on guard duty, pull a shift at the TOC,[33] and continue to work on the yearbook. I haven't heard from Rita but I'm sure the divorce is chuggin' along.

### November 11, 2004 continued

It's evening now. The power is out and the alarm sirens are wailing. Helicopters are filling the skies with flashing lights, their rotors whopping the air about 50 feet above us, their tinny, whiny jet engines tearing away any semblance of peace.

I'm writing this squatting and hunched over in the relative cool of the evening air outside my cell, the red-tinted lens of my Army-issued flashlight illuminating my journal. Soon someone will inevitably come by for an accountability inspection, to see whether there are injuries and to make sure that everyone is where they are supposed to be.

This place is so unreal it makes my head spin, and yet it's reality in its rawest form.

---

33  Tactical Operations Center. They provide facilities for the planning and communication necessary to control operations at theater level. Every soldier from our company had to work there from time to time.

## November 17, 2004

I heard that a woman was executed recently. She was a natural-born American who had lived in Iraq for the past 37 years doing humanitarian work for the needy. She was a legal resident, a Muslim, and had married an Iraqi citizen.

Why would anyone ever want to kill someone like that? My mind can't comprehend it—killing someone because they are a humanitarian. No matter how I twist it, I can't understand. What's the point of all this anger and violence?

I feel like I'm slowly degenerating over here. It's an indescribably horrible feeling to question your own sanity, that all-too-fragile grasp you have on all that is good about yourself. It's a frightening slippery slope and an abyss is waiting below should you lose your grip. It only takes a subtle nudge and then you fall, joining the wretches who fell before you with their insane, twisted grins, the grins of the mad, the wicked, the ones who let go of their sanity and lost their grip on reality. I worry that I'll join them if I stay here much longer.

My self-identity is slipping away like water through my fingers.

How do I survive in America knowing what I know, seeing what I've seen? How will I live now that my beliefs have been twisted? How will I live in our society... or any society at all?

## November 18, 2004

My guess would be that we are all aware on some level of how unjust it is that we're here to begin with. I think that subconsciously affects our thinking in subtle ways we may not be aware of and often manifests itself in erratic behavior. Playing psychologist for a second here, do you suppose you can lie to, suppress, deny, or otherwise repress yourself every day but never be able to truly fool your subconscious? Do you suppose that is at least partially how guilt is formed in people?

I don't know. I *do* know that everyone over here eventually ends up losing it in some form or fashion—it's inevitable. Perhaps it's a result of doing what you're told regardless of the moral implications or consequences. Without a real cause to be fighting for, how can you possibly, truly convince a person that it's right to be fighting?

Then again, we were never asked, were we? We were never asked whether we believed in this war. That was taken for granted. We were simply told to go do our jobs and basically shut up.

Perhaps that is another aspect of this experience that can be troubling for many. It seems to me that forcing someone to do something rarely turns out well. You either generate anger or resentment in a person, which can be counterproductive, or they find some way to skirt what they are being told to do. A better approach would be to *inspire* and validate us, allow us input and weigh our opinions. People often feel better about taking an order when they aren't simply demeaned as if they don't matter, as if their feelings are irrelevant… as if they are merely pieces on the game board—funny how I keep coming back to that.

I don't know. I'm not a psychologist. I just hope we can

make it through this fuckin' nightmare without killing each other. We've been working six days a week under a very tight thumb with the relentless stress of mortars, planted bombs, and tediously long hours for almost a year now. How can anyone not expect to break down eventually?

We were attacked today as always. Things have been really hot around here lately, and I'm not talking about the weather. There have been many planes, mostly F-16 fighter jets, streaking across the sky, conducting search and destroy missions, explosions from the bombs they've dropped thundering in the distance.

Hell on earth.

### November 19, 2004

I'm drinking.

Yes, that's right folks, I am drinking myself into oblivion and I don't care if a goddamn mortar parks itself on my salt-encrusted eyebrows. At least I'll die with a fuckin' smile on my face. Tim had the kindness to smuggle me some tequila, a rather large bottle of it I should say and I am pleasing the palette with that sweet nectar derived from the holy agave plant.

I love tequila.

### November 21, 2004

The latest rumor is that everything, all our equipment and supplies, is going to be hauled back to Kuwait—but not by us. I've also heard there is a push to get most people out of here by mid-December and that there might not be enough space for all of us because the other units have reserved Camp Doha for themselves. Supposedly if we don't arrive south quickly enough, we will be stuck here until March or later.

I find it ironic our government begins a war in a foreign country without even doing the work to house all of its soldiers. Perhaps I really am crazy, but doesn't it make sense to plan for these things beforehand?

I say fuck this place. We've all worked very hard over the past months.

Enough is enough.

### November 22, 2004

I'm beginning to feel that I've experienced all I was supposed to over here. I have learned everything I was supposed to learn. I've seen everything I was supposed to see. My mission that some mystical force set the path for has been completed. Unless of course, there is something more that a divine power has planned for me. I would not presume to debate that wisdom nor resist what it ordains for me. But until I discover that there's something more for me to do over here, I'll just be going through the daily motions.

Things are moving along, or so I've been told. Today we found out the trucks are being line-hauled out of here, which means another unit will be responsible for their transport. We had to wash, scrub, and scour our trucks today and the motor pool is going to be sending them out of here within a matter of days. That is really good news. It means the chances of convoying them to Camp Doha are rapidly fading.

A few moments ago there was a real good blast of thunder that rumbled through our camp. It sounded like a whopper of a storm coming in. The rain began shortly after and you can hear it incessantly pounding on the roof. If it rains hard enough it begins to trickle down the inside of the wall in small rivulets, damaging our equipment.

I'm impressed, oh mighty desert.

### November 24, 2004

I rebuilt another Blackhawk brake today and we have to be at the shops at our regular time tomorrow. No rest for the weary, even on Thanksgiving. What would happen if we *all* said "You know what… we're not fighting today. Today is Thanksgiving and it's time to come together and celebrate."

Can you imagine?

I'm perfectly aware Thanksgiving is purely an American holiday and at least some of its meaning has been lost, distorted by those in power who write history, but would it hurt any of us to find some time for peace, good food, and a celebration of what we're all thankful for?

It seems a daily effort now to not let my anger, disillusionment, and regrets overcome me. I don't want to become so consumed by my rage that I lose my compassion and empathy but it's difficult and I'm struggling. These emotions just seem to burst forth from me; it's kinda scary.

So much for a peaceful Thanksgiving—I can hear the mortars coming in, exploding with their murderous fury.

### November 28, 2004

Gary and many others seem to be walking around like mindless zombies. Today he told me that he doesn't really like anyone any more and that's a sign he is nearing his breaking point. I haven't seen too much of the old boy lately because I've become increasingly reclusive in my spare time. I feel like shuttering the windows to everyone I know.

There isn't much going on in the shops. I just completed the November newsletter for the major and have been thanked for it by numerous people. I must admit, it gives me a real surge of pride that hundreds of people not only read my work but actually *enjoyed* reading it.

So I'm beginning on December's newsletter and according to the major, that's the last one I'll write.

### December 1, 2004

The last two helicopters in our hangar for a phase inspection are coming along just fine. They should be finished soon and will be the last helicopters we'll service—or so we all hope. I found out we missed the extension list. Thank God for that. I couldn't take it if we were to be extended over here. Also, we might have a Christmas party on the 24th.

The last bit of news I have for right now is our shop looks like Santa's workshop. Malcolm and Griffin "acquired" a tree, put it up, decorated it, and put tinsel on the branches. I don't know where they got everything and I'm not asking.

Malcolm was getting a kick out of it and I think he's happy right now. I haven't seen him smile so much in weeks. He was giggling all day. He told me to get presents for Darnell and Griffin. It's a sweet gesture after all we've been through, a sign we're still human and willing to be kind toward one another.

And you know what? The tree makes *me* feel human again. I actually felt a smile creep over my face.

### December 4, 2004

I was talking with a friend today and we both agreed that the longer we stay here, the more we are shying away from people. Relating to others is becoming downright impossible. It's a feeling that is growing by the minute, and I can't control it. I'm like a dog that has been kicked one too many times, cowering in the corner of a room.

This place has been damaging to my spiritual and moral cleanliness. I guess war is bound to harm any rational person's psyche (if I'm rational at this point; sometimes I can't tell) but I feel so dirty inside. Every fiber of my being has been soiled by this goddamn place.

It will be a moral imperative for me to file for conscientious objector when I return home. If I don't, I would have nothing left within me to feel good about; my morals would be so devastated they might not be able to recover.

### December 6, 2004

I woke up today to an ominous sky. It looked an awful lot like there was a storm moving in, swollen, purplish-black clouds covering the horizon, moving swiftly until the entire base was shrouded in a dim overcast light. But nothing happened, no rain, no acrid smell of desert as the first drops attempt to penetrate the cracked sand. After speaking with a few people as I was walking up to the hangar, I realized they were not really clouds. It was smoke from an oil fire that had exploded during the night.

Apparently someone had sabotaged a nearby oil pipeline. Whoever they are, they must have ignited quite a fire. The fumes are permeating everything, blanketing the entire base with a thick layer of darkness and an oily stench that makes it difficult to breathe. It reminded me of a forest fire in the mountains of Montana, how the smoke from the fire clings to the low-lying valleys and a constant haze surrounds everything, burning your throat and nose.

I must say I really enjoy breathing in petrochemical fumes all day.

### December 8, 2004

The smoke from the oil fire is filling my lungs with a heavy, oddly slimy feeling, shortening my breath and clouding my mind. We've seen virtually no sun in the last couple of days, the sky purple with terrible bulging fumes. They hang mercilessly over our heads as if the world were coming to an end.

I received a coin, essentially a token, today for my newsletter work. Malcolm put me in for it and that's the only reason it means something to me.

But, it's too heavy to play quarters with.

### December 9, 2004

This week I packed my belongings, perhaps the only things I own in the world. We have to have our black boxes and whatever else we want shipped home in a Conex located in the hangar by December 23. So I dutifully went through all my stuff, inventoried it for a necessary customs slip, and neatly packed it all up. It was a very gratifying experience.

Now virtually all my things except for a few items I use regularly, such as my gear, hygiene products, and my beloved Star Trek DVDs, are ready to go. My duffel bags are packed as well.

Of course, customs officials, mainly from the Air Force, are going to go through it all anyway, so I'll have to unpack then repack again when they examine us on December 29. I could leave here in a day at most after tying up loose ends at the hangar.

Mike has informed me I might be going to Kuwait to help wash any remaining trucks and equipment, but that's undetermined at this point. I have no idea what's going on or when the chain of command might make a decision. It's also unknown whether I'm coming back to Iraq after I'm finished there.

Mortars landed very close today and my eye twitch is continuing to bother me. It seems to come and go at its whim.

I've found I'm rather casually turning up the volume on my laptop when the mortars land and the alarm sirens start demanding my attention. Sometimes I just feel like screaming "Take me already, why don't you?" to the heavens. "Just do it now and end my suffering."

We haven't had power for a few days now and the reek of the toilets is beginning to infuse everything with a fragrance that would turn even a goblin's nose.

### December 11, 2004

Several thoughts collided in my head today and crashed down on me in one clattering pile. I suddenly became acutely aware that I'm terrified of what the future could bring. If I end up going home, I will have no place to live and nowhere to go.

Oh my God… I'm homeless.

Worse yet, I have no one to come home to, nobody to wrap my arms around. Of course that should have been obvious to me for months now, but I don't think it ever really sunk in with so much force before. The longer I pondered this, the more terrified I was.

When I left for this deployment, I had a home that my wife and I both spiritually and physically had built together. I was looking forward to a warm homecoming and resuming life with my partner. I could start working again, settle into a normal routine. I had friends and neighbors all integral to me—people I felt I could trust. I had a car. I had pets that were members of my family. I've lost everything, even dishware, furniture, all the usual accouterments we take for granted. *Everything*.

Now, all I have left is the *possibility* of a job and given my current state of mind, I'm not even sure I could go back to it. Everything has changed so radically. I'm stuck with the shattered remains, alone in the world with virtually nothing but memories and I feel as if I'm at a crossroads, a four-way intersection. I'm standing in the middle of it, whirling, and trying to find my way.

I would never have thought she would have done this in a million years. I feel so completely and utterly blindsided.

What made her pull a 180-degree turn on our relationship after all these years? Will she ever tell me what she was thinking? I doubt it. Does it matter? Maybe, maybe not, but I would love to step into her head for a while and find out the truth, the mechanisms of her thought process.

None of what I had planned for has come to pass. For years I was completely prepared to grow old with Rita. I almost couldn't think of any other way to live. I know that no relationship is perfect—there is always something that annoys the other person or some unresolved argument—but I honestly felt we had the dedication and devotion to work things through. This has been a betrayal of the deepest trust.

But perhaps there is a lesson here.

Perhaps love is not enough. Perhaps it's not the ultimate

foundation to rely on. I thought Rita loved me enough to want to work on our issues. It's been quite a shock to find out that somehow, somewhere, she changed her mind. Had she been thinking about separating the whole time I have been deployed? Was she thinking of separating *before* I received the notice to deploy?

I honestly think there is something that I'm not aware of. Something has happened that I'm not privy to. I'm at the point of beginning to wonder whether any of it was real. Has my life been just a dream up until now? Was I really married to a beautiful woman with a head full of steam? God Rita, did you mean our vows? Did you really take them seriously or were they just empty words? *I* meant them. That's why I was always willing to work on our issues. How could you just throw in the towel? I don't think I'll ever understand.

Perhaps I should die over here. Perhaps I was *meant* to die here, to be brought home in a black plastic bag. Perhaps I should start praying for a mortar to land near me again and explode into a hundred tiny fragments, penetrating my body with deadly thorns, ripping the limbs from me, snuffing my life out in a matter of seconds. Perhaps it would be better that way. The questions I have would no longer matter.

The idea is gratifying. People would move on with their lives; they always do. There would be no more need for apologies, no more miscommunication and distrust. No more guilt, shame, or sorrow. Perhaps it would be peaceful, tranquil. Perhaps I could rest.

### December 12, 2004

Are adults really adults?

The more I ponder this question the more it seems that a lot of adults are just overgrown children who have never resolved how to handle complex, intimate emotions in a healthy way.

How much time and work does it take to become a well-rounded adult? How many people are afraid to face being alone in this world, afraid to face waking up alone in the middle of the night?

Is every relationship transitory? Is *everything* in life transitory?

A few people here have expressed a desire to keep in touch with me after we leave this place. I'm not sure how to feel about that.

I honestly think we'll all separate for good. I have traditionally had a very difficult time with keeping the lines of communication open. I might hear from them from time to time, but it will peter out the way it always does as people become absorbed with their lives.

Our relationships over here are transitory—nothing more. That is the way of things.

I accept that about people, this place, and this life.

### December 13, 2004

So, today the courts are supposed to finalize my divorce. Rita and her attorneys are appearing before the judge and we will see what happens.

I have yet to hear news from either of them.

## December 14, 2004

I'm amazed there is still no word from Rita or her attorneys. I would really like to know how things went in court.

The suspense is killing me.

I sent the attorneys an email and I'm resentful that no one has had the courtesy of writing me before now.

Should I be angry about that?

## December 15, 2004

On December 13 my wife and I were officially divorced. There was a brief hearing with the judge and then the deed was completed.

Rita's attorneys finally emailed me today. Amazing how someone can be so coldhearted but this type of behavior seems normal to me now.

I sincerely doubt Rita and I will have any further conversations. It is clear that I'm discarded waste to be viewed with disdain.

It is done… over.

I've spent roughly one-third of my life building a world with this woman and with one swift stroke of a pen that era has been wiped away. I can hardly believe the reality of it. I feel as if I should be pinching myself, waking from a slumber to realize that this was just a nightmare.

I don't know if I will ever understand how my life tumbled so wildly out of control.

### December 16, 2004

The oil fire is dissipating now, only small wisps of clouds and smoke are lingering, the air is clearing and I am able to breathe comfortably again. What a relief, yet I can't help but wonder what damage has been done to the environment due to trivial human bickering.

Isn't it amazing how after thousands of years of evolution, the human species is still fighting over the rights to the water hole?

More than 20 mortars came in today. I couldn't hear my movie over the racket. What a fuckin' nuisance.

### December 17, 2004

You know, I really loved her. I always thought Rita and I would be together forever. From the moment I met her, I fell in love with her, her bright brown eyes, her crooked smile framing perfect teeth, the energy that was electric when she spoke. I fell in love with the softness of her skin, the gentle curve of her waist and hips, her passion for nature, her intelligence and wit, even the way her glasses framed her face.

One night spent talking, drinking cheap beers at a local bar, and I knew I loved her.

There was something special about her, a magic between us

that I'll never be able to forget. She was all I wanted in a woman. Sure, I can remember times when I grumbled to myself about her, frustrated with her, angry with her, angry with myself… but not once did I ever stop loving her.

I remember holding her hand when she was sick, making her tea, brushing the hair back from her brow, knowing she was by my side and I hers. What happened to that? What was her final straw? Or was this just the way things happen? Does the flame just die of its own accord?

Why didn't you want to at least *try*? What part of you gave up? We had it good once, baby. We had a great life together and I wanted it to last forever. I felt it. I know you felt it as well.

Or was it all an illusion? Was I just a fool in love? What made it die, baby? Was it all me? Did I extinguish our flame? Oh dear God, am I to blame? Was I that horrible of a husband, that lousy of a man? Am I that unforgivable?

I guess if you don't believe in relationships merely washing out, fading like a picture in the blazing sun, then the finger must be turned toward me. I did this and I have to live with it. I'm so sorry. I honestly didn't do anything intentionally or maliciously.

I wish I could turn back time and go back to the happiest days of my life.

Writing this brings tears to my eyes. We once glimpsed the magic, baby.

I wish we could have gotten it back.

### December 18, 2004

We had another power outage today. I lay on my bunk staring at the ceiling, lost in the murkiness of my mind. And then a feeling of utter hopelessness crashed into me like a big semi doing 80 on the highway.

I fear I'm almost at the point where I can't stand this place any more. I want my life back. I want my freedom, my independence. Thinking about being here drives me to the edge of madness sometimes. Or is it me who's driving me mad? I feel like screaming at the top of my lungs.

My thoughts soon drifted to the people in America, what they might be doing, what it's like to be there. Sometimes the U.S. seems like a dream I once had. But today I imagined all the people going about their lives, pushing and shoving in their local mall, oblivious to the pain and suffering over here.

"You signed up for this," I'm sure some would say. "You're serving your country, making that sacrifice. Now be a good boy and suck it up. You better learn how to deal with it."

"Bullshit," would be my answer. "No one signed up to fight an unjust, unnecessary, senseless war."

Sometimes I don't know how I've managed to survive here for so long. Sometimes the world seems to dim before my eyes. It becomes a grey place where there are only shadows for people and all I can see are blurred faces like distorted horrific apparitions. My heart pounds in my head, thumping against my eardrums. I want to clamp my fists to my temples and sink to my knees. Then I become angry and want to lash out at the people who sent me to this place. I want to lash out at the people I thought were my friends, who spurned me when I was at my most vulnerable and tossed me into an overflowing trash bin filled with other superfluous souls.

I don't know why my friends don't want to talk to me any more but I'm angry with them for betraying me. And that beckons the question: How do you know people are true friends? How do you honestly know the truth about the people you know? How do you know until something happens—such as my divorce—then without warning you become an outcast, someone they feel uncomfortable talking to?

I can picture it now: "Too bad about Scott and Rita. They seemed so happy. God, you know it's such a shame that he has to be part of all that suffering over in Iraq. My heart goes out to those poor troops."

It's all petty, vacant bullshit. They don't care. They mouth some empty words and go back to drinking their eggnog and talking about how the new couch fits in with the rest of the living room. Vain, one-dimensional people—you really do discover who will stick with you when you're in a situation like this.

Who will ride with you to the bitter end? Who will join hands with you and say "I am here and I always will be"—and *mean* it?

Perhaps it's for the best that I'm discovering this now. I'd hate to go through life ignorant of their real beliefs. I want meaningful friends, meaningful relationships. I want people I can trust to stand by me.

I'm tired of the falsehood, the shallowness of it all. I'm going to surround myself with better types of people—to Hell with the rest.

Fuck them all.

## December 18, 2004 continued

I think Gary put it the best way I can imagine. He said he wants to deal with people on his terms and no one else's. I'm going to have to remember that idea and apply it to my own life from now on. Over the years I have put up with so much, always bending over backward to appease people or make them happy, often at my expense. It's not in me any more.

I've had it.

This is the new me—straight up with no ice. I don't want to be a mixed drink. From now on what you see is what you get. I'm gonna do whatever the fuck I want because I have to live for me regardless of who I'm with. I've learned that from Rita. I've learned not to sacrifice my goals and dreams for the sake of the illusion of love. I'm not going to cheat myself out of my life because someone doesn't like some part of me. That's their fucking problem and they are going to have to deal with it.

I'm sick of being treated as if I am less of a man. I'm sick of being berated for decisions I made in a heartfelt way when I was honestly trying to help.

What's worse than knowing you're not being true to yourself? That's the biggest way you can cheat yourself and it's not going to happen to me again. I want to explore my personality, my beliefs, and my interests and get to know myself again.

I've been missing myself for far too many years.

## December 19, 2004

Anger is burning within me.

She cut me with a razor then went on her merry way, justifying her actions with the assertion that I was the one who screwed up our relationship. That haughty bitch.

Obviously I know that I'm not exempt from blame. I bear a certain responsibility for my life, for my relationship—that's only reasonable. But I can't help but feel that without this deployment as a catalyst, things would have been different and that makes it worse. It's beyond agony to know that none of this had to happen the way it did, that I should never have been here—that only fans the flames of my rage.

And I had a thought today that scared me more deeply than anything else as of late. I put so much faith in these people—my ex-wife, my friends—and now, given what's happened, how can I trust myself any more? What does that say about my judgment? If I can't rely on my judgment then what can I rely on? How can I conduct myself with people I meet from here on? It makes me wonder what else in my life I've been oblivious to.

I can feel my heart crumbling… or changing; I can't be sure any more.

Rita never did find the courtesy to email me when the

divorce was final, something I requested and thought was only fair.

The tic in my eye is as bad as ever. We're old friends now.

My shoulders ache. I'm so thin.

I'm so tired and the days seem endless like some vast, lifeless ocean, the horizon unclear, foggy.

Most days I feel as if I'm energized by nothing but sheer adrenal force. I wonder how long it will last.

### December 20, 2004

Today I'm feeling a bit calmer although the undercurrent of tension is still within me. Like striking a match, I could be put to flame in an instant. I'm just glad I have my journals.

I'm glad I'm not the type to express rage with a shotgun as many people have done. The human race has a tendency to take its pains out on others.

Oh my God, that was close. A mortar just landed near me and rattled this hovel like we were in an earthquake. I can see the dust cloud that the impact kicked up. It sounded like a shotgun going off right next to me. My hand is still quivering as I'm trying to hold my pen.

We've been getting mortared consistently for a couple of days now. I have to get out of here. Being penned in with the constant fear of being killed is becoming unbearable. Insanity slithers along my skin, always probing for a way in.

And still America marches on. Millions of them are

Christmas shopping right now, jostling each other out of the way for a good spot in line or the toy that's been selling out this year. Grim faces with clusters of bags sprouting from under their arms, steadily marching to the beat of carols. Woe to anyone who gets in their way. Babies crying, teenagers giggling and flirting— who's the new hot guy on the street or who's got the perfect ass.

Older ladies pushing carts full of stuff that their loved ones probably won't want. There's stuff for everyone—a reindeer sweater for the old man, a tacky tie for the son-in-law, a cute shirt for the daughter, not too low-cut. Old men slouching on benches, grey frizzy hair peeking out from under baseball caps, yawning and waiting for their wives to come out of a department store smelling like 10 different perfumes but didn't buy a single one. Over stimulated little children wailing from fatigue and exasperated mothers chastising them with a pointed finger and stern voice. It's the land of capitalism, where you charge as much as you want in a vain attempt to fill a void in your soul.

Parties, eggnog, turkeys, stuffing, fruitcakes, trees, gaudy Santa lawn displays, grandpa snoring in the recliner, heaps of discarded wrapping paper to burn in the fireplace.

Yes, it's Christmas in America.

Yet I sit here in Iraq, scared that I might never get to elbow my way through a crowd again. Perhaps I'll never see the packed parking lots of the malls or be lucky enough to kiss a pretty lady under the mistletoe again.

Funny what you miss when your life is in danger.

### December 21, 2004

I don't recognize the face that I see in the mirror now—the cheeks are drawn, the bones are showing, and the expression is dull, numb. The eyes are lifeless, unfamiliar—I swear they're not mine.

I don't feel human any more.

Word spread around the camp that 20 or more Americans were killed in Mosul.

### December 22, 2004

We brought our black boxes up to the hangar today, packed to the brim with nonessential stuff. I had to drag mine by hand for a mile along the narrow roadway to the hangar, sweating like mad and taking breaks along the way—the fucker weighed a ton. When everyone was assembled the boxes were loaded into a Conex. Eventually the Conex will be loaded onto a ship, provided the convoy bringing it south into Kuwait isn't ambushed or blown to pieces by an IED.

In a month or so it will arrive in the States, though no one really knows for sure. With any luck my box will be in Montana before I get there, but we'll just have to wait and see. This is the Army after all, and the Army is not exactly known for its efficiency. But all my movies, most of my books, trinkets, and spare clothing are in there waiting to be inspected by customs on the 29th of December.

Supposedly they are going to line up the Conex in the

hangar and customs is going to have us unpack so they can do an inspection to make sure we're not bringing anything illegal home. Then we'll have to repack everything again to be put back into the Conex, which will then be sealed and trucked to the shipyards in Kuwait.

There's going to be close to 250 black boxes, plus equipment, to be readied. It's going to be a long day of standing around and waiting for just a few minutes of personal inspection. I can deal with it though since it's another very good step in the right direction—a step closer to going home. That's my only priority now.

I've developed a little rash about the size of a quarter around my right ankle, probably a symptom of the living conditions we are forced to endure. I found some cortisone in a first aid kit and have been putting some on it every day. There are some strange "cruds" that float around here. People have been coming down with unknown coughs, skin irritations, even lung infections. They seem resigned to living with them, shuffling through the day, hoping to leave here before anything gets any worse. No one has any answers and it's kinda scary.

At least the bruises on my feet have hardened to something resembling calluses. Either that or my feet have just plain become numb to the pain.

### December 25, 2004

Christmas in Iraq. This is the first time I have celebrated this holiday away from the States, the first time in 10 years away from

Rita or our families.

Today, we had a mandatory formation at 0830. There were some promotions and Top played Santa. He even put on a beard, bushy white eyebrows, and a hat. He handed out gifts the major had put together for each person in the company.

I got a copy of the yearbook project I finally finished—I found that pretty amusing.

To receive our gifts we crowded around the tree that had been set up in the hangar. They put out refreshments, mainly Gatorade and water. It was nice, I have to admit. This little celebration represented the beginning of the end of this epic struggle to remain sane and alive.

Yet I felt so distant from everyone. I felt like a phantom, a stranger, emotionally detached from all the chattering faces.

As I floated through the crowd, I realized that the "good me" still exists but it has been soiled, tainted, or as if that part of me is being held at bay by the rage, the disillusionment, sorrow, regret, and self-loathing. Now, only disappointment and sadness have power over my heart and I am helplessly lost to that inner turmoil.

Life seems to be nothing more than a facsimile of something that once meant so much. I've been corrupted by what I've experienced and the hope of experiencing beauty again means nothing. A haze of pain and sorrow fogs my eyes, making the world dim and grey. Things that used to move me come through sounding tinny, like from a blown-out stereo system.

Memories of Rita and better days clutch at my throat like a tightening noose. I feel that I have fucked up what was good in my life. Is it an integral part of me to take my blessings for granted? Or even destroy them? Why do I seem to have this self-destructive attitude? I don't understand anything any more. It's all so hopeless.

I remember when Rita and I would giggle together at the drama of others. How free and easily everything seemed to come for us. What happened to those years? How did we get so lost?

We were always joined, not needing more. Did we grow apart? Or did we grow up?

I remember tasting the mashed potatoes at Rita's parents' house on Christmas Day to make sure they were done. I remember watching her cook, admiring her body, loving her spirit—she never knew. I never let it out like I should have. I kept it tight within me. Why I was so inhibited, I don't know. Why not let the woman you love know how you feel?

I'm listening to people partying a few hovels down from here. Even as the mortars drop and the killing continues, boisterous voices drift over the air undaunted in their quest for peace. Yet I want no part of it. I shy away from people now despite my loneliness. They scare me because I'm all too aware of the violence residing in each of us. Whether it's emotional or physical, it's all too ready or eager to be unchained.

But they party like there's no tomorrow. Who can blame them? There might not be another tomorrow. They're furiously attempting to forget where they are and the suffering they have endured here. Let's drown the beast of sorrow until the bottom of the bottle is in sight, only to wish for more because it's not enough. It's never enough. We drown ourselves, still wondering "How come this void is still within me, how come I still feel so empty?" The response being "Ahhh, that's a buzzkill; fuck it, let's have another drink."

God... help me. I feel so many years heaped upon this weary, bony body and my strength is fading like a sunset. Help me out of this sinkhole of depression that has me caught in its swirling grasp.

Why did this happen? Did *you* do this? Did *you* lead me here? Are you showing me that I've been going down the wrong trail? Did I ignore your warnings? Did you lead me here to die? Should I close my eyes, never to wake again? Should I find the peaceful sleep of forever?

The weight of this year has taken its toll. There is only a whimper, a dying gasp left in my heart and I wish for deliverance from this life. I'm going over the cliff with the engine roaring, gas pedal pinned to the floor.

And I don't care.

Fighter jets roar overhead. Helicopters beat against the air in the distance. The violence of war continues.

No day is sacred in this land.

I am broken.

Merry Christmas.

### December 26, 2004

It rained here today. All the usual sand and dust once again rapidly turned to a sticky goop. Going to the latrine or shower trailer has become a tedious task of revoltingly "shlocking" your way through the mud. Finding just the right path of high ground is a challenge. There's an abundance of spots in the mud where your feet just sink in and you stop, wondering if you've lost a boot or flip-flop, like a beached derelict of a wrecked ship with half of its hull jutting from the mess.

People have put down thin planks of wood, anything they could find lying around, forming a precarious walking path to the showers and latrines. The planks are so slick with mud that you teeter on them like some mad daredevil walking a tightrope between two skyscrapers, arms flapping like a baby bird.

Inside the trailers, tracks of mud cover the floor, spatters of it even on the walls like smears of baby diarrhea. The stalls are clogged with the remnants of soiled toilet paper and someone's unsettled dinner.

Soap for the three sinks is often scarce, so you end up just rinsing your hands, absently gazing at your lifeless reflection in the grimy mirror and wondering "How did I get here?"

You step into the showers, muddy flip-flops and all, to the remains of the last person's mud still spotting the stall. You turn the water on and the brown goop pools around your feet and sits there, refusing to be washed down an already clogged drain. It never wants to leave your side. It's a most loyal mud. And you scrape your flip-flops on the bottom of the stall just as vigorously as you scrub yourself, to cleanse both your body and soul... like some abysmal baptism. But you never really feel clean no matter how hard you try.

On your return to your prison cell, mud cakes the bottom of your flip-flops again no matter how carefully you pick your way across the treacherous wood planking, this time even more carefully because you're desperate to stay clean. The small pockets of gravel look like the bottom of a fish tank that has been drained. When you step on them, they no longer crunch; instead you feel only the agonizing sinking of the mud underneath, like you're stepping on an immense pile of freshly laid manure. The wind blows, wiping your brow of accumulated sweat. It ripples off the puddles and bites into you, cold air that is at least 80 degrees; together with the mud, they both strive to make your life even more miserable than it already was.

When you finally make it to your cell, relieved to have made it with only a few smears of mud to track in, a mortar whines overhead. It arcs over your cell only to land near the mess hall some yards away. The explosion shakes your very soul. You wince, shoulders instantly burning with the stress of anticipating death, your eye twitches, your hands shake, scenes from your previous life flash before you.

You see the picture of Rita hanging on the wall. You see your parents crying at your funeral procession. "That was a close one," you mutter, carefully shaking off your flip-flops on the muddy entrance rug you took from someone else's garbage pile.

You sigh.

You wonder how long your luck will hold out. When will

be the day that a shell drops in on you, not bothering to knock, just rudely crashing through your ceiling and greeting you with vengeful violent glee, your shock only registering for a brief moment before your life is extinguished.

It's just another day in Iraq.

### December 27, 2004

The latest word is I'm leaving Iraq for good on January 7, my 33rd birthday. Mike informed me I'm flying to Kuwait with a large group to be on the wash crew—cleaning trucks and equipment before they're shipped home. I presume that I'll be going to Camp Doha since that's where the wash racks are. If all goes well, we're not coming back. The rest of the unit will be joining us at some point in the future. Some will be leaving here on January 23, the rest after the change of command on the 31st.

After a few undoubtedly boring briefings, we'll fly to Ft. Bragg to demobilize. With any luck my time at Bragg will be quick and painless and then I'll be on my way back to Montana.

On the 29th, Air Force customs officials are inspecting our black boxes.

I have 11 days left in Iraq and I'm never coming back.

My tour of duty is quickly coming to an end.

I got some new boots from Supply today and my feet are in love with me.

I guess I can leave now.

### December 28, 2004

Today we had to stay at the hangar until 1300 for a mandatory formation. It was excruciatingly boring. All told, there are about 20 people at the hangar now and no helicopters to work on. There are no phase inspections, no hydraulic lines to replace, no brakes to overhaul—nothing. They were playing football while the day droned on with explosions and the sounds of fighter jets overhead. I wandered around all morning. We're just waiting for the airplane to whisk us away.

Top had us unload our black boxes from the Conexes to get them lined up for the customs inspection tomorrow. I was more than glad to help out. It means we are one step closer to leaving this godforsaken wasteland of a country.

Tomorrow is the big customs inspection. From what I've heard it's not a big deal. They have two people and 200 boxes to go through in two and a half hours or less. Imagine that.

We've been mortared a few times today—the alarm's been going off left and right. There was a fairly big one that opened my eyes a bit but it landed no closer than a dozen other shells have since I got here. I guess my ticket isn't up just yet.

No matter how loud I've played my Star Trek DVDs, they've never managed to drown out the sounds of killing and violence. I will never look at Star Trek the same way.

Iraq takes even the most sacred of belongings away from you.

### December 30, 2004

I got word today that I am now leaving Iraq on January 5. Supposedly I'm not coming back here—at least so they say. It's exciting to be taking another step in the right direction, although the nervous anticipation of it has me a little on edge.

But in other ways, I'm *used* to it here. This is my *home* now, like it or not. I feel a certain anxiety, as if I'm leaving home for the first time to go out into the world, not knowing what to expect and scared at the prospect of leaving these familiar surroundings. It's funny how the human mind can adapt to any situation and resign itself to a set of once-foreign variables.

I'm used to it here, that's the bottom line.

This is my home and I'm ready to die here.

### December 31, 2004

New Year's Eve and I'm spending it in Iraq of all places, something I would never have imagined. No friends to drink pints with, glasses clinking in a toast as if beer won't be brewed next year. No resolutions, no banners, or crowds pushing toward the bar. No ball dropping in Times Square heralding 2005 with raucous clamor and endless confetti. No kisses or passionate lovemaking as the clock strikes twelve.

There was only another night of attacks. Alarms and explosions standing in for noisemakers and firecrackers, reverberating off the outside walls of the trailers while we passed the night away. Soldiers go about their business, taking showers, wondering if the mess hall might be open, walking up to the flight line for a mission, Humvees and trucks rumbling past on some errand for their superiors.

It's just another day, no looking at the clock to see if it's midnight yet—who really cares. It doesn't matter whether it's 2004 or 2005 because you live from day to day, hour to hour, minute to minute. Those are the only parcels of time that mean anything significant to your life. It's time to go to work, time to go to lunch, time to go back to your cell. Nothing stops the daily routine.

I finished the final newsletter for the major.

Happy New Year, Scotty.

### January 7, 2005

I haven't felt like writing this week, no energy—lethargy has taken root. Time, or anything else, doesn't appear to matter as the days are blurring together like an engulfing grayish mist. An unsettled feeling I can't pinpoint lies in the pit of my stomach making me feel very uneasy, off-balance somehow.

Perhaps it has something to do with feeling as if I'm detached from daily life as I plod through each day. Worse, I am detached from the emotions of my memories. I don't know what to make of it, only that I feel unfamiliar even to myself. I see myself doing things, yet sometimes I can't comprehend that it's actually me who's doing them. I look at my hands and they are not attached to me. My brain hardly recognizes that it's commanding them.

Work-wise this past week, I didn't do anything. I had to go to the hangar as usual up until the third and enduring the hours at the shop was a slow, at times unbearable process. With nothing to do, I paced the floor as always. The mornings slowly ticked by, the seconds of those last few minutes before lunch seeming to last for hours. I remember the long arduous walk home over gravel, the dry crunch of every footfall grating on my nerves and feeling so edgy, so punchy, ever ready to lash out at anything that came my way. But, on the fifth I left Iraq with a small group from my company. I'm now at Camp Doha in Kuwait and we are waiting for our scheduled time to wash our equipment and trucks.

Now that I have the opportunity to rest more easily, I'm finding that I can't. Last night was silent, eerie—the quietest night I can remember in a long, long time. There were no explosions or gunfire—not even helicopters. The tranquility of Kuwait took me by surprise. I'm not used to being able to rest easily with no worry of being killed and it felt odd, unbalanced with life as I know it now.

I'm constantly on edge, always expecting the next explosion or siren, the sounds of war echoing in my head day in and day out. When I lie down at night, or even while I'm having a cigarette, my hands are clenched—my whole body is tense. Relaxing takes a conscious effort now and most times I can't, even when I try. Two minutes after unclenching my hands they are clenched again without me even realizing it. I don't know what I can do about it.

In short, it feels *normal* to be afraid now.

I'm so used to it that this peaceful place feels foreign and ominous not only because my fear no longer has a basis in reality but I'm afraid my mind has been rewired somehow. I can't wrap my head around that one but, it's true nonetheless. The constant threat of death has sunk into my soul and is part of me now. At least when the bombs were falling being afraid made sense.

I loathe Camp Anaconda yet, I miss it. I feel hollow without it, as if I've lost a friend, and I don't understand how this can be. I was completely unprepared for the feeling. It's like I've just been released from prison only to find I don't know how to act in ordinary circumstances on the outside. I don't know how to feel. It's like Camp Doha is a dream... and so is the prospect of returning to the world.

I still feel awkward in my skin. I had thought the feeling would recede when I left Iraq but I feel uncomfortable, always on guard. I watch others go about their business, bustling to and fro and I can't relate. It's a feeling of nonexistence. I feel as if I want to disappear within myself and shut out the outside world forever.

I turned 33 years old today. I was born at approximately 0800 in 1972. Only today I was born again into a strange, unfamiliar life that most take for granted: a world without the constant threat of danger.

I don't feel 33. I feel as if I am a newborn, an infant with a past life of experiences and knowledge buried somewhere within me. It no longer feels like that old life is a part of me now—I'm merely aware of its existence. Oh my God, how excruciating this is, this feeling of detachment even from myself. I'm beginning to wonder if I even *should* go home. Really, who needs a person like me around?

### January 9, 2005

I had the day off. There is nothing to do until we're scheduled to begin washing the equipment and trucks. So I spent the day catching up on laundry, writing, organizing, just trying to catch my breath and acclimate to the feeling of not having to wonder if I'll be killed. In between, I spent some time reliving the memories of leaving Camp Anaconda.

On January 5, I was to have my gear ready for departure at 1830 hours, the ride to the Air Force side of the base to take place at 1930. There were 60 of us from the company in all—the nonessential personnel. So much time has passed, yet everything comes around full circle eventually.

I had nothing to do but wait, wait for the C-130 to transport us to freedom and peace. So I sat in my cell, duffel bags packed and stacked neatly near the doorway, everything clean and fresh as it could be.

It felt so odd, sitting there. So strangely quiet. There were no pictures on the wall any more. They were erased by simply pulling a pin. My wall locker stood open—empty—coat hangers hooked on that horizontal steel bar stripped of their purpose.

The bed was naked. There was no pink comforter, no dismal, grimy sheets, just a mattress.

This room where I had spent so much time, my only sanctuary in Iraq, was now just another empty space waiting Zenlike for the next soldier. It was vacant, yet saturated with memories of the past year, my memories echoing in the walls like ghosts you can't see but know are there.

I wistfully reminisced about the past year, wondering how the time, which had seemed to drag to the point of excruciating, maddening pain, had flown by so fast in the end. A chapter of my life was coming to an end, a period filled with hardship, tribulations, laughter, joy, fear, sorrow, and self-exploration and discovery.

I have to admit, I felt sad about leaving, plausibly attributing that to the syndrome of institutionalization and/or the fact that during the year this small cubicle had been my home, my home where my previous life had been scattered to the wind.

I also felt strangely alive. I could almost tangibly feel my life moving forward again, the next chapter beginning. I felt as if I had just caught a breath of fresh air after leaving a stale-smelling room. I began to feel reborn, as if I was about to emerge from the womb.

It was time for me to embark upon a new path, a path that I have been visualizing for a long time. Now it has only to be actualized, a road to steadfastly tread with thick, solid boots representing the resilience of my soul—a soul that had grown strong over these past few months. It was time for the wanderer to wander again.

When the time came... I was ready. I had prepared myself. I was leaving my home, never to return. With a small frown and steely heart I stepped outside, closed the door, locked it, and walked into the twilight of Iraq. My heavy boots felt lighter with every step I took and the world looked different somehow, familiar yet unfamiliar as if I was smelling, breathing, touching, seeing, and hearing for the first time.

I met a Humvee piled high with duffel bags, the driver waiting. There were no farewell ceremonies, no celebrations, no friends hugging me with tear-stained eyes, no yells and cheers, no banners waving proudly. There was no one to say how proud they were of me for defending America's freedoms, no lover to call my own. I felt that same eerie silence again as I climbed into the back seat and was driven to the plane.

I sat crammed into the back of the Humvee loaded with duffel bags, personal bags, laptops, files—whatever people deemed necessary for the trip south to Kuwait. I couldn't see any of the base for it was very dark. I only heard sounds—trucks passing, helicopters spooling up their engines, people talking at intersections. I saw the bright glow of a single street lamp mixed with red from taillights. A left turn, a right turn, and I shifted my body as a laptop dug into my back, my arm bracing a bag that threatened to fall onto me.

We pulled off the pavement onto a small gravel yard, open except for the latrine trailers starkly standing in the middle, dim light from their lamps illuminating the outside. Palm trees encircled the lot, gently swaying in the cool night air. In front of us were rows of tents protected by the concrete bunkers that surrounded every section of the camp.

The two five-ton trucks containing the rest of our baggage were parked nearby, soon to be unloaded. As usual, there was a standing around period while we waited for the rest of our personnel to arrive, waited for the people in charge to decide what to do with us. So I sat, smoked, and… waited.

We were told to pull the trucks around. It was just like going on leave; the bags had to be palletized for the C-130 that was to carry us out of the country on its sturdy wings. There were two "Chalks," or groups, an early flight and a late flight. I was on Chalk Two—the late flight. It didn't matter much.

So with the accustomed amount of confusion (always so present that without it we would all be lost) the bags were separated. When the bags were finally dealt with, I took a deep breath. I remember it vividly, looking around me at all the people milling around, some quietly talking and smoking under the soft glow of a lamp.

Everywhere was constant activity, the crunch of gravel underfoot, the smell of the dump burning as it had 24/7 since I had come to Camp Anaconda, the glow of spotlights, shadows of soldiers holding the red-tipped ends of burning cigarettes, wisps of smoke drifting through the air. Again memories flooded back. I had stood in this very spot just a few months ago waiting to go home and sort things out with my now ex-wife.

Then we found spots inside a tent filled with cots. It was

early yet and the first flight wouldn't leave until midnight. Some went to the Internet tent, some to the PX. Others immediately lay down, boonie caps over their eyes, combat vests or Kevlar helmets for pillows. Instead of fretting about my lack of control over these situations I have trained myself to mentally turn off and sleep, write, and wait. You get used to waiting in the Army.

Eventually the first flight was called and half of us went out the wooden, creaky door of the tent. I watched them file out then turned back to my slumber. At 0400, the base was still humming with activity as my Chalk was called and we shuffled out to the bus. Collapsing in the nearest seat, lack of sleep burning my eyes, my chin wanting to sink into my chest, I stared blankly out the window at the darkened sky.

It was a short drive around the maze of concrete barriers and down a thin strip of pavement that led us to the flight line. There were a few neatly parked planes, some running, some dark as night, trucks clustered around each of them like worker ants tending to a queen. I listened to the sound of air whistling from the spooled jet engines, the loud whir of a thousand angry bees from the propeller blades. Blue runway lights stretched to eternity parallel to my travel lane and the brightly glowing crescent moon overseeing our departure dimly illuminated the asphalt tarmac.

The bus parked about 25 yards away from the yawning rear of the airplane, gaping like some slack-jawed mechanized monster waiting for the puny humans to willingly step into its mouth and take their seats deep in its belly. Four rows of seats again, blue light barely illuminating the cabin as we filed in. I found one near the front, buckled the canvas belt, and indifferently watched the others settle in, stowing personal backpacks and getting comfortable. As always, the palette came next, riding on the twin spears of the forklift, directed by the rear crewman, the pilots assisting from the front, arms waving, crossing them above their heads: "That's enough, no farther. Wait. Back a little." The mouth of our soon-to-be soaring creature silently closed.

Movement, barely perceptible at first except for a slight back and forth rocking, became more apparent as we began to taxi. I settled in more deeply and looked around, gazing at the faces, some eyelids already beginning to close. There was no talking, no sound but the engines of the airplane. I could feel the wheels rolling across the runway and I listened as the pilots performed a flap check, jackscrews driven by hydraulic whirring. I felt the airplane turn, the heavy wings swaying then steadying as we entered the runway, the monster readying for flight. Stopping with a lurch, I imagined the pilots asking for final clearance to leave… then the propellers and engines slowly began to scream, mad with enthusiasm, louder and louder until we were sprinting down the runway, everyone pushed backward by the force.

I smiled. "I can't believe it," I thought. "Here I am again, only this time I know I'm not coming back."

We left the ground, that momentary floating feeling of leaving Mother Earth quickly relinquishing to the demanding hands of gravity and g-force. The cabin tipped, tipped more, a steep climb, a combat takeoff to avoid mortars and other fire. Air pressure was adjusted. Ears popping, I swallowed. We turned steeply, swayed a bit then leveled out.

We began to climb again, a few minutes later leveling out at the desired altitude, the cabin pressure still being fine-tuned. Looking around, I saw that some of my company were already asleep. Others stared blankly; some sipped on bottled water. I watched the parachutes oscillate from the ceiling like a baby's mobile, emergency oxygen masks swaying in rhythm with the aircraft like a steady pulse.

A whine startled me out of my reverie. The wheels came up, then a dull clunk on the belly as its round rubber feet tucked themselves neatly into their compartments. With another whine the wheel-well doors closed. Another turn, then level flight again. It's hard to tell which way you're going in a C-130, as there are just a few small windows. You have to trust the pilots, the mechanics—you have to have faith. They are trained. They won't fail, not while carrying such precious cargo.

Time passed.

I listened to the whine of the engines. I wanted to feel every dip, every turn—this was the moment I had yearned for, the moment I had dreamed of a thousand times—the dream of leaving Iraq. We dipped steeply, leveled out then dipped again, more gently the second time, more whirring, flaps lowering, steel machinery at work. I began to see small glimpses of sand through the windows—and then we landed, my musings interrupted by the unexpected touchdown, the bellow of the engines deafening me, now shoving me forward with braking action so suddenly I was pressed against my seatbelt and the person next to me.

A small turn and the winged beast came to rest, panting in the morning air. Its mouth opened once again and I winced at the stream of sunlight entering the cabin. Before I knew it, we had been regurgitated onto the pavement and I felt somewhat dazed as I took in the morning air. The sun shone brightly against the sand dunes in the distance and a chilly breeze whipped across the tarmac.

After the baggage palette disappeared around the corner of the airplane, we found two buses waiting to take us to Camp Doha.

We had arrived to the quiet sands of Kuwait. No mishaps. No more bombs or bullets.

No more death.

Ali Al Salem Air Base was quiet in those early morning hours. All the bags were put on one bus and all the people on the other. There was no organization this time, no chain of soldiers collectively helping to load everything. It was just a grab-bag free-for-all. We were all weary from traveling, grimly going about the task with adrenaline-fueled determination. I smiled cynically as I overheard a quiet discussion among the officers—"Where will we be staying? What am I supposed to do with all these guys?"

We climbed aboard, found seats, not wanting to speak. The bus lurched forward with a grinded gear and with squinted eyes

I peered out the smudged windows upon the endless miles of wind-rippled tan sand. With each passing mile my shoulders relaxed just a bit more, drooping with the knowledge that Iraq was behind me.

We made the 45-minute drive, the last bit of it adorned with neatly spaced palm trees gently swaying in the midmorning breeze, leaves fluttering with a light carefree, almost cheerful demeanor, beautifully landscaped with pebbles surrounding the base of their trunks… and then with a final turn the blue rectangular sign came into view, a sign I had seen many times: WELCOME TO CAMP DOHA.

We lumbered past the maze of concrete Jersey barriers, past the guard post, one civilian security contractor waving us by with the swift motion of a rigid hand, another lifting the red-and-white striped gate that allowed us to pass. It all seemed so absurdly subdued compared with the racket of war up north.

Our bus wound down narrow streets between the long, bleak rows of warehouses. As we parked beside one, I sighed—yet another warehouse. How many times had I been an occupant in one of these warehouses?

It didn't look all that different from the others. Inside the stark grey ominous walls were, once again, rows upon rows of bunks. Always rows—rows of warehouses, rows of bunks.

Now a seasoned traveler and soldier, I was quick to grab a bottom bunk at the back of the bay. The farthest corners from the front door are the most secluded and the bottom bunks are easier to climb in and out of to take a piss at night. You can also store your stuff underneath them. You have to act quickly or those bunks will be snatched up. It's every man for himself.

Now it was finally time to sleep. Much to our chagrin, early the next morning we were told to move again, to another warehouse, to make way for another unit.

That's life at Camp Doha.

Lately it has occurred to me how everything in life comes full circle. I stayed here in the beginning of my odyssey and I'm staying here at the end.

Every end sees its own beginning.

Good-bye, Iraq.

**January 13, 2005**

I've spent the last two days working on the Camp Doha wash rack—a fairly well-run organization, all things considered. It began when we had to get up at 0400 on January 10. We had to be ready at 0530 after a quick breakfast and an even quicker formation, ready to walk a mile across the base to an approximately 30-bay, massive, high-pressure, semi-rectangular wash rack.

Cleaning a military truck is a tedious, meticulous task. Slithering under a truck propped upon concrete ramps, you lie in muddy puddles and there is no escaping the water jetting from the high-pressure wand. It seeps under your collar, soaks your uniform top, wetting your neck and back and chilling you to the bone. Water runs down your arms, past your rubber gloves, even under the Gore-Tex sleeves that you have velcroed as tightly as possible. Sheets of water run down your goggles, blinding you.

You have no idea where you're actually spraying—only that water and mist are everywhere, mud is dropping gloppily down on you, and grease is staining your clothes. You spray everything at point-blank range and still the truck is not clean. The customs inspectors (Air Force personnel) come by and poke fingers in the most unthinkable places, leaving you to wonder how you missed that access hole, that joint, that bearing, that wheel.

"I'll be back," they cheerfully say. "Let me know when you've finished."

So you crawl under again, this time spraying with gritted teeth and stubborn determination. It has become a private little war. You spray the bed of the truck, the cab, the engine, the wheels, this time taking your time with it, making sure that everything comes off.

They only give you two shots. If you fail, you and your truck go back to the staging area, the back of the line, holding things up because you only have two days to clean all of these camouflaged pieces of equipment that the Army has entrusted you with. More units are awaiting their turn. There are endless lines of vehicles, some worse off than yours, some better, all to be loaded on ships bound for the homeland, each eventually going back to their respective states.

After spraying again, double-checking yourself and crossing

your fingers an Air Force sergeant sidles over, creeper[34]and clipboard in hand, bright reflective mesh vest with a "CUSTOMS" nametag brightly glowing in the sunlight. He walks around the truck, poking fingers in holes, looking for any missed spot. He's sure you have—everyone does. They've been trained to inspect the most obscure areas you would never think mattered but apparently do.

You're standing there, dripping, watching, waiting with wand in hand to hit the stray spot to ensure your truck passes. Minutes go by like mini-eternities. Then without a word he begins writing, scribbling, filling in empty squares on a form. You've gotten the thumbs up, you're good to go. The paperwork is complete, signed, taped on the inside of the cab window. The truck, trailer in tow, can now be taken to the "sterile lot" to join the other empty monstrosities waiting to be loaded onto a ship and carried across the endless waves of the Atlantic Ocean.

A thrill of joy surges through you. You're tired. Your feet and legs ache. Your hands and fingers are as pale and wrinkled as a waterlogged corpse's. Water is dripping down your back. But you smile, climb aboard, and make the five-mph creep to the sterile lot, ground guide walking ahead, clomping in his muddied rubber boot covers. You park the truck, and it's someone else's problem now.

You go home to the warehouse, the endless aisles of bunks strewn with duffel bags and makeshift privacy barriers

---

34   A wheeled platform that mechanics lie on to slide underneath a vehicle

constructed out of a spare poncho or a smelly Army-issued wool blanket. Like every other warehouse at Camp Doha, this one is entirely open under pale florescent lighting and divided by a concrete wall topped with barbed wire that separates the boys from the girls.

As always there's one completely inadequate heater for the entire building and you shiver in your blanket waiting for sleep to come. There's sand on the floor and mud on your clothes. Stray wires dangle from the ceiling as if the construction workers quit midway through the job, stepped out for coffee and never came back.

But hey... it beats Iraq.

At night you sit on your bunk, green canvas scratching your skin, your shelter from everyone and everything until you wake up at 0400 the next day. For two days you do this until every truck is clean, then you wait again. You wait because the order to go to the shipyards hasn't come in yet. You don't know what's going to happen in the next few days, no one really knows, but it doesn't matter, you've just taken another step toward going back to the United States. The anticipation is like waiting for your college acceptance letter or first driver's license.

You just wish with all your heart you could get Iraq out of your head, that its memories would fade, especially when you find yourself waking up at night in a cold sweat, your eyes wide with fear, heart palpitating, hands grasping the wool blanket, reliving the explosions and gunfire, the whine of mortars still searching for your flesh.

Sometimes you realize you're still alive.

Sometimes you think you're dead.

### January 14, 2005

When we first arrived in the warehouse I grabbed a bunk alongside one wall. As I was unpacking my Army-issued fluffy green sleeping bag, Derek, Gary, and I noticed that a buddy of ours had secured himself a place by the sliding door entrance and had begun a construction project out of the boxes of water bottles that were stacked on a nearby pallet. For the better part of the day he neatly, meticulously stacked each box like bricks until satisfied that his stronghold was complete.

The enclosure was just large enough for his cot, allowing for a foot or so on either side, with a poncho strung up for extra privacy—three walls with a small gap for an entrance. He went about his task with the slow methodical pace of a manual laborer accustomed to years of heavy lifting; the world seemed to disappear for him as he intently, silently went about his task.

Finally he cut up some of the leftover boxes into large rectangular shapes and duct-taped them to the tops of the walls, thereby creating makeshift shelves to store his combat gear. We've nicknamed it "The Fortress of Solitude" and it's where he isolates day and night. It was both endearing and frightful to watch.

I wonder what kind of eccentricities will rear their heads in my new world.

## January 17, 2005

I feel as if I develop a sort of neural constipation when I don't write. I become listless, unfocused, and I want to slap myself in the head for missing those details that could mean so much to me in later years.

So I'm writing again.

At 0730 hours we walked about a half mile across the base to attend our first exit briefings. Naturally the Army had told us to arrive too early. The classes wouldn't begin until 0800, so we stood around, chatted, smoked, and found shade where we could.

The briefings were tedious and devoid of real information. One was a short PowerPoint presentation on how to readjust to civilian life when we return to the United States. They emphasized that this could take some time, that we are different people now and the people we left behind are different as well. Accordingly there are healthy, nonviolent ways to solve any problems that might arise. At the end they gave us a toll-free 1-800 telephone number to call if we ever needed help.

It was hard not to roll my eyes at that.

The JAG gave a briefing as well. It had been tape-recorded by someone who could barely speak English and constantly over-pronounced his s's. He mentioned the elevated divorce rates for returning troops and cautioned us to be watchful of that.

That was enlightening. I promised myself to be on guard.

We attended a medical briefing as well. Doctors interviewed and examined us, then entered our information onto a palm-held device that created what they called a "Smart Card" containing all of our medical information on its tiny microchip.

At least they didn't brand us with a barcode.

The briefings ended around noon. When we filed out of the makeshift auditorium, Gary chuckled at the handprint on my face from leaning on it for practically the entire time.

There's no use writing about it any more; it was so mundane. It was obvious these briefings would be repeated when we got to Ft. Bragg.

We were released to our own whims, and I went to lunch with Derek. When we got back, we discovered it was time to move to another warehouse. So we gathered our stuff as quickly as possible, haphazardly shoving things into our bags, and lugged everything about half a mile to two warehouses down the street. I quickly secured a bottom bunk and set up my cubicle again, using a sheet and my poncho as side walls with a wall locker on one end.

Thus protected and sheltered, I feel much better. My friends are across the way, but I need some distance because I am essentially a solitary creature now. I enjoy people on my terms, not theirs.

I get claustrophobic now when my space is threatened in even the most routine, casual way, my anxiety reaching almost panic levels. Maybe I understand my friend more than I'd care to admit—cases of water bottles or a poncho, it makes no difference.

I think this could be the fourth or fifth warehouse that I've lived in during my tenure at Camp Doha, although I may be wrong. They blend into one another but I have the feeling that this one might be the last.

I am putting my theoretical money on being in Montana by February 16. We've all laid bets on when we are going to be back in the States.

Someone will collect big when the time comes.

### January 18, 2005

I'm finding that I wake up late, usually around 0300, almost every night now. Sometimes it's from a bad dream, a dream with explosions pounding the walls of my skull, sweat breaking on my skin as I awaken with wide eyes and shaking hands. Sometimes it's from a dream of Rita and our life together.

Normally I take a few moments to get my bearings and let the sensations recede. Restless and unable to go back to sleep, I wander outside to watch the stars glittering in the Kuwaiti night. I light a cigarette and revel in the peace of night—it's my favorite time of day now. All is quiet, even in the warehouse, most people sleeping, the occasional snore or shift of a listless body immersed in a dream of home—of green fields or a lover's arms.

A cough breaks the silence as I reach my bunk, pull off my boots, and slip into my sleeping bag, using my laser pen to guide my way. I pull my poncho down from where I tucked it under the edge of the mattress above me, closing the door to my makeshift sanctuary, the left side hanging limply like its partner—a blue bed sheet I had stolen from Anaconda.

I'm sealed in. I feel safe. I have my privacy.

I feel drowsy, yet I can't sleep. My eyes close but soon they open again and I am wide awake. I hear explosions. I feel my bunk rattling. My heart pounds, my breath seizes up, and my eyes search the darkness, frantically attempting to find something solid for my sanity to grasp onto. A moment passes and I realize there were no bombs or explosions. There was no reason to be afraid. It was just another dream. I can hear the silence of Camp Doha. I wipe the sweat on my brow and close my eyes again, hoping not to dream.

The next thing I know it's 0730. The sun has come up. I can hear the shuffle of flip-flops as men make their way to the shower trailers, scraping their way along the sandy concrete floor, fluorescent lighting from the ceiling lamps casting a cold glow upon pale skin. I hear the drowsy mumble of a waking soldier groaning with lack of desire to face another day. Deadpan looks of the lethargic killing time.

I hear the slam of a wall locker door. Life is brewing again, stubborn life, determined to endure the routine of another day, to get coffee, poke around the PX, buy things no one really needs or wants, the falsehoods of external stimulus emptying the spirit.

Who cares, it passes the day.

I sit up and pull my boots on. Hands clasped, forearms between my knees, I gaze vaguely at the floor, images passing before my eyes, my brain flooded with emotion and memory. I muse on the turns my life has made that I never would have dreamed of, the hardships I have endured, the good times, the traveling I have done. Something within me says it will be all right, that I was meant to survive this war, that I was meant to do something better than I had done before. But I am doubtful.

After gathering my necessities, I head to the shower trailer, over the gritty paved rough road and cracked sidewalk, past the leering red and white–striped smokestacks from the nearby power plant forever puking their dark smoke into the veil of Mother Earth, past the twin outdoor basketball courts with no nets, their backboards chipped by time and abuse, past a dilapidated gazebo with peeling white paint that sits at an angle to the rest of the base, the floor planks rotting from pools of water.

I am under a golden, lightly clouded sky, a cool breeze smelling vaguely of sewage and rotten vegetables from the mess hall as I stroll past a high-ranking officer's mud-streaked SUV to the empty concrete lot, a few broken-down trailers in the middle looking lonely in all that space.

I walk up the black grated steel steps of the shower trailer and am greeted by the conflicting stench of day-old shit and shaving cream. The floor is somewhat clean today, someone, probably a Kuwaiti or Filipino worker, has at least attempted to mop. I find a stall with a yellowed shower curtain and soap-stained walls but it's the best of the lot and I'm thankful for it.

I go to relieve myself and find a toilet overflowing with someone else's meditations, discarded toilet paper rolls on the rotting wet linoleum. All the stalls are this way or worse.

Someone's dinner didn't agree with them, evidenced by the smears and stains on the walls and floor. I find a lone toilet in the corner that's seemingly untouched by human foulness. The hunt for a roll of toilet paper begins, and just as I'm beginning to accept that I might have to hold it this morning, I find a scrap on a shelf, just a few sheets but enough to conduct my business.

Turning on the shower, faintly odorous, mildly hot water sprays my tired body with decent pressure. I make sure to close my mouth, a habit from Iraq. To my surprise there is no water bubbling around my ankles today. That brings a wry smile to my face.

Thank God for small miracles.

I scrub vigorously as if I am scrubbing the past away, as if the scrubbing will cleanse me of this life, as if I am dirty in some way beyond the usual day-to-day grime. I want to wash away the stains of the year and something inside me believes that a bar of soap will do it but I'm afraid to close my eyes when I wash my face. I'm afraid that I'll hear the mortars again if I do, that they'll come back and finally get me.

Two other showers come on, sapping my water pressure. Now there's only a forlorn dribble from a sorrowful faucet, just enough to rinse a few inches of my body at a time. I grimace. All pleasures are fleeting here. Just enough to torment you with their momentary embrace. It fuels anger—the stony glaring faces that walk by me every day as I roam Doha, myself glaring back.

Painstakingly, I rinse my body. The water pressure is rapidly decreasing. I'm afraid I'll lose it all together so I rush in the most efficient manner I can. Efficiency and speed are a matter of habit now, routine.

I get the last few drops out of my shower, rubbing them over my body, using every molecule to finish the rinse, and towel off. Lightly padding back to my sanctuary, I change on my bunk, sheet and poncho closed—at last some privacy again.

Soon it's time to complete the morning routine—coffee and a cigarette, probably one of the most satisfying aspects of my day. It's a time to breathe and relax, a few moments of reflection before embarking on the day's duties, whatever they may be.

It's peaceful watching the new day dawn, a few scattered soldiers crossing the streets, SUVs filled with civilian contractors or other more important people driving by on some errand, the sun casting sharp rays on the camp between drifting marshmallow clouds, the warm morning breeze ruffling the leaves of the occasional palm tree, the smell of the sea mingling with the stench of the power plant and open sewers.

There aren't many people out yet as the days often begin late at Camp Doha. My mind bends toward home again while I walk. I imagine the peace of the U.S., the freedom of being a regular Joe again, the warm embrace of loving arms, gentle laughter that floats on the breeze like a melody.

The Starbucks is crowded; it's where everyone seems to be at this hour. I see eager faces, people pushing ahead, crowding one another in their rush to get what they want. Immediate gratification is the American way.

Push away anyone trying to cross the same finish line that

you are. Heedlessly breathe down someone's neck because *you* are what's most important. Talk right in my ear, I don't mind. I always wanted to know about the guy you were dating. It's all about the "me" in America. I'm astonished at some people's behavior yet I do it too.

I get my coffee and stroll back to the warehouse to find everyone awake now, towels slung over makeshift clothes lines, music playing from portable boom boxes. The younger guys are talking about the hot girl they could have had last night at the nightclub on base but they've always a convenient excuse for why they didn't.

Obviously she was a bitch because who could ignore the brilliant one-liner they threw her way? They boast, they brag, tell stories… and lies. Everyone knows they're telling tall tales but it's all a part of the scene and the others smile and go along with it.

I go to my bunk and sit, a dry look of disgust inadvertently creeping across my face as I listen. I've heard it all before and have no desire to hear it again. So I read *Stars and Stripes*[35]and drink my coffee, shaking my head as the news is always grim and my horoscope never makes any sense. George Bush is in hot water again. Uh, oh.

I consider taking a nap. Why not? There's nothing else to do. I have no responsibilities right now and am thankful for that. But I'm so used to being under orders that a restlessness has formed within me that I can't quite explain. I'm just used to the constant

---

35   A daily newspaper serving the United States military community

activity, forever on guard for the unexpected.

I keep listening for the sound of mortars and gunfire but they never come. It's strange, this peaceful quiet. I'm left with a nagging feeling that there must be something I have to attend to. I consider sleeping but know I won't be able to. I only get fleeting bits here and there now— nothing meaningful.

Rest is precious in the military. You learn to take advantage of it at any opportunity, in any spot. Usually you're so exhausted that rest comes easily no matter the circumstances, but not here at Camp Doha. Here rest is not only a privilege, it's almost a right. I lay down, gazing at the steel grate holding the mattress above mine at bay.

I'm interrupted from my daydreaming by Derek rapping on my poncho and asking if I want to go to lunch. Lunch already? Wow, how the time passes when your mind drifts.

I give an apathetic shrug. "Sure."

I haven't really eaten since yesterday afternoon; my appetite just not what it once was. It's partly because the food is so unhealthy, but it's also due to how melancholy I feel.

So I prop myself up and walk with Derek to the mess hall. I get in the line for the main entrée, the same prepackaged, unidentifiable slice of meat. The sauce is supposed to resemble gravy but reminds me more of the stains I saw in the latrine. Canned vegetables are the side, all part of the mass production of feeding thousands. I go looking for my friends, crisscrossing my way through the crowd, my pile of meat steaming in the stuffy air.

As we silently scoop up forks of rice and beef, news headlines roll by on the 37-inch widescreens mounted on the stark walls. We watch images of violence in the world, an analysis of the war effort, and George Bush's latest gaffe—which seems to affect his confidence not at all. He is proud of America's fighting men and women. He's proud we are defending democracy and liberty. We make snide remarks under our breath. We don't care for the dog and pony show any longer.

Everything's provided for, my government once claimed. Your sons and daughters have everything they need to fight the enemy, yet I can't even find a roll of toilet paper in the morning, to say nothing of larger issues such as no armor for our vehicles.

Dinner is a repeat of lunch. You're thankful for another day ending—and frightened of the terrors the night will bring.

After I am finished writing this, I will be struggling to close my eyes, knowing another day has been ticked off the calendar.

I'm frightened because night is when the mortars come in.

Night is when I dream.

I used to love my dreams. Now I'm afraid of them, afraid I'll wake to find that being here was just a dream and that I'm back at Camp Anaconda, in that hell on earth. I'm afraid if I go to sleep, the mortars will begin again, relentlessly marching nearer. It seems as if every night I wake up trembling, eyes wide in the dark, curling up in a ball on my side and rocking back and forth in my sweat until the sounds of explosions leave my rattled skull.

Sometimes I feel like there is something wrong with me.

I don't know what it is but I can feel *something* in me that's growing, blooming. I'm scared because I don't know who I am any more. What is happening to me?

I have to have hope and faith. Hope for a chance to rebuild what I have lost and faith that I'll have the wisdom and courage to do it.

It's the only thing you can cling to when all else fails.

### January 21, 2005

The mission for the day was to convoy the trucks to the shipyards so they could be loaded for the voyage home. Ammunition was scarce due to most of us dumping it in an amnesty box when we arrived at Camp Doha. What was left was split up, some of us ending up with a mere few rounds, five at most. Everyone was saying "Make it count—one shot, one kill" that morning. We were all very concerned about this situation considering there had been a few attacks as of late.

Kuwait *does* have its dangers. Although it's nothing compared to Iraq, there are insurgent forces in this country and I won't let my guard down. But five rounds or so is what we had to work with.

Sarcasm, that ever-present defense mechanism soldiers use when they know they are being short-changed, set the tone for yet another excursion upon the highways and byways of this corner of the Middle East.

Shortly before 1000 we were guided out of the yard by the

civilian workers and hit the highway for the 45-minute ride along the coast to the shipyards, each of us hoping to avoid an encounter with insurgents.

We drove at an average of 40 mph. The ride was slow and uneventful. I remembered the "old days" in Kuwait, the smokestacks eternally burning, the endless maze of piping and steel stairways, the barbed-wire fences, and stark red signs forbidding photography ominously protecting the precious black gold that is Kuwait's only real claim to prosperity.

We drove past the Department Of Oil Protection building sheltered by a grove of palm trees, down the narrow roads, and past the numerous checkpoints until we finally reached a gravel parking lot, the grey hulks of ships, including one American battleship in the near distance.

I must say, I was impressed with the battleship. It was impossibly big. Obviously not as large as a carrier but impressive nonetheless. A mighty symbol of American power, its guns, antennas, bridge, and hull all combining to lend a very imposing presence to anyone unfortunate enough to get in its way.

The lot was full of other trucks, some tan, some green—all camouflaged—impossible to estimate the number, rows upon rows of the wheeled Army war machine lined up for their turn to be hoisted into the vast holds of even vaster ships. There were trucks of all variety and shapes and trailers of every sort. There were even tanks, muzzles plugged by large funny-looking caps. Navy personnel in reflective vests and hard hats scampered every which way, each one on some important errand fueled by caffeine and an innate sense of urgency.

Then we waited again, engines idling until we were directed by the workers to form two rows. We found our spots, parked, and milled about at the end of the lot, wondering where lunch was—we'd had little to eat this morning.

Eventually we were allowed to go over to the yard mess hall and had a very bland lunch of pork chops and scalloped potatoes served on the usual plastic plates. Whoever supplies those plates must be making a fortune—they have a monopoly, that's for sure.

Then two buses came to transport us back to Camp Doha, the drivers blaring Arabian music, the melodic crooning of a woman serenading my ears. I fell asleep, waking only when we arrived. The day was done; it was 1500. Weapons turn-in was at 1700, dinner at 1800.

Our job is done now. There is nothing more to do except twiddle our thumbs and grow more restless by the hour. Even the officers admit it and leave us alone—a wonder and a gift. People sleep constantly. Video game gunfire pierces the bay walls. Movies intermingle with one another, combining in a grotesque conglomeration of sounds and dialogue. People stay out late, prowling for some sort of excitement, something or someone to help pass the time, wild looks of expectation just behind eyes dulled by boredom and a year of bullshit.

We're so close I can taste it. Sweet impending freedom is bursting on my taste buds like the vanilla shake I just bought at the Baskin Robbins here on base. I can hardly believe such luxuries exist—my mind is still adjusting to the fact that civilization is real, that I'm not in Iraq any more. It all feels foreign to me now.

It's a new world.

I feel as though a paradigm shift is taking place within me, a whole new world is opening up. It's a world filled with violence, anger, killing, greed, corruption, and betrayal—human beings at their worst. But it's also a world of wonder, of the smallest of luxuries such as ice cream, a quiet night, of being clean… of being alive.

My eyes have been opened and it's impossible to close them again. Does every person who has experienced war feel this way? I know I was blessed with things in life I have overlooked, things I dismissed because I was complacent enough to think they would always be there for me. I won't do that any more.

Talk of when we are actually going home touches every conversation at some point or another. I understand the official word is February 16. Then again, I've also heard it might be February 8. I've heard that's what our superiors are pushing for—they're anxious as well—but the latest buzz is that it's February 5.

I saw on the news that George Bush was inaugurated again. I caught some footage of him in his tuxedo dancing with his wife at a glitzy multimillion-dollar party they threw complete with champagne and plate upon plate of all the gourmet food they could eat.

I heard that Anaconda got hit really hard with mortars

yesterday. They're thinking of closing down the mess hall and living off the MREs they have on base.

**January 25, 2005**

At formation this morning, we were told that we are scheduled to leave Kuwait on February 8. Two more weeks here and we are done. The plan is as follows: There is an advance party leaving ahead of us on February 2 that includes all the officers and most of the higher enlisted ranks—the bottom of the barrel, myself included, will be left behind. On the eighth, the rest of us will fly to Germany or Ireland via the military's charter company and then take another flight across the big pond to Ft. Bragg. After we're demobilized—which should take about four days or so—those of us going to Montana will take another plane to Helena where this journey will finally conclude.

Isn't it amazing?

Now that the time is rapidly approaching, I almost don't know what to do with myself. I fear that as the time grows ever closer I will become progressively more antsy. I have to discipline myself to remain calm and not become irritable simply because I'm impatient. Our exodus will come in due time just like everything else in life.

It seems like it's been so *long*. So much has happened. I scarcely remember what the U.S. looks like. I still feel as if I'm having a bit of separation anxiety from this place, from war, from my prison for a year. I suppose I'll try to ease into this process the best I can and I can't help but speculate what will happen when I am home in Montana and wondering what to do with myself.

We were also issued our rifles at 1000. At noon we were sent to another warehouse to put them in an industrial bath, a huge washer of sorts that supposedly works pretty well. But when we got to the cleaning warehouse, we discovered that only half of us could clean our rifles as it was only equipped to handle a few at a time. So, most of us trickled back to our living quarters to come back another time, perhaps later in the afternoon, to accomplish our task. I'm pretty sure I will have to go back tomorrow to finish, but it should all get done eventually.

Derek admitted to me today, in a rather pained tone, that he hates everyone around him. I found myself empathizing with him although I was a bit surprised by his outburst.

We're all just plain sick of each other and want nothing more to do with this disgusting business. I'm not entirely sure how to reconcile this feeling yet as it is completely contradictory to the propaganda that there is no greater bond than between those who have lived through a war together. It goes against everything I was brought up to believe in since I was a child playing "war games" in the back woods of my parents' house with my friends. We had air rifles and baseball hats for helmets. We scarcely knew the real-life consequences of what we were playing at when we plotted to overrun the enemy hiding behind a tree.

I guess the reality is that everyone's experience in war is different and mine will always be different from any other combat veteran's experience.

Tomorrow I'll try to clean my rifle again. We'll see how it goes.

### January 26, 2005

So the latest and the greatest is we are now leaving on February 9 with the 10th through the 13th as back-up dates if anything happens.

I managed to make it to the rifle cleaning facility. There were these three large cylindrical containers standing upright and opening vertically with two huge doors. Inside were two circular metal grated racks with a pole.

We were instructed to completely disassemble our rifles and safety-wire the main components together, with the exception of the smallest pieces and the softer plastic ones, and put them on the grated shelves inside the tank. Then we sprayed them with a lubricant and the doors were closed so the great machines could go to work.

About 20 minutes later the parts were cleaned and lightly oiled. We had to wear protective gloves to pull them out because they were so hot. While these parts were in the machine, we hand-cleaned the smaller, more sensitive parts. When the process was finished, we wiped everything down with clean cloths, dried the parts with compressed air, and reassembled our rifles.

And that was that—rifle cleaning finished. It gave us something to do for a while.

**January 29, 2005**

Life tends to be easier when you accept that you're a mere twig floating on the currents of time and destiny. Throughout hardship and strife, it's encouraging to have faith that they will ultimately carry you to where you need to be and instead of fighting the inexorable stream, you begin to revel in everything that comes your way for their own unique lessons, truths, insights, and overall pleasure no matter how brutally they're presented.

If you don't accept this concept, it seems that all too often you end up hurting yourself. Worse, you could hurt others due to your own confusion and angst and I believe you have to find an inner tranquility that only comes when you allow time and destiny, perhaps a higher power, to guide you. The unexpected surprises that enter your life could reward in ways you might never have imagined.

So I am going to be patient and revel in the fact that I'm still breathing and alive. I've been so convinced I was going to die, even *wanting* to die, that I can hardly begin to comprehend what it means to actually live again.

I'm constantly astounded by how fresh everything can be— the colors, the smells, the sounds. It's as if I have come out from a long black tunnel and am suddenly blinded by sunlight. I can begin the process of rebuilding myself with a stronger, clearer vision of what I would ultimately like to be.

So much has changed. But change doesn't always have to be shied away from. Sometimes change can be a good thing.

Sometimes, it can be your savior.

Change can be feared, at times with ferocious, damaging energy, but I think it's important to keep in mind that change sometimes doesn't present its benefits until long after the fact, instead preferring with some mystical wisdom to hold out until the appropriate time. And when the benefits of change finally do become apparent, we often have a much greater appreciation for the lessons we were meant to absorb.

Perhaps that's the way it's supposed to work, that the meaning would be lost if it didn't. Sometimes it's hard to have faith but I've found that acceptance is a golden key to healing and growing.

When life is sweet, we all revel in it. When it's bitter, we stagger under its weight. But overall life is wonderful. It's ever-changing with challenge and it can bring joys such as we've never seen before. It's pretty damn cool when you think about it that way, how you can be propelled into experiences you never dreamed possible, wondrous experiences that you'll treasure for the rest of your life.

Then again, what do I know?

I truly hope you find happiness Rita. For a long, long time I wished it could be with me. Now I accept that it wasn't meant to be. Find yourself my old, sweet darling. Find yourself and know I was happy to be a part of your life. You will always be in my heart and I don't want to lose that. We may have been hurt and resentful, but I know there will come a day when I'll look back and appreciate the gifts we gave each other during our time.

I will always love you.

**January 31, 2005**

We had a meeting today. The officers (our demobilization team) called us all together in the auditorium.

On February 2 the last remaining members of our company (there's only five or seven left at Camp Anaconda, including Capt. Davis) are supposed to fly down to Camp Doha.

On February 9 we are supposed to fly to Ft. Bragg, but they're leaving a three-day window in case of an unexpected change. We were told that demobilizing at Ft. Bragg should take about five to seven days of medical examinations, finance briefings, what they call "readjustment briefings," and the like.

Then we fly home. Whether by commercial or military is still up in the air, the details to be worked out during our stay at Ft. Bragg. Most of us are betting on being home by February 17 and I believe that's a safe bet. That's where my money is.

When we arrive home in Montana, the 38 of us Montanans will have about two or three days of demobilizing in Helena to look forward to, consisting mainly of turning in our gear and more briefings. I've been told that Capt. Davis wants to release everyone as quickly as possible. I have confidence in him. He is a solid, smart officer with the best of intentions for the men under his charge and he's always been the real leader of our small group from the great white north.

I've also been told the state of Montana is paying for us to stay in a hotel in Helena, something I find gratifying. And Capt. Davis wants to bypass the whole formation ceremony crap when we get off the plane, which I find even more gratifying.

So there you have it.

So much for Iraq.

So much for Kuwait.

So much for the war.

It almost seems anticlimactic.

### February 27, 2005

I flew into Montana on February 18—losing my bet by a day—my deployment over except for gladly turning in any property of the state and sitting through briefings on how to appropriately handle ourselves as we reintegrate back into a normal life.

We spent the first part of February sitting in Camp Doha bored to virtual tears. At times it seemed like pure anguish, the days wasted with nothing to do but wait and think. They say the last few minutes of a wait are the worst and they are right.

I think all of us at one time or another wanted to jump out of our skins with impatience. I remember lying in my bunk, staring at the flat grey paint on the springs above me and feeling the minutes tick by like hours, wondering if the day would ever actually come.

But it did.

It was around February 11 when we actually boarded a plane to leave Kuwait. I looked out the window of the aircraft as we climbed in altitude, approaching the Persian Gulf, banking steeply, and turning north as we headed for Europe.

Silently saying a final good-bye to that region of the world where my life had changed so radically, I settled back in my seat and closed my eyes.

As usual, I slept a lot on the flight, only opening my eyes for a meal or to watch the west coast of Italy, the famous "boot" peninsula so prominent, serenely drifting by from 30,000 feet. After flying for what seemed like days we landed in Ft. Bragg.

I don't recall very much of Ft. Bragg. Much of it was spent waiting and enduring more briefings but eventually we, the Montana contingent, were able to hitch a ride on a Montana Air National Guard KC-135[36]out of Great Falls that just happened to be in the area.

We clambered aboard with our gear, relieved that the last leg of our adventure was coming to a close. I sat in the cockpit for a while during the flight, at times making casual conversation with the pilots as they checked their instruments, but as the now unfamiliar scenery of the Midwest drifted by, I became silent. I watched as the snow-capped peaks of the Rocky Mountains came into view... and with them... a new adventure.

---

36    A military aerial refueling aircraft

# Epilogue

# Aftershock

*If the present world go astray, the cause is in you,*
*in you it is to be sought.*

—Dante Alighieri, *The Divine Comedy*

DISEMBARKING FROM THE PLANE IN Montana, we were greeted by celebrations, banners, cheers, and music. Families were waiting and there were plenty of happy tears, warm embraces, and welcomes. For me, as I wandered the tarmac alone, it all seemed hollow and empty. I found myself oddly out of my skin, eerily without emotion, strangely without form as the world closed in on me.

I shook hands, looked into the faces I knew from the Montana National Guard (the ones who had stayed behind), and they now seemed unfamiliar. I felt a deep sense of disconnection, the eyes of people I had known, no matter how well, seeming remote, even alien. I don't remember much after that, only vague images and flashes that are difficult to grasp to this day. That was the beginning—my first real sense of not feeling normal.

Being homeless with nowhere to go, I began living out of my sleeping bag on the concrete garage floor of a couple Rita and I had known, the only people kind enough to help me. As I lay there on the concrete, huddled in my sleeping bag night after night, constantly turning the events of Iraq and my divorce over in my head, the profound gravity of the losses I had experienced began to sink into me.

With each passing day I became more and more convinced that I had lost not only my wife, house, car, job, cat, and savings but my morals, judgment, and beliefs—my very soul. I had been abandoned to reconstruct some semblance of a life on my own, to sweep up the rubble from the blast of Iraq. I felt as if I was standing in an empty field with a solitary brick, a brick that could help rebuild my life but with no guidance as to how or where to lay the first foundational cornerstone. It was agonizing. I had nowhere to turn, no one to talk to.

It began to dawn on me that the real battle I would have to face would be readjusting to life in the United States. I also began to realize I had contracted a healthy dose of post-traumatic stress, otherwise known as PTSD. I found myself besieged with a number of symptoms, emotions, and after effects of the Iraq War, some of which I had little comprehension of how to rationally handle.

It made my head spin, a jumbled mess that seemed impossible to untangle, and the Army hadn't adequately prepared us for what we would have to deal with. I'm not convinced that *anyone* could have, but my government's paltry effort was almost as pathetic as the war itself. It's no wonder to me now why so many veterans have so much trouble when they come home.

The symptoms manifested themselves slowly over a period of a couple of months. They began to emerge through my actions and thoughts, sometimes subtly, sometimes with such volatile force that I could hardly control them. They would sneak up on me, blindsiding me like being unexpectedly tumbled by a wave in the ocean. And when the wave had washed me up on the beach, I was dazed, with no idea which way was up or down.

It was often only then that I realized I had just passed through another "wave" of PTSD. Sometimes I couldn't remember what I had done during the wave, as if I had left my body, entered a dream state, and only when the wave receded did I reawake to everyday reality. It often took days to fully recover only to be triggered by something and get slammed by another wave. It seemed relentless and never-ending.

The turbulence of depression, anxiety, hyper vigilance, suicidal ideation, recurring nightmares, rage, isolation, detachment, survivor guilt, difficulty relating to even those closest to me, and the loss of interest in things I had previously loved coursed within me as if they were in my very blood.

Nothing made sense to me any more.

Because I felt so odd, so out of body, so out of joint, I began to withdraw and isolate myself. When I did emerge from the garage, I would often feel exasperated by a conversation with a person because they seemed to have no idea how to relate to me—my ideologies and the way of life I had acquainted myself with in Iraq—nor could I relate to them and their own worries. Worse, I found I had no idea how to relate to civilian life in general.

Sometimes I felt so filled with anxiety that anytime a person came near me I felt physically uncomfortable, even threatened. I felt as if I had to continually look over my shoulder, always waiting for something dangerous or bad to happen. It was overwhelming and similar to the same claustrophobic feeling that I had developed in Iraq.

Rage would often surge through me. I found myself ready to explode at the merest whim, triggering a further need to isolate, to not hurt others with some spontaneous outburst I knew I would surely regret later. It happened one night a few months later when I was living with Beth, a woman I have known for 20 years. We had been friends since childhood, but at the time, I was vainly trying to have a healthy intimate relationship with her. I remember the night fairly well, although I don't remember exactly what caused me to detonate with such volatility.

I had been drinking and Beth had said something that upset me for some reason. It sent me into a self-loathing rage, a self-deprecating rant that quickly escalated out of control. I remember feeling as if no one understood the pain I was in. I felt I was a lowlife, a loser with no hope of redemption or happiness. Iraq had taken my soul, my moral fiber, parts vital to my existence that were never coming back.

I blamed myself for the dissolution of my marriage. I thought I had failed miserably at being who Rita wanted me to be and therefore had failed as a person. I had let her down because I was never as successful as she wanted. I felt hopeless, helpless against the onslaught of the tattered remains of my life. I remember screaming at Beth that it was entirely my fault and there was no hope. I picked up a lounge chair and threw it across the living room, missing her by a few inches.

The next thing I remember there was a knock on the door and I found myself in the hands of the police. They were kind to me, however, knowing I was recently home from Iraq, and allowed me the time to cool off and reflect upon my actions. The matter was settled and I was allowed to go home, but the damage had been done. Our relationship suffered greatly from that point on although we did manage to hang in there a while longer, mostly due to commitment, but over time we drifted away from each other and no longer speak.

I found myself turning more and more to alcohol as a means to soothe my soul, as a means of escape and self-medication— just to be able to look at myself. Week after week, for years in fact, I would spend endless days doing nothing but downing the largest bottle of vodka I could find in the liquor store, often beginning the morning with a drink and continuing until two in the morning.

I felt as if it was the only way to deaden the raw nerves of my warped brain. They burned with visions of Iraq, of the memories, sounds, and smells of the desert, of Rita and my previous life. Even a helicopter flying overhead was enough to trigger a memory of Iraq, plunging me back into the war, the present world literally disappearing for minutes at a time, the chop of the rotor blades echoing in my ears as I broke out in a sweat, rocked back and forth, and swallowed another shot of vodka. It felt as if I had left part of my soul in the desert, as if I was not a complete person any more and as a result was floating in an endless void of sorrow, a netherworld of jumbled emotions.

It's strange how alien you can seem when you look in the mirror in the morning. Most days I didn't recognize that it was actually me staring back. I vacantly watched myself as I tried to go about my day—an eerie out-of-body experience. I had no idea what was happening to me. I felt as if I was on a distant planet when I tried to relate to people, desperately screaming for a voice only to find a void—a hollow feeling that pervaded every molecule of my body and soul.

There's just no way to adequately describe the feeling.

I remember when I went to pick up my remaining belongings from Rita—the things she deemed were mine. She had saved my books, some clothes, and a few other trinkets for me. I remember stepping into her new house and seeing all of *our* belongings—the furniture, our laptop, the entertainment center housing the television we had bought, the paintings, the decorations—things she now claimed were her own—and it felt completely foreign to me. If I remembered using a frying pan or sitting at our dining table, the *feeling* of me actually living those memories was beyond reach. It was as if those memories were someone else's memories. It was as if my memories were a film of someone else's life.

I began to feel a need to connect with my past in some way, partly due to nostalgia but mostly in a desperate attempt to ground myself and find something tangible to tie my sanity to. I had always felt a deep fondness for our friends and wanted to know how their lives were progressing. For years we had spent significant time together, throwing dinner parties, spending nights grilling and drinking, and sharing our joys and concerns. Connecting with them would have helped me feel human again. It would have helped me realize that my previous life hadn't been just a dream.

I remember driving out to Idaho to see a couple Rita and I had known for years. I called ahead of course, and they welcomed me into their home but within ten minutes they claimed they were busy. I was welcome to stay but they wouldn't be back for quite some time. I felt abandoned, betrayed, and I promptly left.

I've never seen them since.

Another time I was pulling out of my friend's driveway to go for coffee (I *did* get the remaining car), the friend in whose garage I was staying. It was a couple of weeks after returning home and I happened to see Rita's brother driving by. I recognized him instantly as we had spent so much time together, hiking, bowling, dinners at Rita's parents' house. I was elated to see him, again wanting to connect with someone whom I had known who could perhaps, through no will of their own, help ground me. I drove after him and at the next stop sign, rolled down my window, waved, and honked my horn. He looked into his rear-view mirror and then, much to my horror, gunned his engine and rapidly sped away. I was left sitting there bewildered, hurt, and abandoned.

I won't lie and say that the pain I've experienced hasn't almost driven me to the point of losing it completely and wanting to end it all. I obviously haven't ended my life, but the thought was ever-present.

I have survived two suicide attempts, the latter in 2008. It landed me in the hospital, handcuffed and drunk, ranting and raving about how pathetic my life was. I would have welcomed death compared to the hell I was living in. The pain was too much to bear.

I felt utter despair.

Despair had led to helplessness, a feeling of hopelessness compelling me to load a pistol. I stared at it for hours while drinking martinis and contemplating what it would be like to blow my head off. I felt as if I was beyond hope of ever being human again. I had texted Beth of my intent and she called the police, but the real savior that night was my cat. I remember him looking at me, wondering when he was going to get a good belly scratch or his next treat.

I was filled with a vivid image of the shot going off, him being startled by the blast then returning to me, sniffing my dead body, perhaps even sniffing my blood splattered over the couch. I began to wonder what it would be like for him to be suddenly homeless and abandoned like I was. He would be subjected to the whims of some authority, taken out of his loving life, and away from his father.

It was at that moment when I put the gun down.

I did it for him, not myself. Because he deserved better. I had an obligation to care for him, to be his dad. Once that sense of responsibility kicked in, I realized it would be selfish to take my life. Ironically that's when the police arrived but maybe it was for the best, for I could've been willing to change my mind.

I guess we get caught up in these messes before we realize what's happening. While in Iraq, I had realized my folly and things began to crumble under their own weight. I learned how twisted and lost we can become while completely absorbed by a failing relationship. I learned how violent people can be, how terrible war is no matter how much it is glamorized in the movies or political propaganda.

The feelings I had were so intense. Some might call me dramatic, some might shrug it off, but I remember praying to myself in Iraq that when I went home I would have some shred of humanity left. Some of that prayer came true, but my soul was beaten almost to the point of no return.

I remember the first time I summoned the guts to reread my journals. It took three years, even longer to find the courage to write this manuscript, and as I thumbed through them I was amazed at how intense the experience was. But I was dismayed at how little I could remember or feel. Why? Have I blocked out those memories?

I do remember some things. The day I was shot at. The man I aimed my rifle at. The mortar that flew over my head. The day the PX was bombed. The smell of the desert and what my shop looked like. But these are only snapshots, not a narrative, and if I hadn't chronicled the experience I'm not sure I would have anything solid to convince me that I was really there.

Even now, years later, I am still struck by my tremendous sense of detachment from the experience. It just doesn't seem real, that it was actually me who frantically scribbled on those pages. It's as if I am reading someone else's story and when I look at pictures of myself from the past I'm continually overwhelmed by how I can't identify with that person. I don't feel like a veteran, I don't feel like a divorcee, and this feeling of detachment from my own life has been one of the most troubling aspects of living with the consequences of Iraq. It's as if a circuit in my brain has been unplugged and there is no way to plug it back in. That, coupled with being exposed to shadowy parts of yourself you never knew existed, is enough to turn anyone upside down.

I remember when I was driving through Baghdad and I aimed my rifle at that man on the side of the street. To this day, I can vividly recall his eyes—I don't think I'll ever forget them. I was ready to kill him. All it would have taken was the smallest move of my finger and the trigger would have been pulled. After a time, it began to dawn on me just how frightening that mindset was and still is.

I became afraid of myself.

That can be one of the most traumatic things for veterans to deal with—the realization that you are perfectly capable of killing. It's like discovering a demon within yourself. It's even more troubling when you realize *every* person might have this beast inside them. It only takes a certain situation, whatever that might be, to transform a once pretty easy going person into a killer.

That realization is often difficult to reconcile. I think it's one reason why veterans tend to isolate. For me, it just felt better if I stayed away from other people now that I'm aware of what I'm capable. Naturally this fear of myself was enhanced when I came home and slowly discovered myself behaving in even more unfamiliar ways.

When I threw that chair at Beth, I was not the person I had known. I had never behaved like that before in my entire life. It's scary when you see yourself doing these things and you realize how little self-control you have. What was invading my psyche and compelling me to act out in ways I could never have imagined before the war?

At the time, I took on the entire blame for the destruction of my marriage and the situation I had found myself in. I was the one who had allowed myself to be deployed to Iraq and was forced to face aspects of myself I didn't want to recognize or even know existed. I was the one who had been turned into a potential killer poisoned with spite and anger. I saw myself as an utter failure, which in turn led to profound feelings of despair, self-deprecation, and a fear that I was unworthy of any sort of compassion, love, tenderness, or forgiveness. The combined weight and intensity of these emotions are what ultimately led to my suicide attempt.

Perhaps I don't have a right to complain. I didn't see any real, heavy combat, the kind you read about in magazines or news articles or see on the nightly news, the kind that earns Purple Hearts, Medals of Honor, or Silver Stars. Perhaps I don't have a right to complain about my woes because I *did* come home with all my limbs intact. I will never have to face the burden of my sacrifice every time I attempt to walk or pick up a pen or even write this manuscript. You could say I'm one of the lucky ones, but I don't think anyone is lucky in war.

Shortly after my suicide attempt, I remember waking up one day and staring at myself in the mirror for what seemed like hours. My heart began to race, sweat broke out on my brow and I realized that my suicide attempt had brought me to my knees, emotionally and spiritually. I knew that I would end up permanently broken if I didn't do something and as the day wore on I began to feel an insistent desire to reconnect with my past, my folks, to begin afresh. So in the summer of 2009, I decided to come home to New England where I spent my childhood. I felt that moving might help me feel more normal, help me reconstruct my identity and find some solid ground on which to rebuild my life. So I packed up my belongings and spent four days on the road driving to New England to begin a new life.

It was the best decision I've ever made. Since coming home, I have embarked on a whole new set of adventures, learning quite a bit about myself along the way. I have met people who are compassionate, engaging, and thought-provoking, people who appreciate and love me without judgment; people I can share myself with without reservation, who respect me for my experiences and insights. I can only hope to do the same for them.

I have begun studying music and am becoming an accomplished guitar player, fulfilling a dream I've had since I was a child listening to old blues and rock 'n roll tunes on my record player. I have created a garden in my backyard, spending hours tilling and planting little seeds and watching my plants grow. It thrills my soul to nurture them to maturity, taking great care with their welfare and they in turn have provided nourishment for my soul and body. I cannot describe the thrill of plucking a pound of pesticide-free zucchini and cooking a fantastic dinner for myself. In fact, cooking has become a favorite pastime and much to my delight, I've discovered I'm quite good at it.

I've seen a counselor at my local Vet Center regularly since I came home and we have built quite a friendship and rapport, being kindred spirits and Iraq veterans. Through patience, understanding, and support, my counselor has guided me, fostered my internal growth, and helped me to realize that I am not hopeless, that I am not a loser, not worthless, that there is something within me worth having around, worth embracing and loving—a novel concept still new to me but one with which I am slowly but surely coming to terms.

We go to Red Sox games together, ride our mountain bikes all over New England, and find mutual support with each other. I've found comfort that there are people in the world who feel the same as I do.

They are my kin, my brothers and sisters.

They are veterans.

As I look around my house now, what I've created, a comfortable home filled with my life, memories, travels, and experiences, I realize that I'm very different from that raging pain-consumed alcoholic teetering on the brink of either suicide or insanity five years ago. I've realized everything in life is transitory, that Rita and I were meant to be transitory. For a brief moment in time we were meant to learn from each other and enhance and broaden our lives from a shared experience.

I've learned that life itself is a perpetual driver of change. At some point I'll tear everything down again and build something new. It's not unlike when winter is on the run and spring is breathing down its neck, beckoning for a fresh start. I think the real trick is to be comfortable with that and we must realize that we too are cyclical. If we miss part of the cycle, we're missing out on our lives as they were meant to be. We'd be missing valuable lessons about life and there is always something new to learn.

I've learned that the present is the only thing that truly matters. The past is of value to the extent that it brings us to any given point in life; it exists for us to grow upon. And the future will never be known, there are just too many variables. Given this, moments are how we should concentrate on shaping ourselves and treasuring our worlds. I knew this in Iraq but it took me quite a while to fully integrate this way of thinking, years of abusing my body, my mind, culminating in my suicide attempt, and finally making a drastic change. Now, I'm no longer afraid to die nor am I afraid to live or love myself.

I've often found it ironic that violence, war, and fear of death could ultimately conclude with me living in peace, love, and openness. I've found that by doing this, my demons are being chased away, that the darkness that held my heart for far too long is turning into light. I believe that is God's way of showing me that I've never been truly abandoned or betrayed, that I have always had a companion who loves me. Sometimes tragedy can bring a gift and I've been given a spiritual one.

I'm also beginning to learn that my participation in Iraq isn't something to be ashamed of. While preparing to go overseas, I had the opportunity to file for conscientious objection status and stay in the United States. I had a chance to stand for my value system—my abhorrence of violence, my repulsion for warfare and the effort of killing. But when I overheard that conversation between the command sergeant major and the warrant officer who notified me of the deployment, I realized it wasn't that simple.

In an instant, I was torn in half. I realized that raising my right hand and taking the oath of enlistment as every service member is required meant much more than defending my country against all enemies foreign and domestic. It meant more than bearing true faith and allegiance to the same. It meant more than obeying the orders of the president of the United States and my officers. It meant that when you give your word to something, when you raise your right hand and take an oath, you must uphold it, if for nothing else than to serve alongside the people who make the sacrifices of war.

Within two minutes, I realized there was no choice—I had to go. I had to go, not for me, not for my president, not for the war effort, not for the citizens of the United States, but for the people who would be deployed. As I told my friend and counselor one day in his office as we were discussing the senselessness of the Iraq War, "There was honor in honoring them." I committed myself to upholding that honor.

By standing by the men and women who were going I made

the biggest sacrifice of my life. I lost everything—my marriage, my home, my belongings, my friends, my career, my car, a cat I dearly loved, even to a large extent my value system. But it was the right thing to do and regardless of the consequences, I accept what happened. I've realized that my integrity ultimately would never have allowed me to do anything different.

I raised my hand. I took a vow. And Iraq devastated my life.

But that devastation is nothing compared to how I would have looked at myself in the mirror for the rest of my life if I hadn't gone. With that knowledge, I rest more easily when I think of that terrible year in Iraq.

As for Rita and me, these days I no longer care to debate about who was more to blame or who caused more damage to our relationship. The simple fact is we were young, we tried, but it didn't work out the way we had hoped. I guess sometimes the best intentions don't always produce the best results. In the end, we both drew our lines in the sand—her through action, me in my mind. We had matured and in the process had defined what our boundaries were within an intimate relationship. Tragically, we found those boundaries to be incompatible and were forced to separate. Iraq was merely the catalyst.

But she was a tremendous influence in my life, an influence I feel to this day, and I have much to be thankful for no matter how destructive our relationship ultimately became. Regardless of how much we might have hurt each other, I refuse to cling to hard feelings instead preferring acceptance and forgiveness for both of us. In some form I will always love her, if for nothing else than for the wonderful years we spent together, traveling, exploring, experimenting, and learning from each other. I don't feel that those experiences were a waste of time. They were a gift and they helped form who I am today. I couldn't be more thankful for that.

What I've ultimately realized is that my perspective has changed. I've undergone a gradual paradigm shift with regard to how I view myself, of what transpired in Iraq, and even my relationship with Rita. Destructive self-blame has shifted into an ownership of my choices and thereby an ownership of myself. By accepting that responsibility I have reclaimed power over my life. Now I own the choices I've made not with self-blame, but in a positive way that's allowed me to realize I can love and not live in fear of this world, of myself, of my sense of inadequacy, worthiness, or helplessness, a way that's both liberating and empowering.

To this day, I continue to grapple with the effects of post-traumatic stress including anxiety in public places, isolative tendencies, hyper vigilance, even flashbacks. It's still a struggle to blend the personality of my previous self with the person who was formed in the combat theater, the person who I see in the mirror today, and I often don't fully understand or even remember who each of those personalities may be at any given time.

It can be very confusing and I think it's important for people to understand that an actual physiological change takes place within the body during prolonged exposure, or even an isolated incident, to trauma. It essentially "rewrites" a person's thought processes and neural chemistry.

You're never the same.

Because of this physiological change, the symptoms of post-traumatic stress endure. It can often be nearly impossible to rewrite the body yet again—to go back to who you were. Given this, the only way forward for survivors of trauma is to learn how to cope with their new wiring. It's imperative to integrate their new way of thinking and behaving in a productive way.

All this sounds straight forward and logical... but it's *hard*. It's no wonder that it takes veterans years to reconcile their war experiences. It takes a tremendous amount of time for the body to adjust and for the mind to understand what has happened. Time and support from the people around them are the keys to a successful life living with trauma. Most veterans I have met struggle daily and often feel "separated" from people, misunderstood, even shunned and abandoned by people they felt they could trust and look to for support. As a result, veterans often find themselves alone to deal with issues that no one has any solid answers for.

Until I moved back to New England, I was one such veteran. I've stared into the abyss of despair my experiences have generated. I've spent ten years grappling with the effects of PTSD. But I'm also confident there is a way back from the experience of war. There *is* a way to live with trauma. There *is* a way to find the light at the end of the tunnel. There *is* something worth living for and that life can be grand if we allow it in.

My body was tested, my mind was tested, my life was tested, and I still have a long way to go. The wounds of that year in Iraq haven't quite scarred over, even after ten years. But I am confident that I'm in a better place now and forward motion has been a friend of mine. I couldn't be more thankful.

I feel the enormity of all the decisions I've made, the weight of the years on my shoulders. All the places I've been, people I've known, and things I've experienced have moved me, inspired me, saddened and maddened me, and occasionally conspired against me. Yet I still find myself in awe of my life—of life itself.

Every moment matters.

Every sensation is important in its own right.

Every flower has a right to bloom.

I write my stories, I play my guitar, and I tend my garden.

I smile and I think, "Whew. What a journey… and it ain't over yet."

I'm in Hog Heaven… or so we said in Iraq.

# LINES IN THE SAND

*The darkest places in hell are reserved for those who maintain their neutrality in times of moral crisis.*

—Dante Alighieri, *The Divine Comedy*

I FELT COMPELLED TO SPEAK my mind when I came home from Iraq, to stand up for what was left of the tattered remains of my values. I knew beyond certainty that if I didn't I would be betraying what was left of my shredded soul.

I submitted the paperwork for conscientious objection status within two weeks of coming home. On July 20, 2005, I was honorably discharged under Army Regulation 600-43. When I was given the official notice of my discharge I felt as if I had struck a victory for my soul, as if I finally had a voice. It was a relief to express my wholehearted disagreement. It was invigorating, and I took it one step further.

I joined Iraq Veterans Against the War, a nonprofit organization dedicated to promoting peace and why we feel that the Iraq War was unjust, propagandized, and a tragedy for the American people. I soon found myself in Texas and connected with my fellow members who were also protesting. Our goal was to attempt to hold George W. Bush accountable for his actions, for what we felt were crimes against the citizens of the United States, against the families and soldiers who suffered the violence of a senseless war.

We spoke out about why the Iraq War was not only a waste of time, money, and resources, but wasted the potential of those who were devastated while they served. As a result I spent most of my time during the summer of 2005 participating in photo shoots and media interviews to speak about why war is inherently wrong, about why the Iraq War was unjust and served only a privileged few.

The summer eventually waned and I found it was time to concentrate on rebuilding my own life. It would ultimately end up being a long road, but one I have stubbornly walked, no matter how many times I have stumbled. In the process, I've discovered that life is just as much about failure as it is about success. They stroll hand in hand and you have to reconcile the two to find some inner peace.

I realized that nothing is permanent. Life is fleeting, precarious, often balanced on pure luck or random chance. That, as much as anything else, has allowed me the freedom to experience an appreciation for life in its unparalleled incredible magnitude. But it also made me acutely aware of how fast it can be taken away. We should be reveling in every moment of it regardless of our differences in race, gender, creed, politics, or religion.

For a long time I was convinced that people were nothing more than dangerous beasts under a thin veneer of civilization. I was resolved to living in a world of ridiculous vanity and shameful violence. But slowly my worldview began to change again. Out of the blue, I would see an act of kindness that moved me. Or I would see something beautiful that made me smile, like the hawk that enjoys visiting my backyard. These experiences began to shake my resolve that everything was hateful, spiteful, angry, or violent.

Are these signs? Are they miracles?

I don't know, but it's a reminder to me that there is both good and bad in the world. Again, they stroll hand in hand. We can get so wrapped up in our own life's bubbles that sometimes it can be difficult to see the grandeur and poignancy of the wide world outside them.

I don't have all the answers. Hell, I don't even have all the questions. One thing I know for sure is that a deployment into a war zone changes people, both the people going and the ones left behind—the unforeseen consequences are incalculable and impossible to predict. I have changed in innumerable ways that are continuing to this day, the memories of those experiences continually forming who I am and beckoning me to be a better person.

A pundit on a cable television news program the other night argued that Iraq was a senseless war that should never have been fought.

Perhaps they're right. Perhaps it was all for nothing.

I really don't know any more. What I *do* know is the older I become, the more I realize that I don't know anything. I know that the future is uncertain but even in the worst of times, the future may provide something good out of suffering. There is no telling what we perceive as bad now might someday be perceived as good, even to the slightest degree. I know that when people learn I am an Iraq War combat veteran, they want to shake my hand and earnestly tell me, "Thank you for defending my freedoms."

I appreciate their words but I don't know *what* that means. I never have. I've never defended anyone's freedoms. I've never felt as though I was furthering a noble cause or fighting for justice, for liberty and maintenance of the American way. I certainly wasn't fighting for the Iraqi people. There were no weapons of mass destruction, not a single one found. I never met a single "terrorist." I merely met insurgents who were baffled by the American presence and resented it as an unjustified occupational force.

It's my belief the Iraq War was purely a politician's war. Many people made a terrific amount of money from it. Others profited in other ways. Many more suffered greatly. Spread among the many, there seemed to be more casualties than benefits. Although it taught me much about the human condition, about how I would like to present myself to the world, and about how I would like to approach my own life, I too can't say with certainty that the war was worth the effort, the expense, the lives, and the tragedies. But then again, it is through these trials that we learn the most. Without them I'm not convinced the lessons would be fully understood—if not by ourselves, but by future generations as they examine our conduct. Perhaps it is through suffering that the best is brought out in people.

My time in Iraq opened my eyes to a broader world, a world both filled with life *and* with death. It's given me a greater appreciation for the remarkable gifts we have been given, no matter which country, province, county, city, or town we come from. Perhaps we all need to realize that we're part of a greater experiment and it's only through our combined strength as a species that we will find the determination and compassion to survive.

When I see the bickering, greed, ambivalence, apathy, arrogance, and ignorance of not only politicians but some of the general populace as well, I can't help but want to cry. I truly wish they could see that broader world I have been exposed to and I'd like to believe that we are better than we seem to resign ourselves to be. We *can* forge a world filled with compassion, tolerance, and understanding. We *can* move forward as a species and not implode. We *can* come together and solve our problems. No matter how different we may perceive others to be, we're *all* just people.

I never imagined I would participate in a war.

I never imagined I would write a book about a war.

I never imagined I would protest a war while my countrymen drove by in their air-conditioned cars, flipping me off and screaming that I was a traitor to the United States of America.

I never imagined I would end up homeless, divorced, and hopelessly confused.

I never imagined the strange twists this life has surprised me with.

I can't imagine what strange twists are left for me to discover—but I *can* imagine a brighter future and a happier life.

The story you just read is based on the fullest account of my experiences as I could possibly chronicle while I was actually there—or as we say in the Army, "with boots on the ground." It's my sincere hope this work helped shed some light onto why we shouldn't blindly leap into the idea of judging, hurting, or killing others before taking the time to understand them or even ourselves. I hope these journals provided a new way of thinking about life, the lives of the people around you, and the world in general.

Did I do the right thing in ultimately deciding to go to Iraq?

Was America justified in invading Iraq?

I ask you to ask yourself, "What would I have done? Would I have gone? Is war ever worth all the suffering and pain that inevitably comes with it?"

I would ask you to consider where you would draw your own lines in the sand with regard to your morals, values, and beliefs—what you would be willing to live with and perhaps do without.

I pray the world will find a better way to solve its differences. I pray we may yet find the strength to carry on the way we are intended to: filled with empathy and love for every person, every animal—for every form of precious life on this small blue ball we call Earth.

We have, after all, nowhere else to go…

F. Scott Service

April 2014

# Author Bio

F. Scott Service lives in New England with his adopted cat Walter and is a full-time author. In his spare time, he tends his garden, cooks, plays guitar, backpacks, travels, and rides his mountain bike. You may connect with him through his website: www.scottservicewrites.com.

CPSIA information can be obtained at www.ICGtesting.com
Printed in the USA
LVOW07s0743280116

472645LV00001B/19/P

9 781634 135740